IMAGES
of America

Trigg's Ozark Tours at Shawnee National Forest

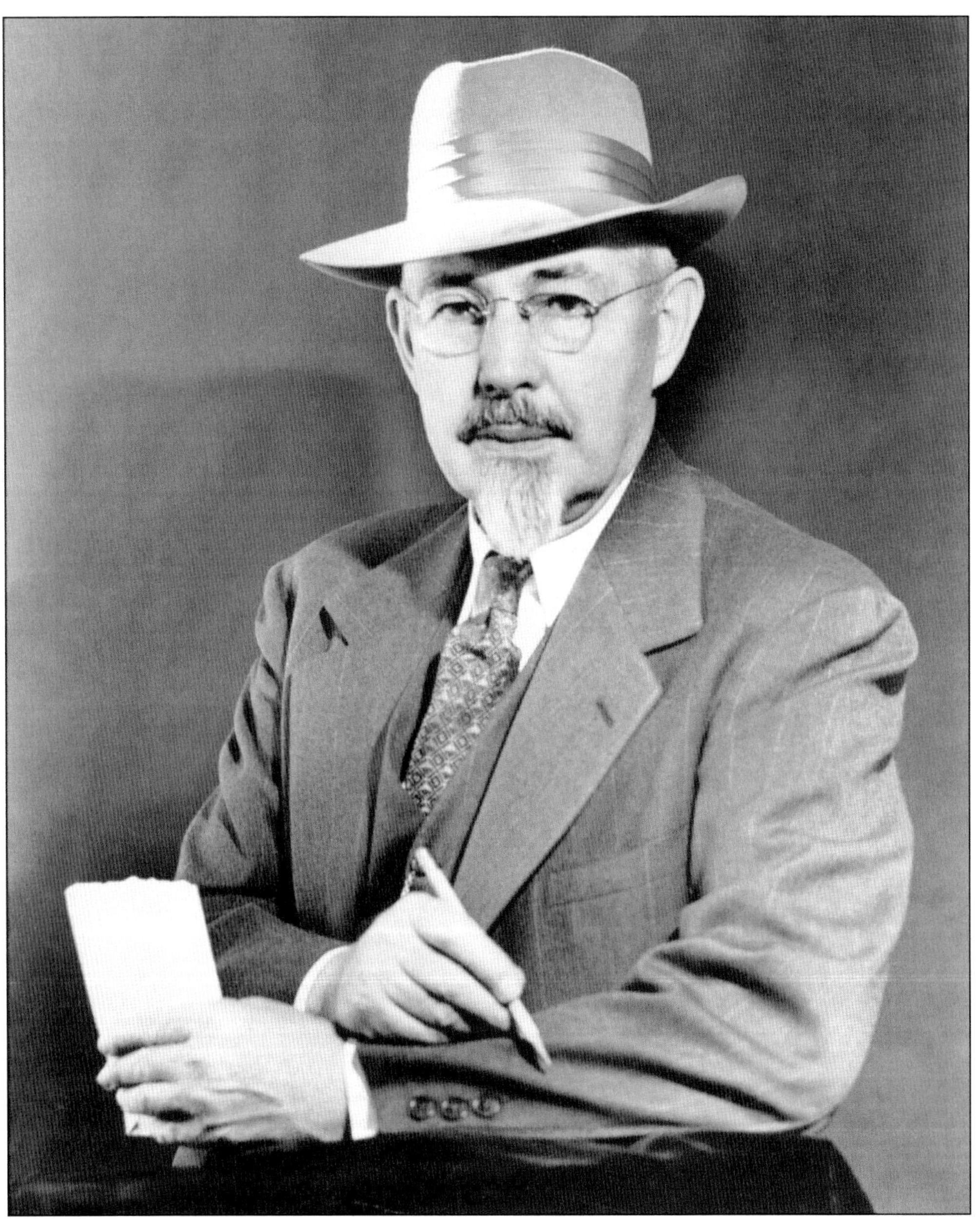

"When we take too seriously the little things that make up our daily lives we lose our perspective and our sense of humor and soon we are spreading gloom instead of cheer. There are times when every man must lay aside his serious and perplexing problems and play a little. These Ozark Tours afford him that relaxation, takes his mind off his worries and shows him the way to more happiness and rest of mind. These trips will assist you in balancing the mental budget." —Lindolph Oscar Trigg (1879–1949). (Trigg Collection.)

On the Cover: L.O. Trigg first led his Ozarkers to these unique rock formations on the 1933 Ozark Tour on a trail cleared for the tour's use. Trigg called the place Anvil Rock Area, from a reference in J.M. Peck's 1837 *Gazetteer of Illinois*. Now called Garden of the Gods, this is one of the most visited scenic overlooks in the Shawnee National Forest. (Trigg Collection.)

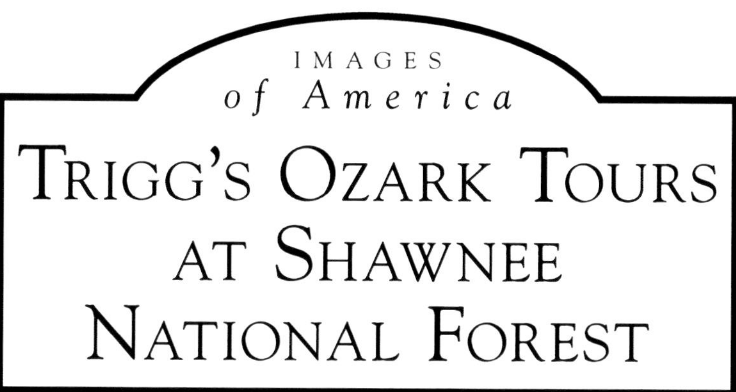

Todd Carr
Foreword by Janet Trigg Davis

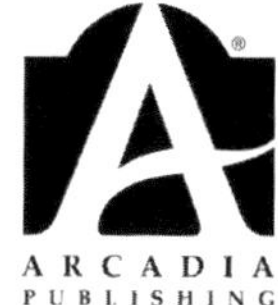

ISBN 978-1-4671-2503-1

Published by Arcadia Publishing
Charleston, South Carolina

Printed in the United States of America

Library of Congress Control Number: 2016950465

For all general information, please contact Arcadia Publishing:
Telephone 843-853-2070
Fax 843-853-0044
E-mail sales@arcadiapublishing.com
For customer service and orders:
Toll-Free 1-888-313-2665

Visit us on the Internet at www.arcadiapublishing.com

To all the explorers who have found themselves traveling Trigg's Trails, Tours, and Detours.

Contents

Foreword

L.O. Trigg was my granddad. I was the youngest grandchild and a tomboy. He was always seeking out people in the hills and talking with them. Some of the places they went, they had to make their own road. He carried a little travel book and "golf" pencil, and he wrote down everything—what he did, where he was, whom he saw, what he ate. It was amazing all the things he put in those books. I still love reading them.

I would always go down to the farm Granddad called Resthaven to see them off when the Ozark Tours were there. The spring trail was my favorite. We would make boats out of half acorns and float them on the spring. It was beautiful and cool down in the hollow. The family and kids would go down there for picnics.

My most vivid memories of the Ozark Tours are going to the farm and the churches for meals. Grandma Inez loved to cook and was on the cooking team. I could ride in the car and go to the meals, but I never got to ride in the back of the trucks.

When it looked like Illinois was not going to get a national forest, Granddad started writing letters and talking to people in Springfield. It was his mission. He was so pleased when Pres. Franklin D. Roosevelt signed the Shawnee National Forest into existence. It was ironic, because Granddad was a lifelong Republican and did not care for Roosevelt at all. He even had a sign on the outhouse at Resthaven that said, "Franklin House."

I knew it was a great thing Granddad did and was really proud of him, but I did not really get interested in the Ozark Tours and his involvement in the Shawnee National Forest until my later years. He was something else. He really was. Knowing him then, I did not appreciate him as much as I should have. He just loved the outdoors, but he was a character—I always said he was before his time.

—Janet Trigg Davis
February 6, 2016

ACKNOWLEDGMENTS

But ask now the beasts, and they shall teach thee; and the fowls of the air, and they shall tell thee: or speak to the earth, and it shall teach thee: and the fishes of the sea shall declare unto thee. Who knoweth not in all these that the hand of the Lord hath wrought this? In whose hand is the soul of every living thing, and the breath of all mankind.

—Job 12:7–10

Very special thank-yous go to my wife, Alene, and her unwavering encouragement, and to my daughters Rachel, Allison, and Leah, who looked over my shoulder and marveled as I did at the collection of photographs and paraphernalia; I thank you for allowing the Trigg Collection to spread out over several rooms of our home on multiple occasions.

A great debt of gratitude is owed to photographer Charles Hammond's meticulous research and care in scanning, preserving, and archiving the Trigg Collection. Charlie, this book is a direct result of your labor of love, and it definitely could not have been possible without you.

This book also would not have been possible without the cooperation and resources of the following individuals and groups: Heather Carey, Janet Davis, Gillum Ferguson, Mary McCorvie, Mark Motsinger, Kenneth Price, Jeff Robinson, Mark York, the staff of the Harrisburg Public Library and Rosiclare Memorial Library, and the Hardin County Historical and Genealogical Society.

The following groups partnered to make Trigg's Ozark Tours a reality to a new generation of explorers: Shawnee National Forest; Friends of the Shawnee National Forest; Gallatin, Hardin, and Saline Counties' tourism groups; Hardin County Main Street; and River-to-River Trail Society. This book is the result of renewed interest in the story of Trigg's Ozark Tours during the early years of the Shawnee National Forest.

I offer a final thank-you to the staff of Arcadia Publishing and my title manager Caitrin Cunningham for providing a venue for this story to be told.

Unless otherwise noted, all images appear courtesy of the Trigg Collection.

Introduction

Newspaper publisher Lindolph Oscar Trigg was born on January 12, 1879. He was surely born with printer's ink in his veins, as he made newspapers his life's calling. At the age of 14, he built his first printing press from parts and pieces he cobbled together in his family's smokehouse in Ozark, Illinois. His first print job was printing "berry tickets" for his neighbors. His first newspaper—the *Sullins School News*—was created for his school.

Trigg worked in printing offices in the Illinois towns of Creal Springs, Carrier Mills, Vienna, and Ewing. In 1904, he purchased the *Thompsonville Tribune*, publishing weekly papers in Thompsonville and Galatia, Illinois. In 1911, he moved operations to Eldorado, Illinois, and founded the weekly *Eldorado Journal*. The paper became a daily in 1921.

On August 16, 1901, Trigg published the first issue of the *Ozark News*, an issue now lost to time. He would return to printing the *Ozark News* in 1935 as the principle publication that reported on—and advertised—the annual Trigg Ozark Tours. The *Ozark News* became an annual yearbook of the various groups and individuals working toward conservation and reforestation within the Shawnee National Forest.

Spending his boyhood within miles of Cedar Falls, Bell Smith Springs, Burden Falls, Clarida Springs, Sand Cave, and Gum Springs, Trigg grew to love the scenic wonders of southern Illinois—an area he called the Illinois Ozarks.

Prehistoric Native Americans left their marks on southern Illinois with ceremonial and burial mounds, ancient stone "forts," and flint quarries, but the great forests of southern Illinois were left relatively intact. This changed during the late 16th century with the coming of the Europeans—first, the French missionaries and trappers, and, later, British colonizers. Early settlers arriving overland remarked what a relief it was to reach the Ohio River and finally see sunlight overhead after traveling through the thick overgrowth of trees.

Shortly after the Louisiana Purchase and the breakup of the Northwest Territory in 1803, Americans from the Carolinas, Georgia, Virginia, and Tennessee followed wilderness roads through mountain passes and floated on rivers to the Illinois Territory. Land was cleared for farming and two major industries: salt production (at the United States Salines) and pig iron production (in the hills of Hardin County). Steamships plying the waterways had little need for coal when vast amounts of fuel were readily available in the forests lining the Ohio and Mississippi Rivers. Coal mining and the railroads claimed their share of the forests, and by the early 20th century, most of southern Illinois's timber had been harvested several times over.

By the time of the Great Depression, much of southern Illinois was void of trees and overworked farmland no longer produced crops. Hillsides that should never have been cleared of growth were washing away, choking the rivers and streams with sediment, hampering navigation, and leading to catastrophic flooding. Wild game had all but left the area for lack of habitat. Many farming homesteads were abandoned as families fled to urban areas looking for work.

A number of national forests were created as part of the Roosevelt administration's New Deal. In an attempt to protect and reforest land around major navigable rivers, Congress enabled government purchase of lands in private ownership under the Weeks Act of 1911. In a May 25, 1930, editorial, the *Chicago Tribune* strongly suggests that one of the new national forests should be in southern Illinois.

When the Central States Forestry Congress met in December 1930, E.W. Tinker, regional forester for the US Forest Service, asked L.E. Sawyer, forester with the University of Illinois Extension, if he felt there was enough acreage available in southern Illinois for a national forest; in Sawyer's opinion, there was. Sawyer then met with W.W. Wheatley, president of the Harrisburg, Illinois, Kiwanis Club, and J.E. Whitechurch, Saline County farm advisor, to tour the area and discuss with businessmen and landowners the possibility of a national forest.

In February 1931, William L. Barker Jr., of the US Forest Service, spent a week touring southern Illinois. Accompanying him was Sawyer, extension forester. Barker compiled a preliminary report on establishing the Illini Forest Purchase Unit in Alexander, Jackson, and Union Counties on the west side of southern Illinois and the Shawnee Forest Purchase Unit in Gallatin, Hardin, Pope, and Saline Counties to the east.

The Harrisburg Kiwanis and Rotary Clubs foresaw the need for an organized effort to insure that a national forest was established in southern Illinois. The effort was called the Illinois Ozarks Reforestation Unit, and nine men from the four counties of the Shawnee Purchase Unit were chosen for the committee: B.F. Anderson, president, from Golconda, Illinois; L.O. Trigg, vice president, from Eldorado, Illinois; Clarence Bonnell, secretary-treasurer, from Harrisburg, Illinois; W.W. Wheatley, from Harrisburg, Illinois; W.H. Brinkley, from Shawneetown, Illinois; E.F. Wall Jr., from Elizabethtown, Illinois; A.A. Miles, from Rosiclare, Illinois; A.C. Pickering, from Equality, Illinois; and C.B. Wheeler, from Dixon Springs, Illinois.

Barker's preliminary report on the Shawnee and Illini Purchase Units arrived at the National Forest Reservation Commission in March 1931. The chief forester did not approve the recommendation, declaring that funds were not available for lands such as those found in southern Illinois.

The Illinois Ozarks Reforestation Unit was tasked with securing support from local communities and justifying the forest to the National Forest Reservation Commission through the region's legislators, particularly Rep. Claude V. Parsons of Golconda, Illinois.

Trigg took much of the responsibility of promoting and publicizing the need for a national forest in the region. He prepared a slide show presentation of the scenic wonders and historic sites of southern Illinois and presented to every women's, civic, and community group that would have him. At each presentation, he would ask the club members to send petitions and letters of support to Washington, DC.

The Illinois Ozarks Reforestation Unit decided that people of influence should see for themselves what southern Illinois had to offer as a national forest and proposed a series of three-day camping adventures exploring the region. In those early tours, Trigg was referred to as the "Old Guide" because he made all the necessary preparations for food, lodging, and transportation. He scouted locations ahead of the tour and found interesting people to visit along the route.

In subsequent years, Trigg was called "captain," as he led his Army of the Ozarks into the little-known areas of southern Illinois. From his printing office in Eldorado, he printed flyers and cards announcing his annual "Good Will Trip." The annual camping excursions came to be known as the Trigg Ozark Tours and, later, Trigg's Trails, Tours, and Detours. At a gathering of Trigg's family and friends in 1948, Captain Trigg was promoted to "colonel" in acknowledgement of his efforts in publicizing the Illinois Ozarks.

On June 18, 1931, the Illinois General Assembly approved the act officially inviting the federal government to acquire land needed for a national forest. A month later, on Monday, June 27, the first group of Ozarkers departed from Harrisburg, Illinois, on the first Ozark Tour into the proposed Shawnee Purchase Unit—Gallatin, Hardin, Pope, and Saline Counties. The Harrisburg *Daily Register* reported: "From this trip it is hoped that enough pictures, stories, and publicity is given the section that the National Forest Preserve [*sic*] Commission will see fit to establish their unit in the four counties."

In March 1933, Dr. H.N. Wheeler, chief lecturer of the US Forest Service, was present in Harrisburg to give a talk to representatives from throughout the region. He stated that seven million acres of land currently being farmed or in pasture could be better used for timber production and stressed the need for erosion and fire prevention if a national forest was established. A stack of petitions two feet tall in favor of a southern Illinois national forest was then forwarded to the National Forest Reservation Commission in Washington.

In August 1933, the commission approved the Illini and Shawnee Purchase Units. In October that same year, John O. Wernham, of the US Forest Service, arrived to begin acquisitions. Within a week of his arrival, 16,000 acres had been offered, and by the end of the first year, the US Forest Service had purchased 48,800 acres.

On September 6, 1939, President Roosevelt signed the proclamation for the southern Illinois purchase units to become the Shawnee National Forest. At the time of the designation, the government and private lands acquired for the forest totaled 173,829 acres. Today, the Shawnee National Forest contains approximately 286,000 acres of land.

At Trigg's funeral in 1949, his fellow Ozarkers gathered in the church basement to determine how to best honor him. They decided to complete Trigg's plans for the 1950 Ozark Tour by going "river-to-river" from Battery Rock on the Ohio River to Grand Tower on the Mississippi. As usual, scenic stops would be made between the journey's start and end. At Trigg's Resthaven farm, his son-in-law, Jack Cook, a florist, wove wreaths from cedar branches. A cedar wreath was thrown into each of the rivers in memory of Trigg.

The Ozarkers put forward plans to develop a scenic highway between the two rivers along the ridge of the "Ozark Uplift" with signage and spurs to the various historic and scenic wonders adjacent to the route. They intended for it to be called the Trigg Memorial Ozark Trail; however, that development was never completed.

For the 1947 Ozark Tour, Trigg published a small booklet, *Along Triggs Trails and Tours in the Illinois Ozarks*. The following poem, written by tour member Bill Davidson, appears in the book and was also published in the *Ozark News*:

"The Ozarkers"

It was my privilege once to know, a varied bunch of men;
Who, once each year were wont to go, and rove through hills and glen.
Varied, yes, and varied, no, to their vocations that applied.
Yet heart to heart they blended so, true friendships were firmly tied.
Like boys when free from a term of school, duties, cares; and dull routine
Were left for someone else to rule; their unleashed joys became supreme.
They rode and roved and hills were climbed, relaxing, as from cool springs they drank;
Swapped jokes and stories as they dined; and then to well earned slumber sank.
Thus, for three happy joyful days, each better than the last.
The Old Guide led o'er scheduled ways; and the slowest seemed too fast.
For unbounded beauties these Ozarks are, it is said so few of our people know;
No need to travel miles afar, just to the Ozarks go.
To us we know, for we have seen these diamonds in the rough.
Just as God made them. Grand, serene; each dell, each stream, each bluff.
And, equally so, I also found in that fine bunch of men,
"Ozarkers," we who love the ground, from whence comes all that's been.
Yes, down to earth. No stern formality. Just men who love and do.
Who thrive on grim reality; just men whose hearts are true.
My pleasure is to treasure up each one as all; and all as one.
And hope each year to drink this cup; until our Ozark trips are done.

One

Background

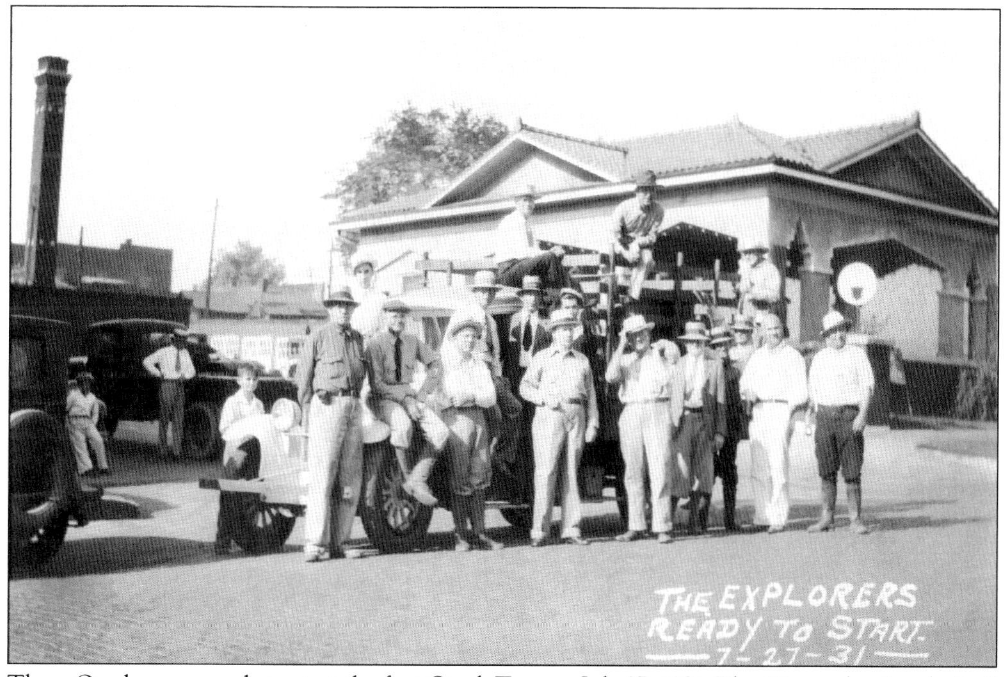

These Ozarkers are ready to start the first Ozark Tour on July 27, 1931. The 20-member "exploring" party followed the recommendation of the book *How To Camp* and left 45 minutes late to "insure success." They started from Aug Zvara's Hudson-Essex Garage on East Poplar Street in Harrisburg, Illinois. With feet dangling over the sides of a flatbed truck, they traveled very poor roads—when there was a road at all.

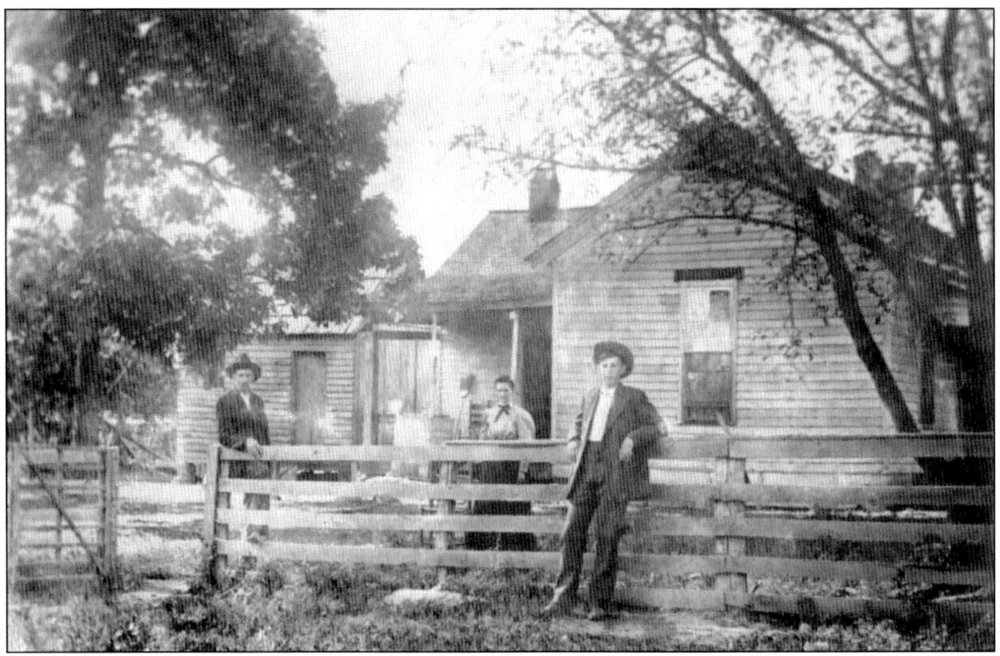

This is L.O. Trigg's family home in Ozark, Illinois. Pictured are, from left to right, Trigg's father, William Anderson Trigg; his mother, Mary Isabel Trigg; and his brother, Lon Trigg. Many of the wonders Trigg would later take his Ozarkers to see were just a few miles from the home in which he grew up.

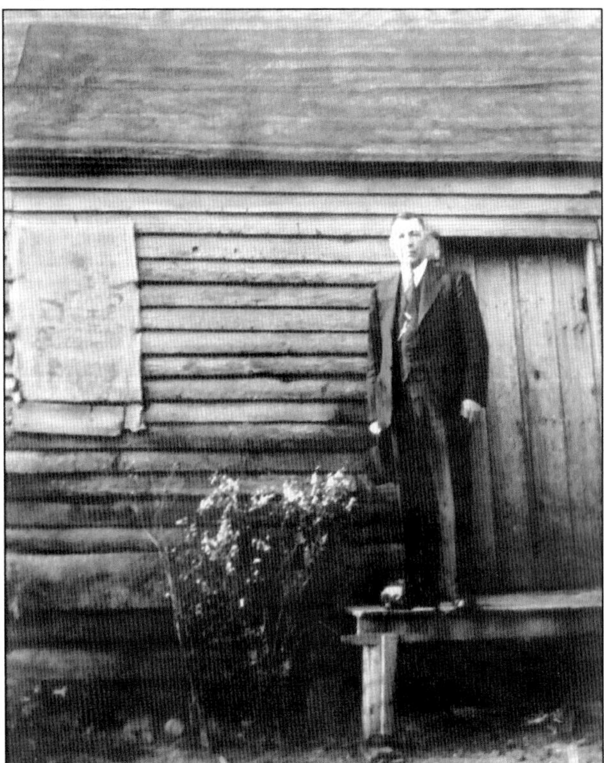

L.O. Trigg stands in front of the family smokehouse, where he built his first printing press at age 14. Trigg's printing press was made using a roller from an old flour mill and a flat marble stone. Trigg printed the first volume of the *Ozark News* here on August 16, 1901.

THE SULLINS SCHOOL NEWS.

"EDUCATION IS TO FIX THE TENDENCY OF LIFE UPWARD."

Vol. I. Sullins School, Jan. 26, 1900. No. 3.

Educational Column.

By S. J. CHOAT, Teacher.

......It is often said (truthfully too) that we are creatures of habit. Most of the routine of life becomes largely automatic, and we do the things we have long been accustomed to do without giving them any special attention. If then we are so far controlled by habit, it is better that the habits formed, even in childhood, while in the school room, be those which will not require undoing.

......In this age of free schools, it is the DUTY, as well as the privilege, of every boy and girl to secure at least a good common school education. It is not a question of can or cant but simply a matter of will or wont. Those boys and girls who absent themselves from school because it rains, another because it snows, another because it is cold, and still another because it is muddy, and repeat this from time to time They need not expect to keep pace with their classmates, who are regular and prompt in attendance at school.

......School life affords many oppertunities for instruction in morals and manners, and certainly each teacher is responsible for the moral training of the pupils placed under his (or her) care. But, how often it is the case, that the labors of the teacher, along this line, are counteracted and overbalanced by home influence. Take for insance, those pupils (we are glad the number are few), who have little or no moral training in the home; children who hear the name of God used in vain. Children whose father will swear in the presence of his children; in the home and at the table, while the meals are being served; and will allow them to curse and swear in his presence. Under such circumstances, the work of the teacher is not as effective by far as if the environments were such as they should be.

......Nothing can be better than the taking up, each day, of a definit program of work and accomplishing it. The effects of this discipline will last far beyond the school life of the pupil. Industry will become a fixed habit. Parents

.......Continued on page 2.......

L.O. Trigg published the *Sullins School News* in 1900 while attending the Sullins School in Johnson County, Illinois. The teacher who provided articles for this edition, S.J. Choat, later joined Trigg on many of his Ozark Tours. At 80 years old, Choat was present during Trigg's promotion to "colonel" at the Fairy Cliff Café in Herod, Illinois, in the summer of 1948.

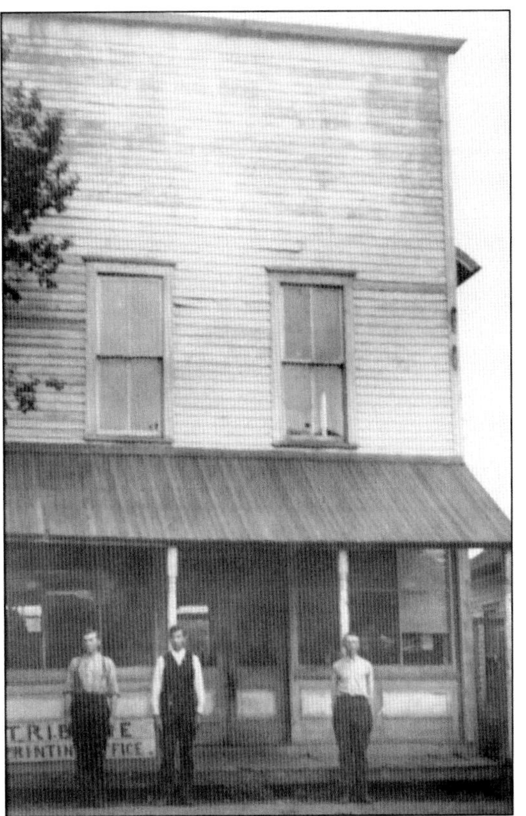

L.O. Trigg owned and operated the *Thompsonville Tribune* from 1906 to 1911. In addition to printing the weekly in Thompsonville, Illinois, for a while, he also published a weekly for nearby Galatia, Illinois. Pictured here are Charles B. Hines, Trigg's brother-in-law (left); L.O. Trigg, owner and publisher (center); and Paul Parker, assistant. (Kenneth Price.)

This photograph of the interior of the Tribune Building shows the printing press in operation. Paul Parker is at left. Trigg, wearing a hat, is hand-feeding the press. At right is printer Charles Hines. Note the hornet's nest hanging from the ceiling and the kerosene lamps on the workbenches.

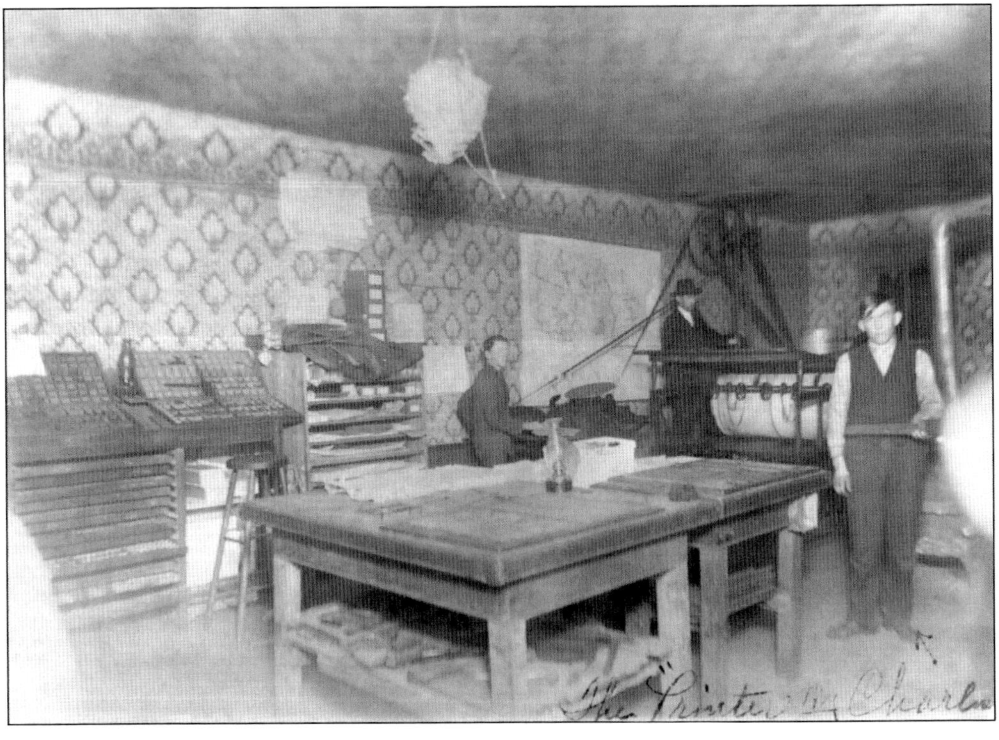

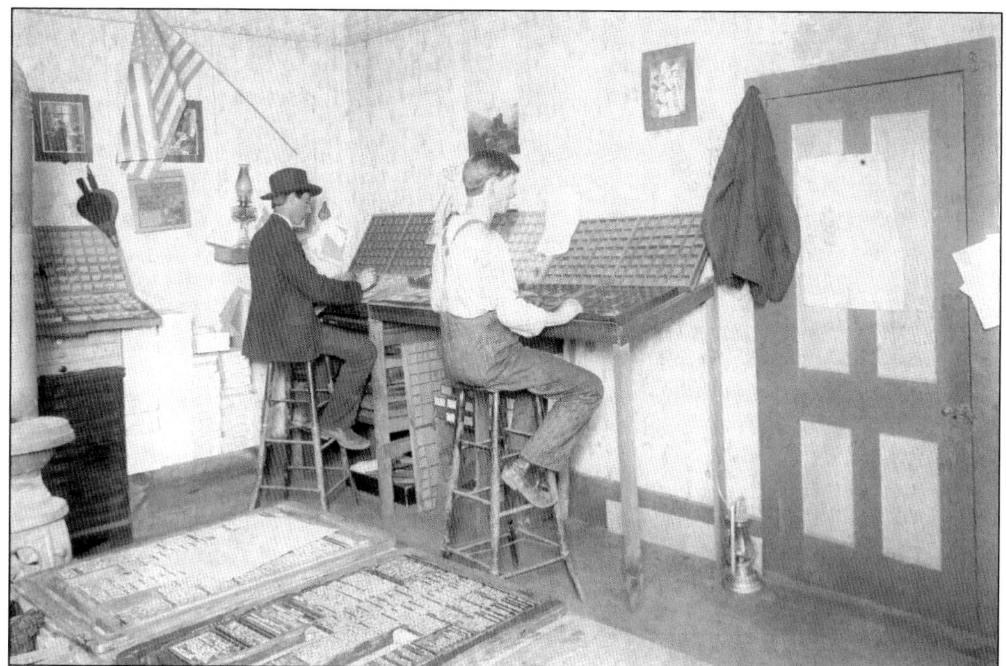

L.O. Trigg (left) and an unidentified assistant are shown setting type by hand. Note the galleys on the table filled with type—one is full and ready for a galley proof. The other galley has empty columns waiting for the typesetters to prepare.

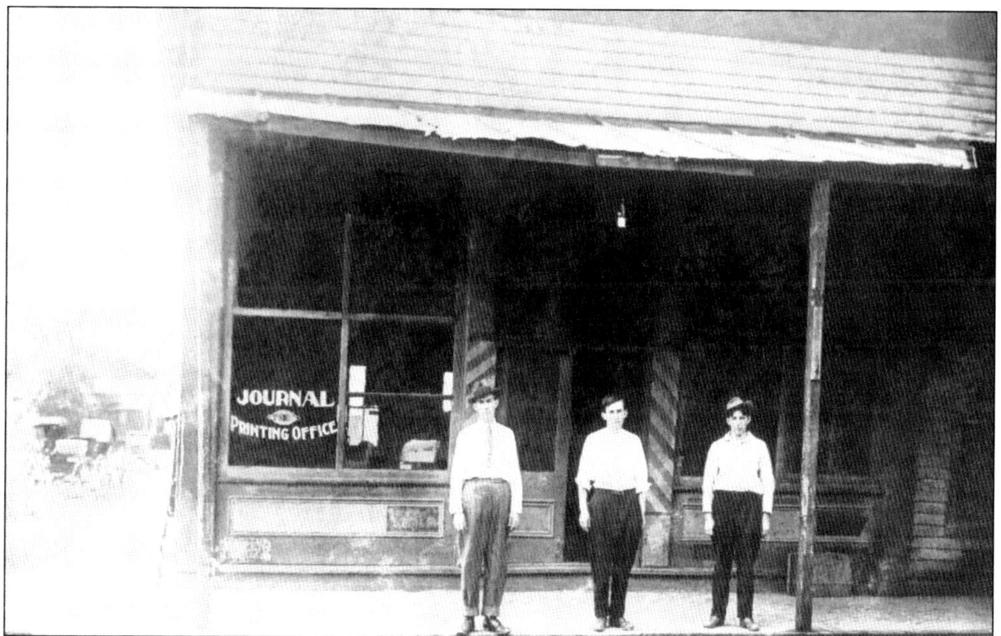

In 1911, L.O. Trigg moved his equipment to Eldorado, Illinois, and started the weekly *Eldorado Journal*. In 1918, fire destroyed his equipment. He bought out his competition, the *Saline County Republican*, and soon started publishing twice per week; he began printing the *Eldorado Daily Journal* in 1921. Pictured are Trigg (left); his brother-in-law Charles B. Hines (center); and Trigg's brother, Lon Trigg.

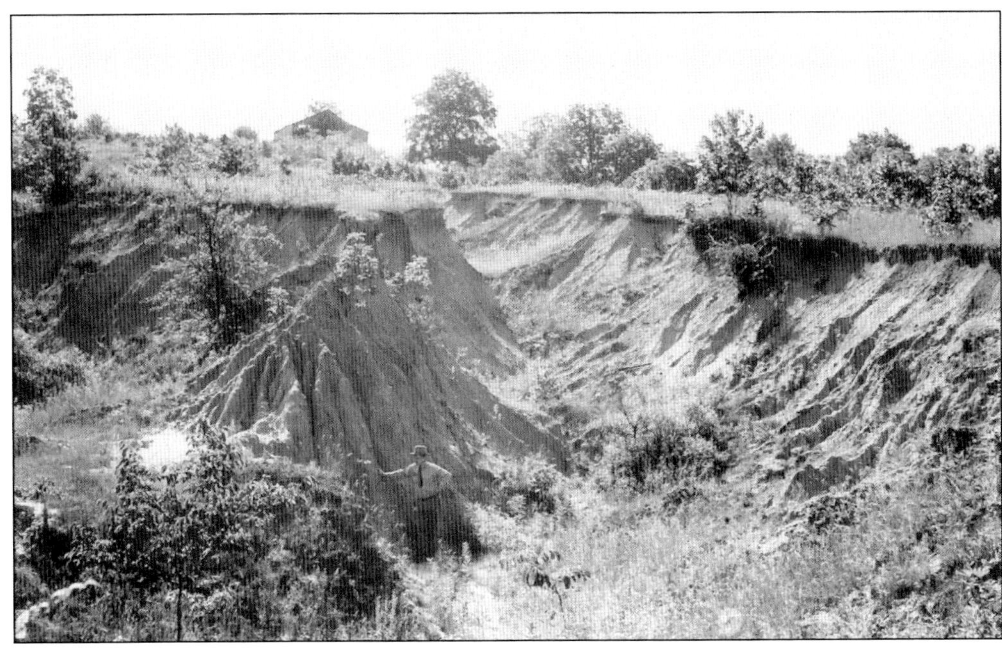

These photographs show the extent of erosion across southern Illinois in the 1930s. Topsoil loss ruined the potential for agriculture, and runoff filled streams and rivers with silt, which made navigation difficult. Land erosion was believed to have led to frequent severe floods on the Ohio and Mississippi Rivers. Forester Rufe Maddox is pictured surveying deep gullies in abandoned fields and erosion on the rural roadsides of Pope County, Illinois, in 1935. (Both, US Forest Service, Shawnee National Forest.)

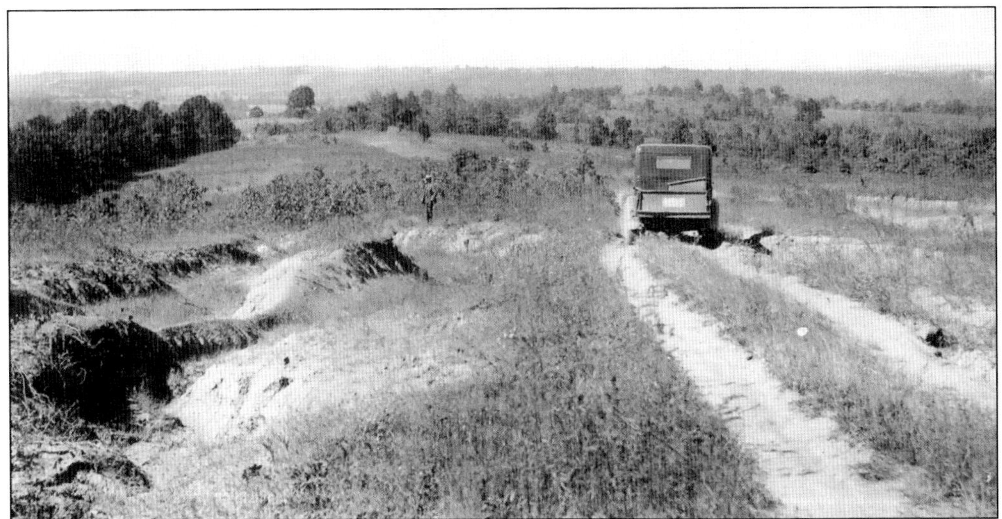

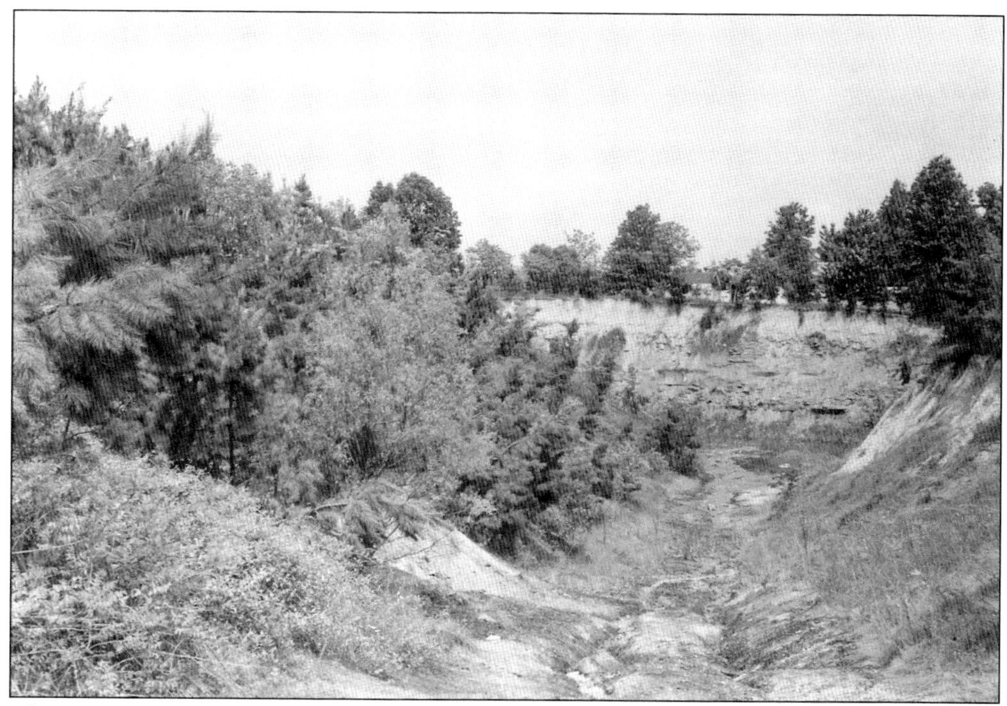

This image shows abandoned strip-mining operations needing reclamation work in southern Illinois. (US Forest Service, Shawnee National Forest.)

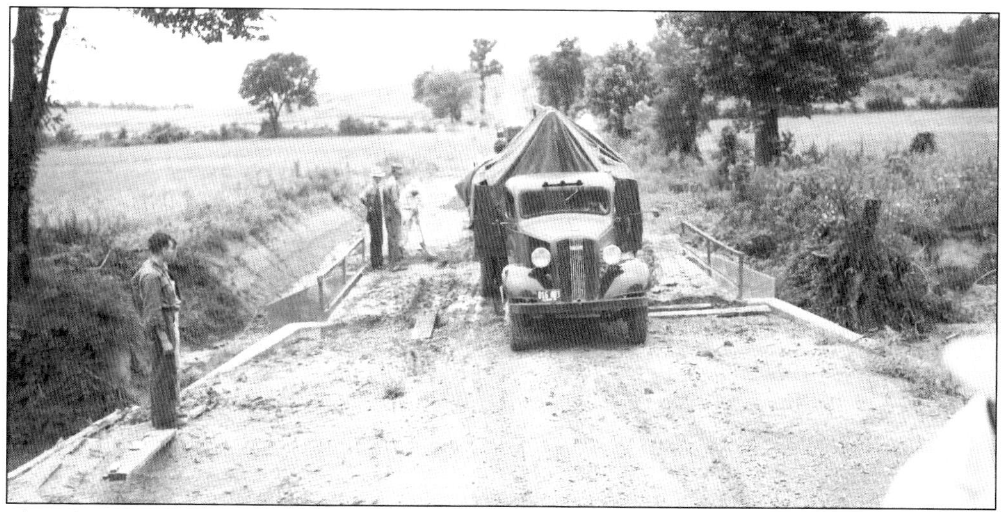

This photograph shows a typical southern Illinois rural road in the 1930s. Here, the 1938 Ozarkers are using shovels to help their truck across a bridge. Most rural roads lacked gravel and became nearly impassable in wet weather. The tarpaulins covering the truck bed suggest the tour had experienced rain that day.

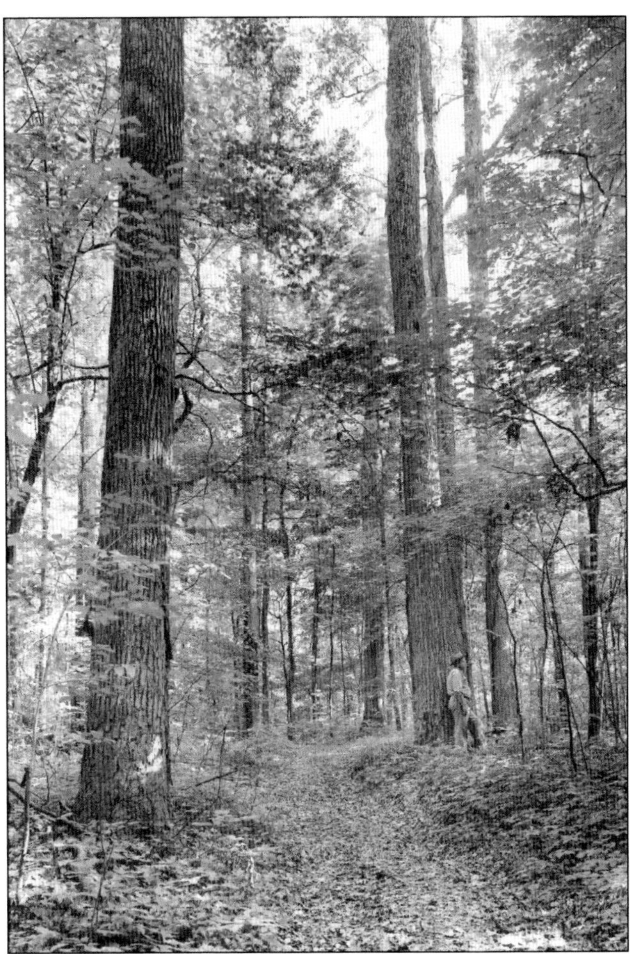

John O. Wernham stands among the towering oak and hickory forest of Kaskaskia Woods, an 18-acre tract that was one of the few tracts of virgin timber still standing in the Illinois Ozarks in the 1930s. Wernham, the first member of US Forest Service personnel to arrive in southern Illinois in October 1933, was tasked with making land acquisitions for the forest. (US Forest Service, Shawnee National Forest.)

This promotional material for Ozark Tours was produced by L.O. Trigg at the *Eldorado Daily Journal* printing office.

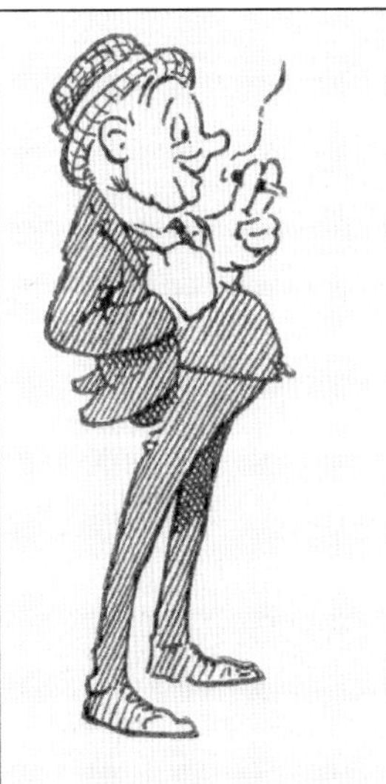

A LITTLE SERMON ON OZARK TOURS

Happiness is largely just a state of mind. Many a poor man is happy; many a rich man is miserable. To be happy defy your troubles or cares by going on an Ozark Tour.

Troubles or cares simply can't follow you on these tours. The scenery and fellowship licks 'em every time. As a general gloom chaser and promoter of true happiness an Ozark Tour has the world beaten.

An Ozark Tour is in fact a short vacation from daily life that inspires, refreshes, rebuilds and revitalizes you. Annual tours are necessities just like medicine, food, clothing and shelter.

They satisfy the human need for fellowship, inspiration and enjoyment as no entertainment in history has ever satisfied it.

To promote your own good health and happiness, plan for periodic, systematic relaxation, and . . . go on an Ozark Tour regularly.

For Ozark information, write L. O. Trigg, Eldorado, Ill.

Ozark News

Vol. 35. No. 2 Ozark and Eldorado, Ill., July 13, 1935 500 Copies

Annual Ozark Tour Under Way Soon

Will Start From Horning Hotel, Harrisburg, Morning of July 22nd.

TRIP INTO ILLINI FOREST

Includes Visit to Union County State Forest Preserve, Spectacular Bald Knob—700 Feet Higher Than Cairo—Alto Pass, Giant City Park, Riverside Park, Fountain Bluff, Pine Hills Skyline Drive Overlooking the River 500 Feet Below.

Plans are fast being completed for the fifth annual Ozark Tour of Southern Illinois—July 22-23-24.

You have already received literature giving full information. Those who have not responded are expected to do so immediately after receiving this Ozark newspaper pleading "the last call for breakfast." True it's not time to start, but it's high time to make reservations. Please give us your final answer.

The number going each year has increased which is very encouraging. Last year thirty-thee responded. Present indications are for a further increase in number over all previous tours, which are becoming "nationally" known.

The Ozark tourists have established a good reputation in these parts and receive the best of treatment and are accorded a royal welcome wherever they choose to roam in our scenic hill country. The Old Guide has blazed the trails and the natives are expecting us. Here's hoping that you wire today that you will meet the party at the Horning Hotel, Harrisburg, Monday morning, 8:30 o'clock, July 22nd.

You will enjoy this healthful outdoor exercise, the fine scenery, pleasant surroundings and appetizing meals. It will prove restful, delightful, educational and beneficial. You will see the CCC camps, see the boys busy at their tasks—road building, landscaping, planting, building, improving and converting this region into a great national forest, numerous parks and recreational places.

Transportation, as previously stated in the "annual invitation, will be made by motor trucks, provided with long seats on either side. Your bedding and baggage will be bundled and piled in a heap in the center space. Bring blanket, or quilt, and pillow, as the party will sleep outdoors in the great open space. One of our regular vacationists sleeps in a hammock. The overnight stops will be made where there will be easy access to shelter in case of rain. This is a camping party, so don't wear your best clothes, even though we are to be treated to a banquet.

You will have pleasant memories of the things you see and the places visited in the Illinois Ozarks, which will include Fern Clyffe Park, Union County Forest Preserve, the State Turkey Farm. Alto Pass, Giant City State Park, lookout tower on Bald Knob (1,030 feet above sea level), "Tom Cat Hill," Kuehle Chicken Farm, Riverside City Park at Murphysboro, Kinkaid Hills, the Pine Hills, Fountain Bluff, Scenic View, Grand Tower, Big Muddy and Mississippi rivers, site of Lincoln-Douglas debate in 1858, Logan's Memorial, etc, etc.

Your donation to the expense fund including transportation and meals, is Eleven Dollars. It's too late to write, so wire L. O. Trigg, Eldorado, Ill., for reservations.

One of Our Prize Letters; It Reflects That Fine Ozark Spirit

"Dear Mr. Trigg: I have your letter of June 3rd, relative to the annual trip July 22nd-24th, starting from Harrisburg at the Horning Hotel at 8:30 o'clock on the morning of Monday, July 22nd.

"I hope to be "among those present", although it looks now as if I will have a pretty busy schedule for July. I am not sending the eleven dollars today but you can count on me to make my contribution even though I may not be able to attend, or be there for more than a part of the time.

"The tours have been in the past so enjoyable and in my opinion have accomplished so much that is really worth while in connection with the development of the Ozark Hills, that I am willing to join with you and the leaders of this organization in boosting it along.

"You will hear from me again in a few days.

"Yours truly,
Walter W. Williams."

Much as we'd like to visit Ed Rosson at Pomona, we can't do it this time. This would be on the way to Natural Bridge, but this is not to be included. Sorry that no CCC road has been provided here. Maybe next time.

Prof. Clarence Bonnell, secretary of the Illinois Ozarks Reforestation Unit, expects to be among those present on this year's trip. He has been obliged to miss some of these trips on account of looking after his peach crop. We are glad he plans to be in the party. He has done much in the upbuilding of this section.

After a 34-year break, Trigg brought back his *Ozark News* publication to promote the 1935 Ozark Tour. He had printed the first volume in 1901 in his parents' smokehouse in Ozark, Illinois. Each year, from 1935 through 1949, Trigg printed at least one volume of the *Ozark News*. Trigg's son and publishing heir, Kenneth, completed the last volume, in which he eulogizes his father. L.O. Trigg encouraged his Ozarkers to write in with personal reports of the tours. He also printed news of happenings in the forest and in the general area of conservation and reforestation. Many of the pictures in this book were first published in the *Ozark News*.

Announcing Ozark Tour . . .

Monday, Tuesday and Wednesday, July 22-23-24, 1940, are the days and dates for the TENTH Annual Ozark Tour—recreation, education and good will—a visit to scenic and historic places of interest in the Illinois Ozarks. Starting from the Horning Hotel in Harrisburg, Ill., 8:30 o'clock a. m., July 22nd, or immediately after the arrival of the Big Four passenger train from Chicago.

Fifteen Dollars donation to the good will and publicity fund entitles donors to meals and transportation for the entire three day tour. (Round trip to Harrisburg.) Your necessary baggage will be transported without extra expense. The tour party travels by trucks provided with seats on either side.

Meals (seven) are served at convenient places enroute. Tour members sleep on cots outdoors. Overnight stops are made at places where shelter can be had in case of rain, or if any one is ailing or pansy-like.

Each year the tour is over a different route to new places, with new scenery, and some new faces, new jokes by the Ozark Sheriff, coupled with a complete change of program makes each trip a little more inviting.

The 1940 tour will include visits to places in Saline, Pope, Johnson and Union counties; also the east and the west side of the Shawnee National Forest, Union County State Forest, and the Thompson State Nursery, and westward to the Big Muddy and Mississippi valleys.

Reservations should be made early to insure accommodations. Annually there is an increased number participating. Last year forty-seven registered for the trip. With your reservation send Five Dollars; the balance is to be paid when you sign the Tour Register and get your credentials.

For further information see, write or wire

L. O. TRIGG, Eldorado, Illinois.

This 1940 Ozark Tour flyer sent to prospective attendees advertised the dates and route of the upcoming tour. A $15 donation to the "good will and publicity fund" entitled an Ozarker to transportation and meals for the duration of the tour. L.O. Trigg requested that Ozarkers include a $5 deposit when mailing in the registration. Early-bird registrants received praise in the latest issue of the *Ozark News*. Although Trigg encouraged participants to "leave your collar and tie at home," he often wore dress clothes. In the "what to take" information, he specifically bans firecrackers; this was a result of the 1936 Ozark Tour, when a few Ozarkers reenacted the "Battle at Fort Massac" at midnight after everyone else had bedded down for the evening. Up to this tour, five Ozarkers had attended all nine of the previous tours.

Additional Tour Information

What to take—

Your folding cot, or sleeping bag, blanket and pillow, hand towel; and if desired—a flashlight, field glasses, kodak, marbles and whatnot to play with. But no fire crackers.

What to wear—

Your everyday clothes and old shoes. Leave your collar and tie at home. Don't bother to shave. Be comfortable. Feel free and easy.

What to do—

Make new acquaintances and see all the scenery and historic places possible. Have an enjoyable and legitimate good time, with fellowship and friendship to all.

Every one travels at his own peril. Care will be taken to prevent accidents but will not be responsible should any occur.

Who Go On An Ozark Tour:

Forestry officials, state officials, senators, representatives, judges, educators, civic club members, Waltonians, archaeologists, geologists, scientists, tree and flower lovers, and those interested in historical and scenic places. And too those enjoying good fellowship and acquaintances among people of similar likes. It is a reunion and picnic tour for all who participate. Five have been on all of the annual tours, and several have been on three or four of them. Jake has a hundred per cent record—for attendance and otherwise.

The LAST of the series

TENTH ANNUAL OZARK TOUR

Monday - Tuesday - Wednesday

July 22 - 23 - 24, 1940

L. O. TRIGG : : : : Eldorado, Ill.

This promotional card announces the 1940 Ozark Tour. The federal government had designated the Shawnee National Forest the previous year, and this was expected to be the last of the annual tours. Early in 1941, veteran Ozarkers began petitioning for a reunion tour into the forest with the "Old Guide," Trigg, leading the expedition. (Jeff Robinson.)

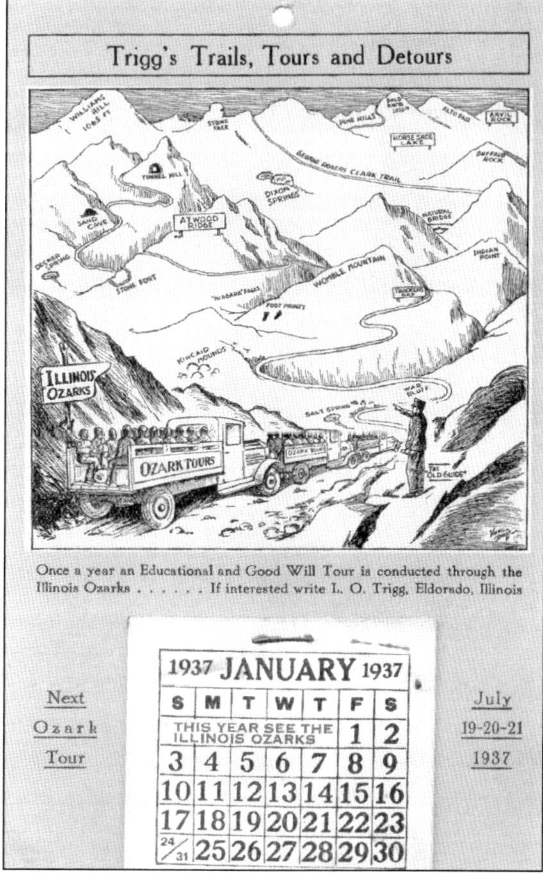

Trigg began passing out promotional calendars in 1937. Each year, the central image celebrated another "wonder" of the Illinois Ozarks. The map on the 1937 calendar was drawn by Vachel Davis of Eldorado, Illinois. Images featured in subsequent years include Horseshoe Lake and the custodian's home, a river scene near Cave-in-Rock, the Natural Bridge in Jackson County, and the towering white cliffs in the Pine Hills of Union County.

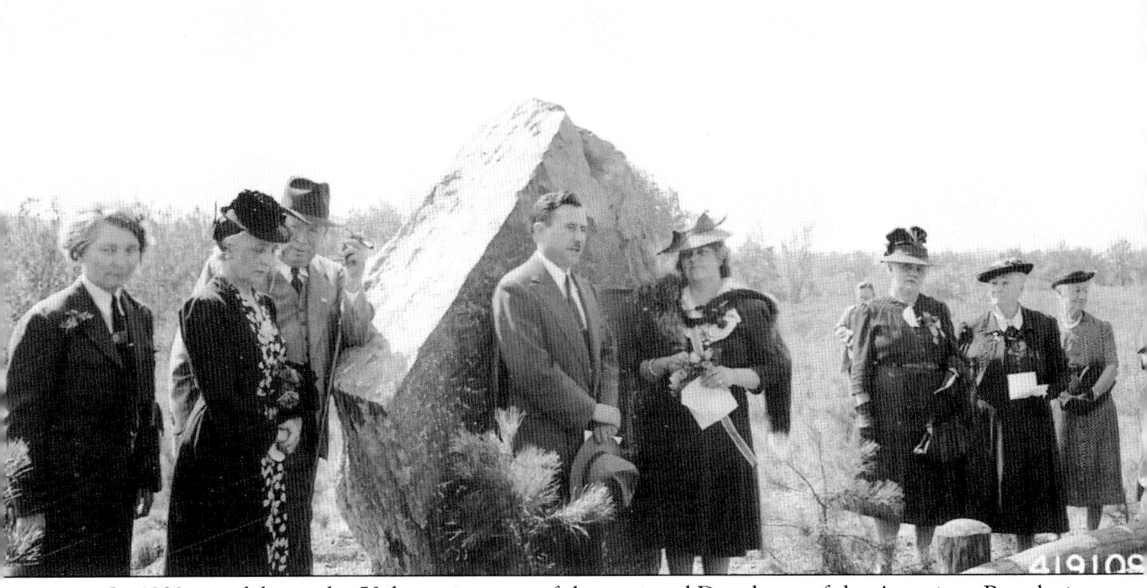

In 1939, to celebrate the 50th anniversary of the national Daughters of the American Revolution (DAR), Mrs. Henry M. Robert, the president general of the DAR, chose the Penny Pine Program as a Golden Jubilee project with plans to designate a memorial forest in every state. The project chosen in Illinois involved reforesting 1,000 acres of Shawnee National Forest land near Pounds Hollow in Gallatin County. Trees planted by the DAR included shortleaf and pitch pines, gray ash, black walnut, and black locust. The US Forest Service planted 1,000 trees per acre at a cost of $4 per acre. The dedication ceremony for the memorial forest was held on October 5, 1940. A new bronze plaque was installed and rededicated in 1981 to replace one that had gone missing. Please see page 116 for photographs of the plaque then and now. (US Forest Service, Shawnee National Forest.)

Forest

Service

Party

May 26, 1934, 6:30 p. m.

Harrisburg Country Club

Illinois Purchase Unit

These images show a program book for a US Forest Service party held on May 26, 1934, at the Harrisburg Country Club. All the dances on the program were named for southern Illinois landmarks. The menu for the evening included tomato juice cocktail, chicken croquettes, dressing, escalloped corn, green beans, spring salad, rolls, butter, angel food cake, and strawberries. Several of these parties were held to acquaint the community with the Forest Service.

DANCES

1	Rattlesnake Ferry	Fox Trot
2	Hunting Branch	Fox Trot
3	Raddle	Two Step
4	Stillhouse Hollow	Waltz
5	Bean Ridge	Fox Trot
6	Fountain Bluff	Fox Trot
7	Horseshoe	Two Step
8	Burden Falls	Waltz
9	Illinois Furnace	Fox Trot
10	Womble Mountain	Waltz
11	Bald Knob	Fox Trot
12	Hicks Dome	Fox Trot

See Them!
Know Them!
Enjoy Them!

They're Yours—
the Illinois Ozarks...

Roads to romance and adventure!
Highways to happy vacation haunts!
Trails that lead to scenic and historic places!
Or to the healing silence of the great outdoors!

A land of many Strange, Curious, Odd and Unusual Things: Nature's Rock Garden, A Scenic Wonderland, wherein is located Cliffs, Caves, Caverns, Underground Rivers, Numerous Springs, A Stone Face, Anvil Rock, Natural Bridges, Mounds, Pre-historic Stone Forts, Shelter Bluffs and Houses of Nature. Also where the Shawnee National Forest is being developed—with reforestation, game preserves, recreational areas and improved roads.

A country worth seeing—a field for unlimited exploration, historically, scenically and otherwise.

This Illinois Ozarks promotional material was produced by L.O. Trigg for his *Ozark News*. (Kenneth Price.)

Editor Eldorado Daily Journal

L. O. TRIGG, SALESMAN

FOR THE ILLINOIS OZARKS

BUT NOT IN THE
REAL ESTATE BUSINESS

ELDORADO, ILL

On his business cards, L.O. Trigg cheekily billed himself as a "salesman for the Illinois Ozarks," stressing in the fine print that he was "NOT in the real estate business." Trigg spent the last 20 years of his life promoting and sharing his knowledge of the hills and hollows of the Illinois Ozarks, often at his own expense.

Two

SCENIC WONDERS

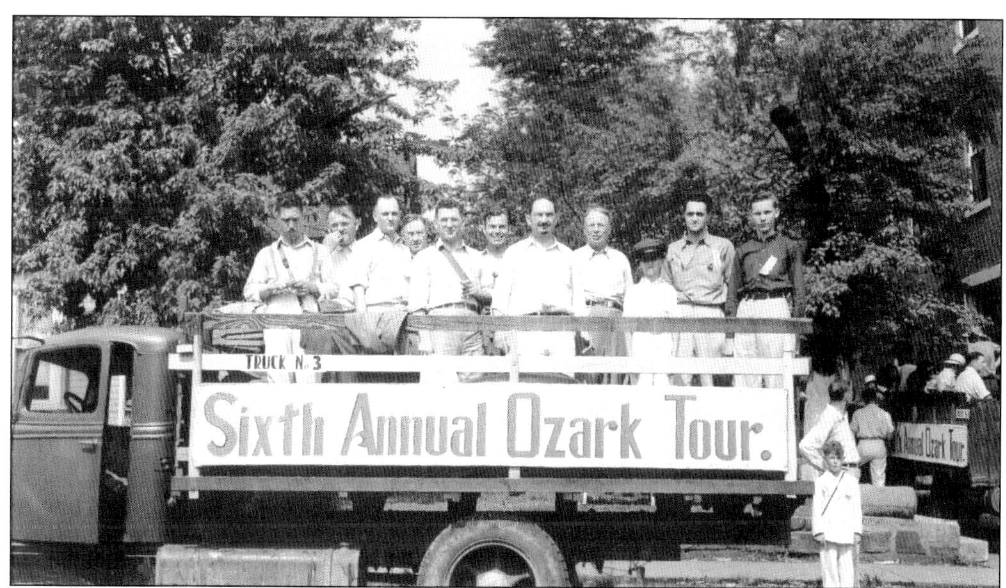

The sixth Ozark Tour started from the Horning Hotel in Harrisburg, Illinois, on July 20, 1936. Three trucks were used to haul the 48 registered Ozarkers through Johnson, Massac, and Pope Counties. Highlights included visiting Boy Scout Camp Pakentuck's Cedar Falls, an active archeological dig at Kincaid Mound, and Bell Smith Springs.

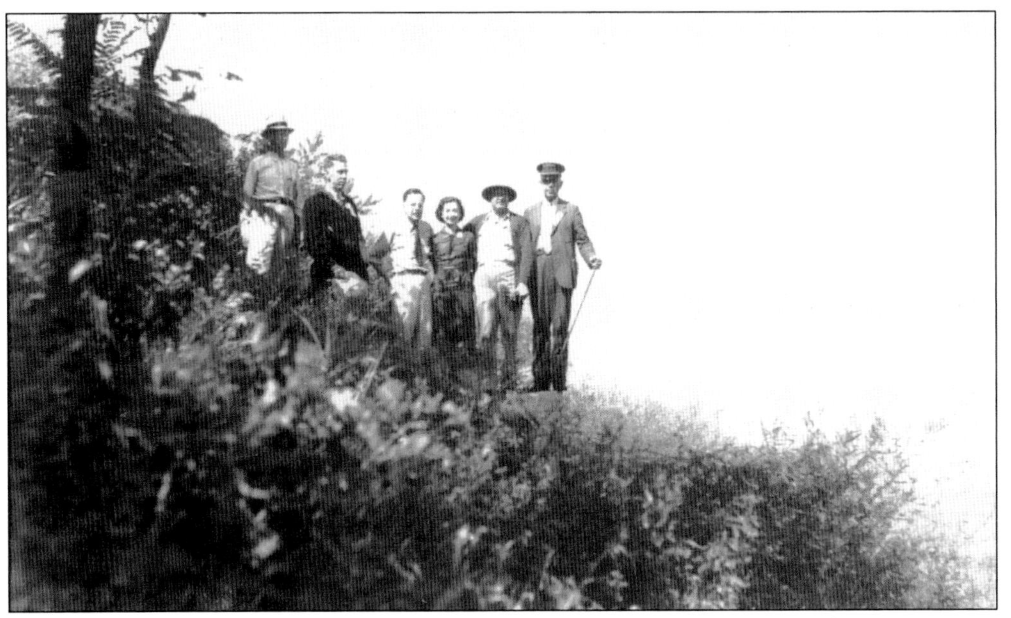

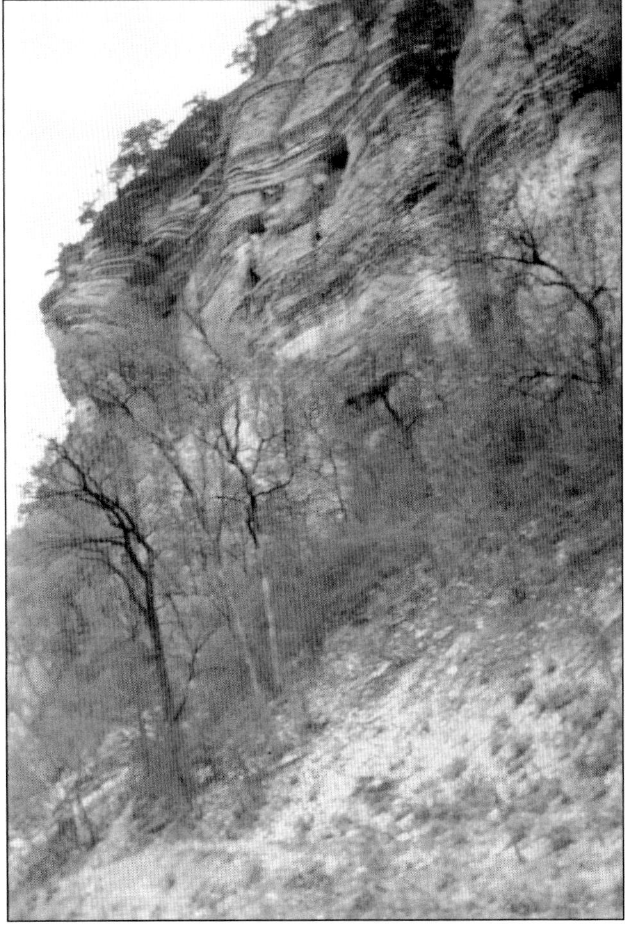

These 1937 Ozark Tour participants climbed to the top of Indian Lookout east of McClure. The woman in the middle of the photograph is freelance correspondent Anne West, the only woman ever allowed to go on one of Trigg's Ozark Tours. Rather than ride in the trucks, she rode in the "errand" car accompanying the group. Sleeping arrangements were made so that she could sleep separately from the men. (Jeff Robinson.)

The 1940 Ozark Tour stopped at the 150-foot limestone bluffs of LaRue-Pine Hills in Union County. Capt. Meriwether Lewis documented seeing the nearly five-mile-long bluff while traveling up the Mississippi River in 1803. "Snake Road," at its base, is closed to vehicular traffic twice a year for reptile migrations. The LaRue-Pine Hills Ecological Area was designated a National Natural Landmark in 1974. (Kenneth Price.)

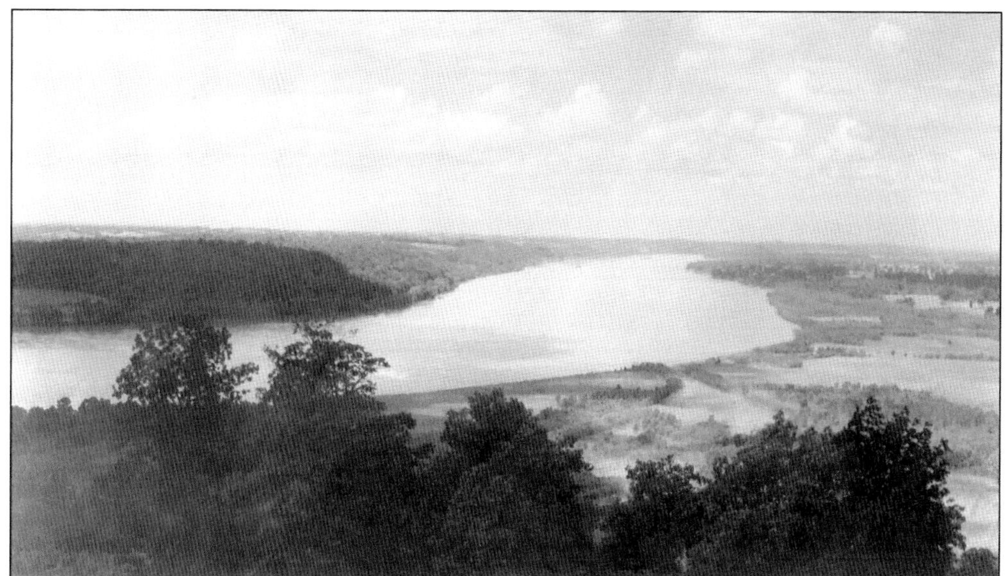

The above image shows a view of the Mississippi River and Missouri from the Fountain Bluff lookout tower (pictured at right) near Murphysboro, Illinois, during the 1939 Ozark Tour.

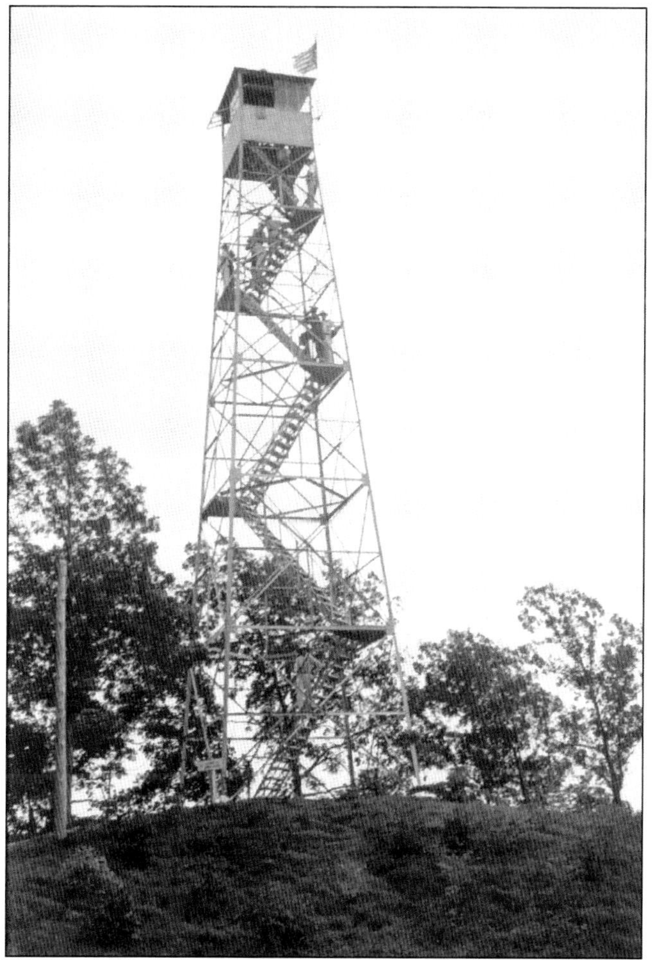

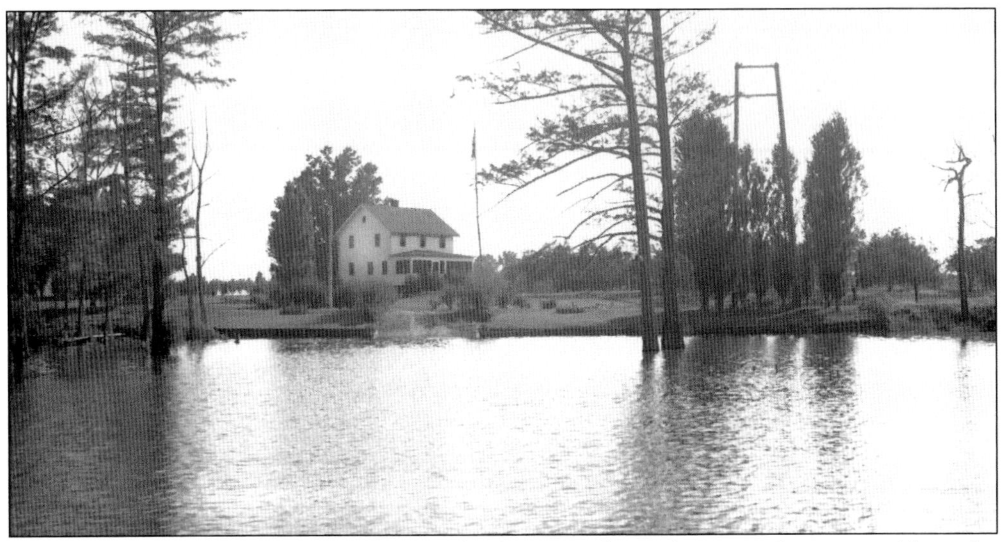

Pictured here is the caretaker's house on the island at Horseshoe Lake Nature Preserve in Alexander County. A ferry was used to reach the lake island when the 1937 Ozark Tour stayed overnight. The Illinois Department of Conservation bought the first 47 acres of the property in 1927 for use as a Canada goose sanctuary. The lake is a remnant of the Mississippi River channel left behind when the river changed course farther west.

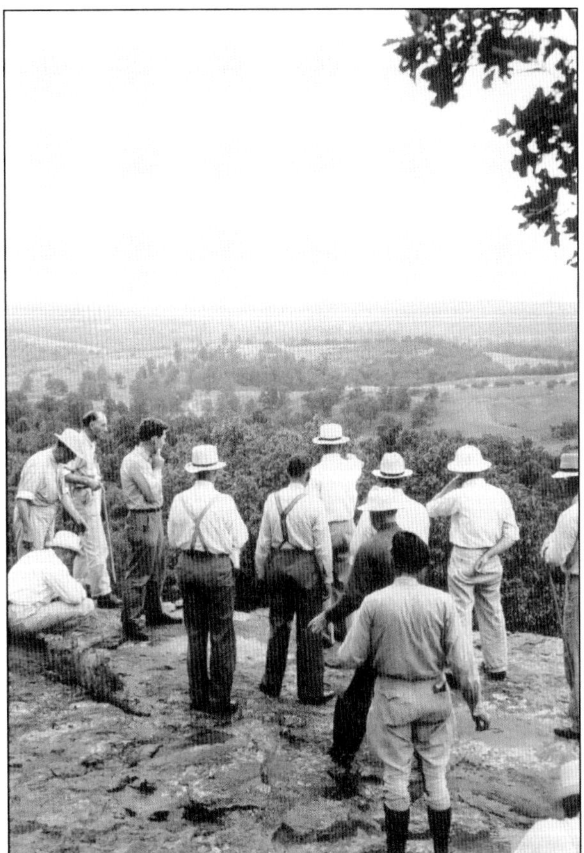

The 1935 Ozark Tour looks west from the scenic overlook on Skyline drive between Cobden and Alto Pass. Just to the right, and out of view, is Bald Knob, the second-highest point in southern Illinois. A fire lookout tower was built on Bald Knob in the 1930s. Today, it is the location of the 111-foot-tall Bald Knob Cross of Peace.

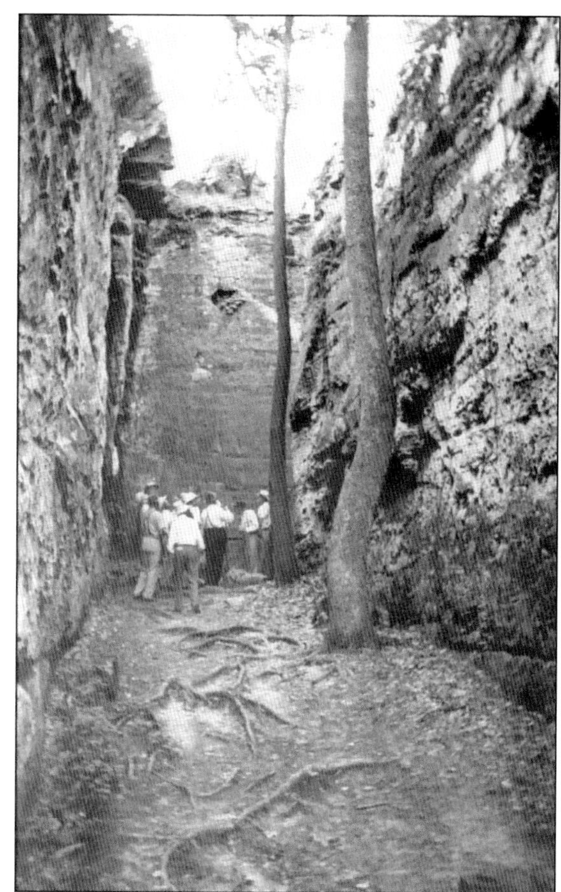

The 1942 Ozark Tour viewed rock formations in Giant City State Park near Carbondale. Giant City was named for the formations that look like streets. Pictured at right is Wall Street, and below is Balanced Rock. The Ozarkers first viewed the park on the 1935 Ozark Tour and ate lunch at the on-site Civilian Conservation Corps camp.

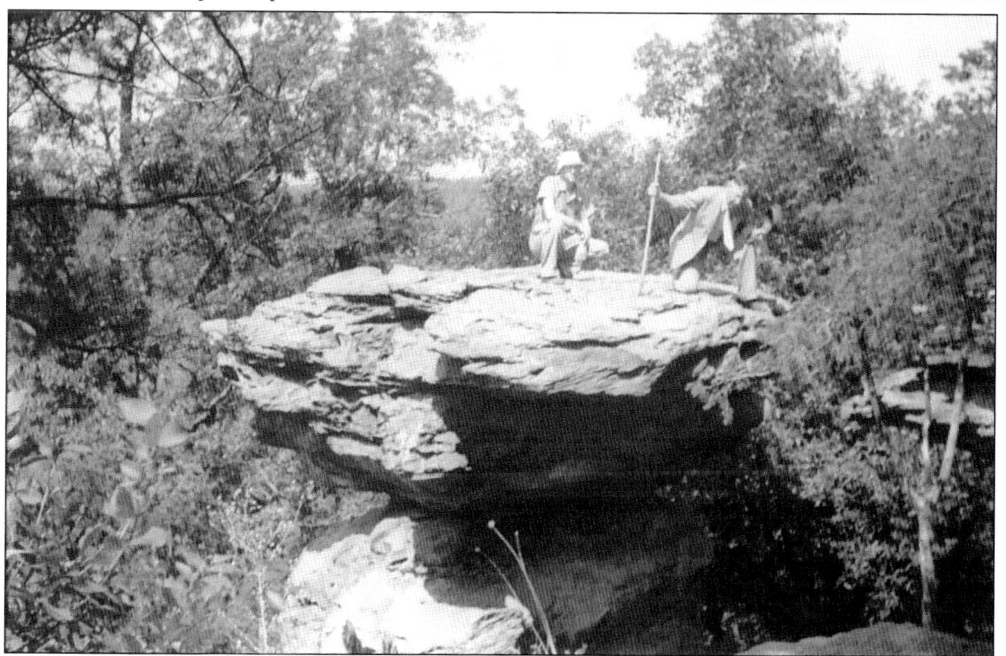

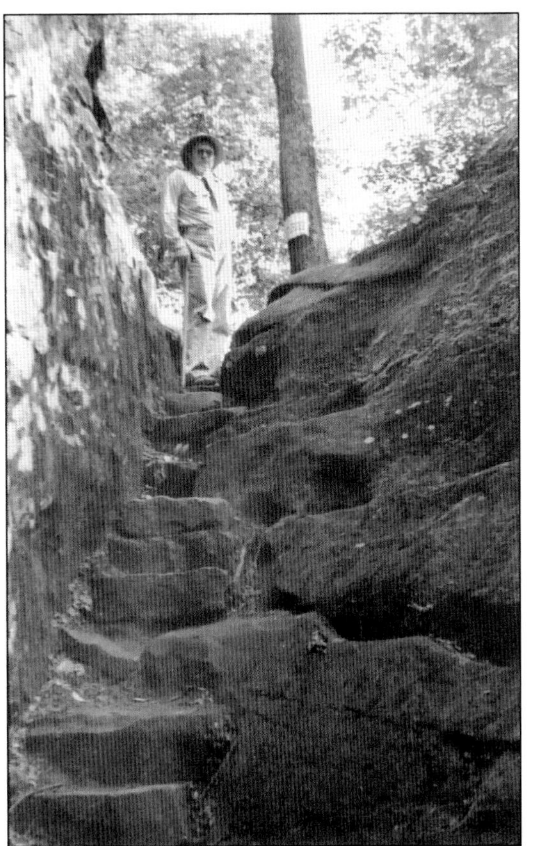

Ozarker Jacob "Jake" Myers, an attorney from Harrisburg, stands atop stairs in a rock formation in Giant City State Park during the 1935 Ozark Tour. Myers was declared "sheriff" on the 1935 Ozark Tour; it is uncertain how much law and order he maintained. He participated in all of the Trigg Ozark Tours until his death in November 1944.

Hawk's Cave, located in Ferne Clyffe Park near Goreville, is shown on the 1935 Ozark Tour. At the time of the tour, it was privately owned by Emma Rebman; it did not become a state park until 1949. Hawk's Cave is a sheer cliff of stone with an opening 150 feet wide. L.O. Trigg speculated that if it were used as a natural amphitheater, 2,000 people could sit in it.

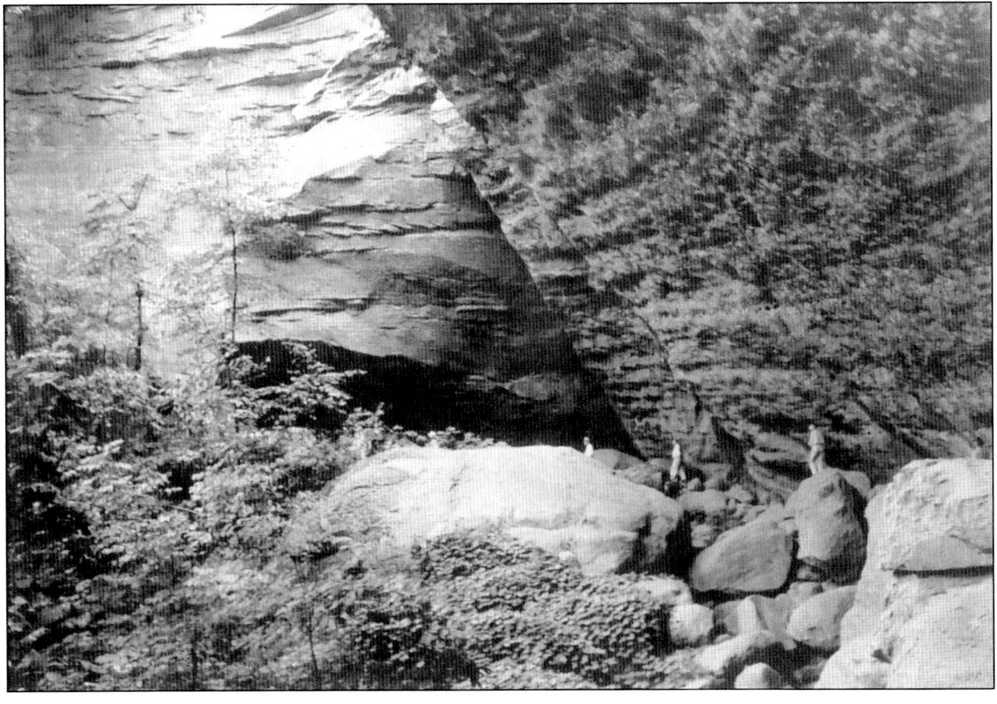

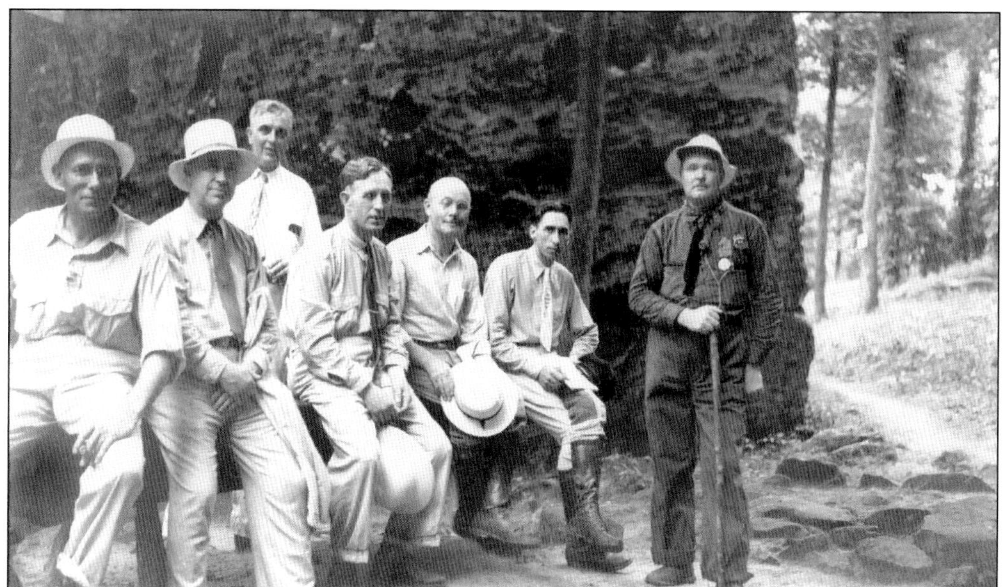

Pictured above on the 1935 Ozark Tour at Swallow Rock on the trail to Mohawk Spring are, from left to right, Otis Lamar, Charles H. Thompson, George Davenport, W.W. Wheatley, M.M. Leighton, Norman Moore, and "Sheriff" Jake Myers. Swallow Rock and Mohawk Spring are located in Emma Rebmans's Ferne Clyffe Park near Goreville. At right is Mohawk Spring, one of the eight springs in the park that Rebman named for Native Americans. During the time she lived in the park, this spring was the water source for her home, located on the ridge above, and was carried up a set of steep stairs a bucket at a time. Rebman purchased the park sometime after 1910 and sold it to the State of Illinois in 1949.

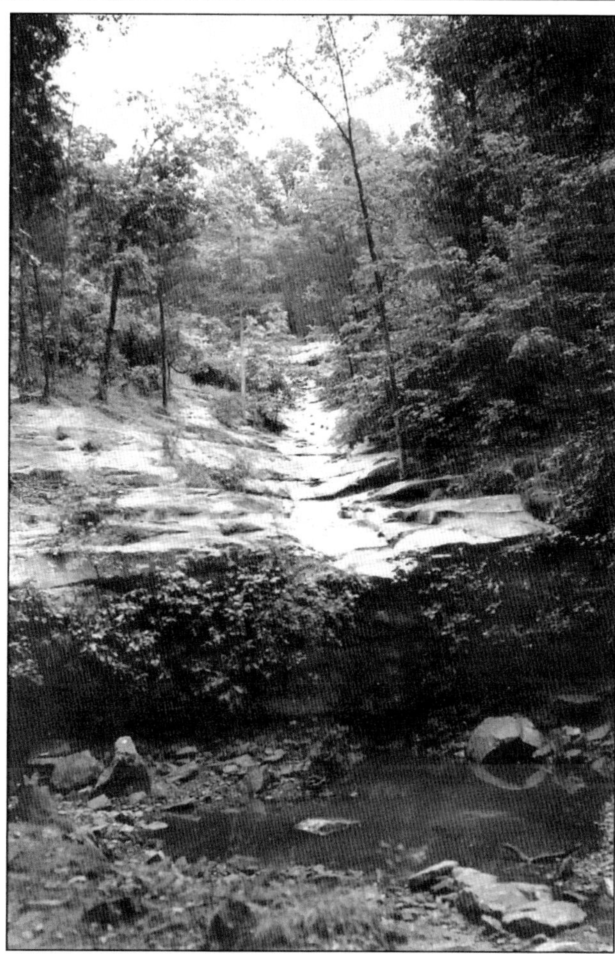

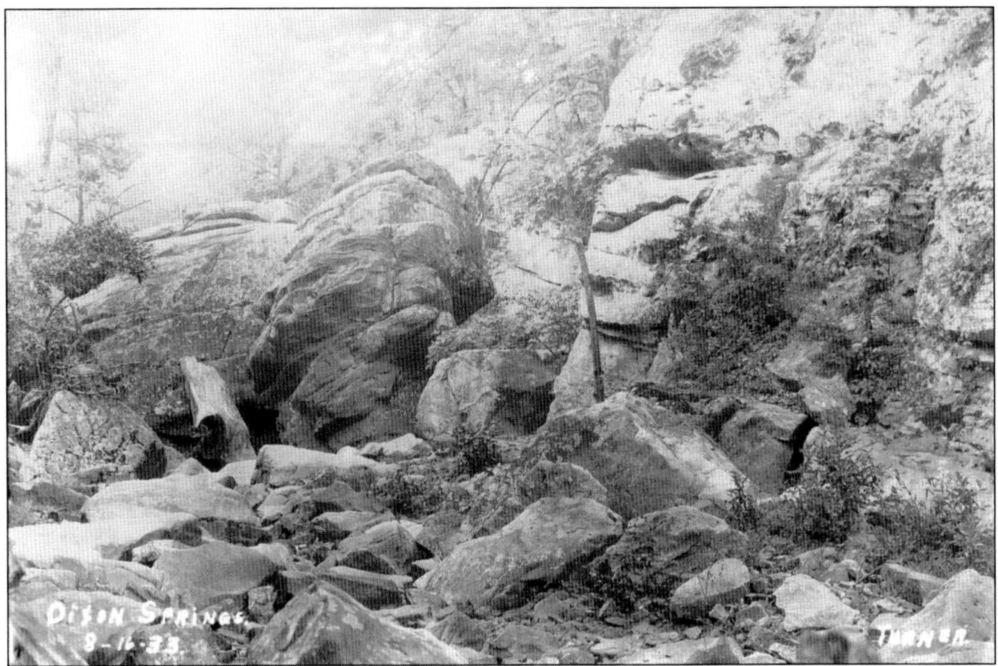

The 1933 Ozark Tour visited Ghost Dance Canyon in Dixon Springs in Pope County. The canyon trail follows a stream as it cascades over large automobile-sized boulders. The canyon is believed to have been the result of a large bed of rock that dropped in a fault line. At the time of this tour, Dixon Springs was a mineral spring resort and not the state park it is today.

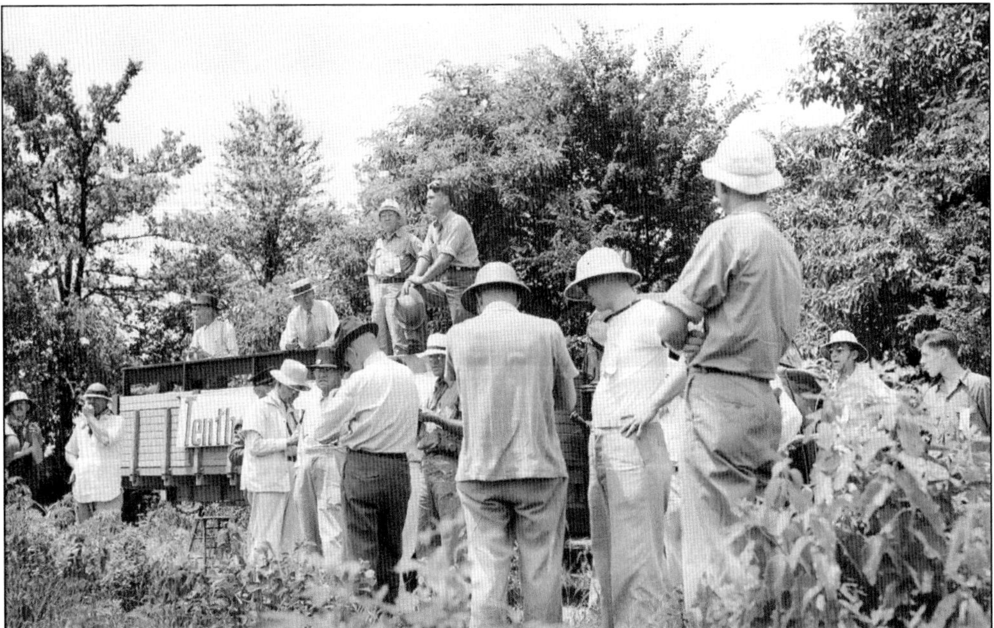

The 1940 Ozark Tour is shown visiting the Eddyville Forest Plantation, one of five forest plantations established during the early years of the Shawnee National Forest. This forest plantation was sponsored by the Illinois Federation of Women's Clubs Cooperative and contained 1,300 acres, most of which were covered with shortleaf pine.

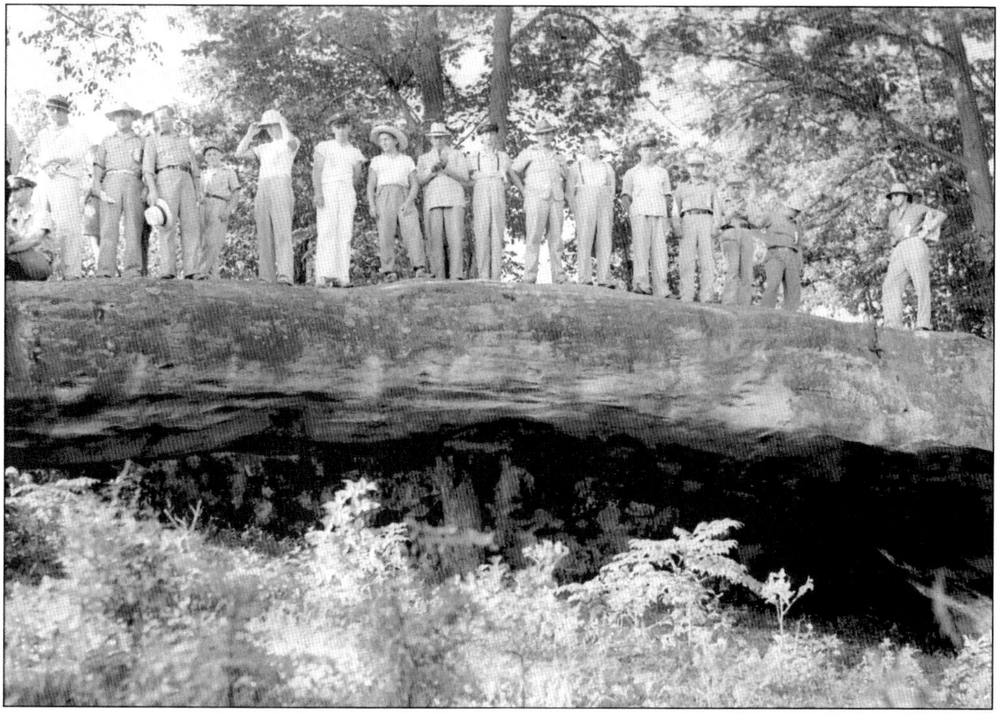

Members of the 1940 Ozark Tour stand on Rainbow Arch, a natural bridge west of Cypress. This natural bridge spans forty feet and has a height of six feet, a width of five feet, and is six feet thick.

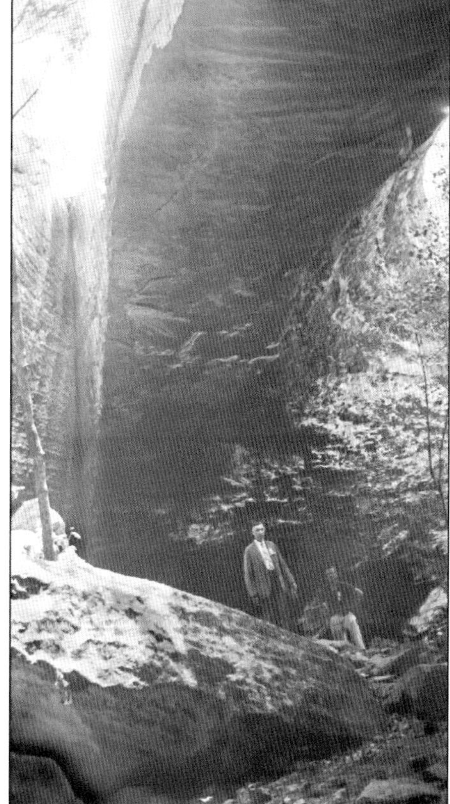

L.O. Trigg (left) and "Buck" Sawyer stand beneath the natural bridge at Bell Smith Springs, near Eddyville, on the 1936 Ozark Tour. This is the largest natural bridge in the Shawnee National Forest and has a span of 125 feet, a height of 30 feet, a width of 8 feet, and a thickness of 20 feet.

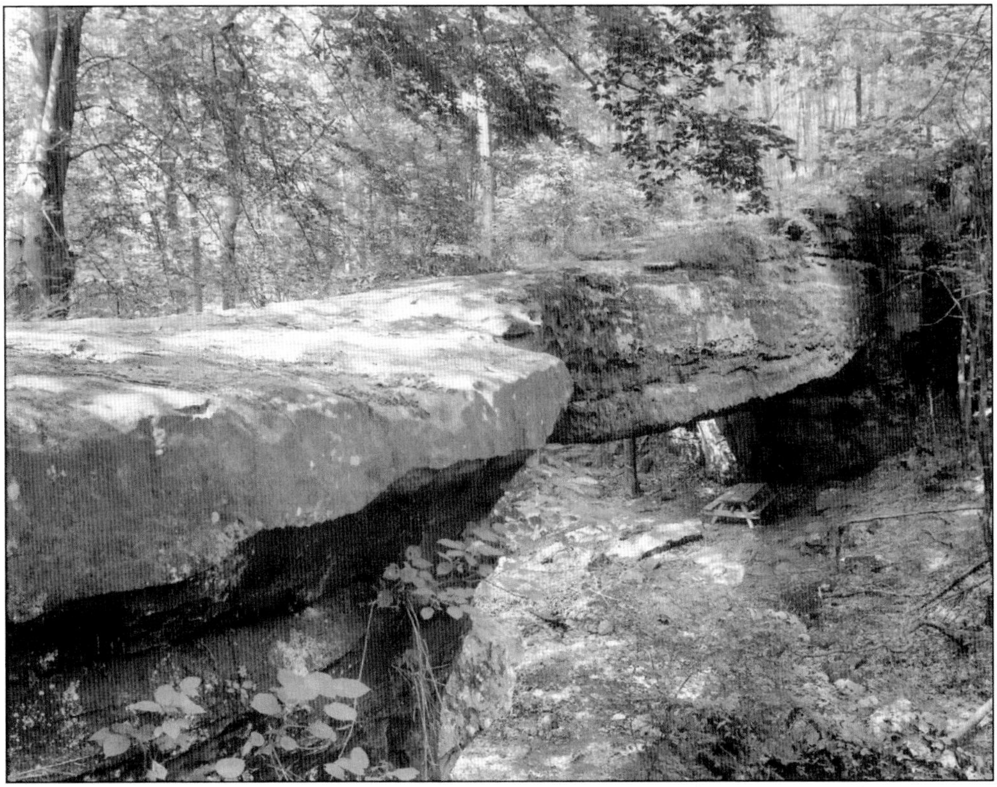

The 1939 Ozark Tour visited Pomona Natural Bridge, located in Jackson County. This attraction was skipped for some years due to poor road conditions after rainy weather. Pomona Natural Bridge has a span of 75 feet, a height of 30 feet, a width of 9 feet, and is 9 feet thick. (US Forest Service, Shawnee National Forest.)

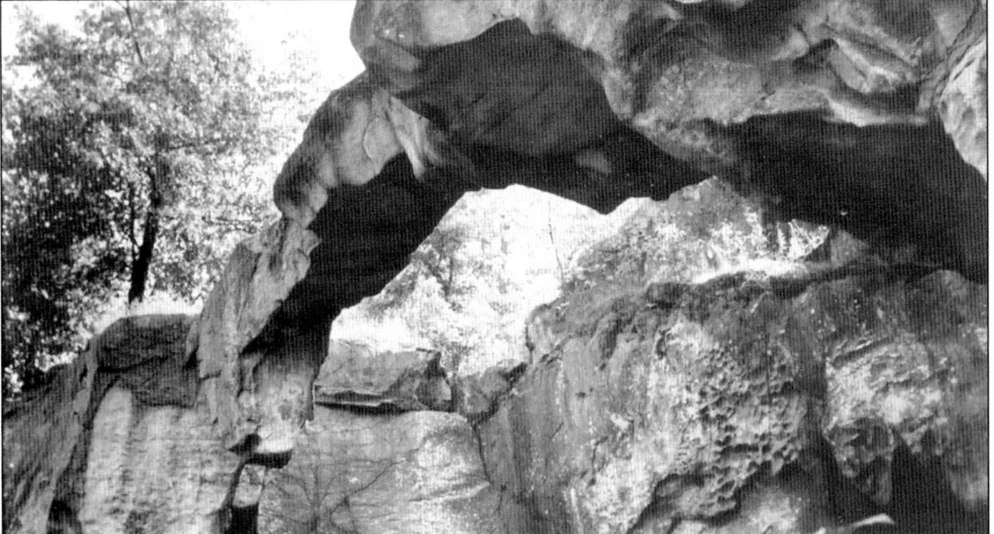

This is the natural bridge behind the Christian church in the village of Cypress, Illinois. This fragile-looking bridge has a 60-foot span and a height of 30 feet, but it is a mere two to three feet wide and only two feet thick at its narrowest point. (US Forest Service, Shawnee National Forest.)

This pool and cascade are located at Hayes Canyon near Eddyville. Ozarkers toured the canyon on the 1940 and 1949 Ozark Tours. (Kenneth Price.)

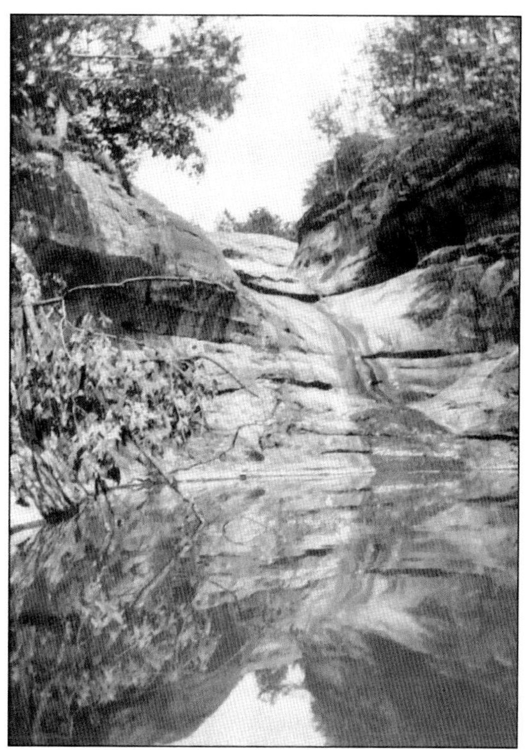

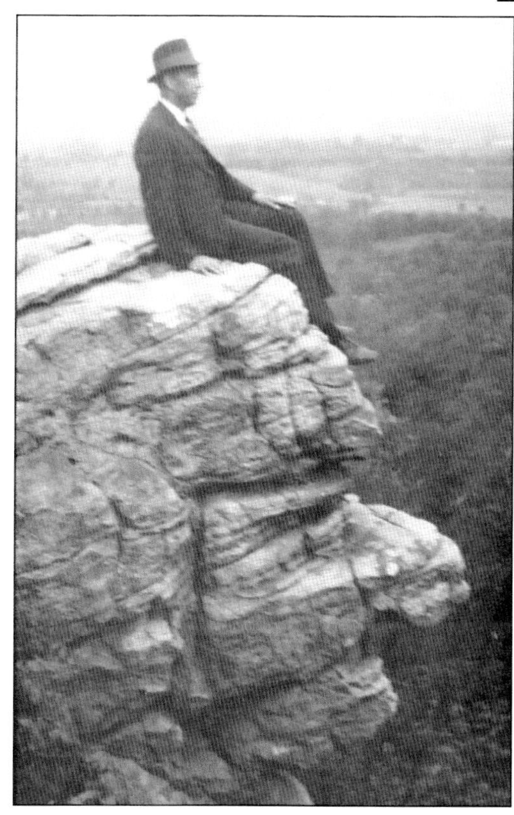

L.O. Trigg sits on top of old Stoneface near Harrisburg in 1934. Located on the Eagle Mountain range halfway between Cave Hill to the north and Womble Mountain to the south, Stoneface was first discovered and described by Ozarker Clarence Bonnell of Harrisburg in 1915.

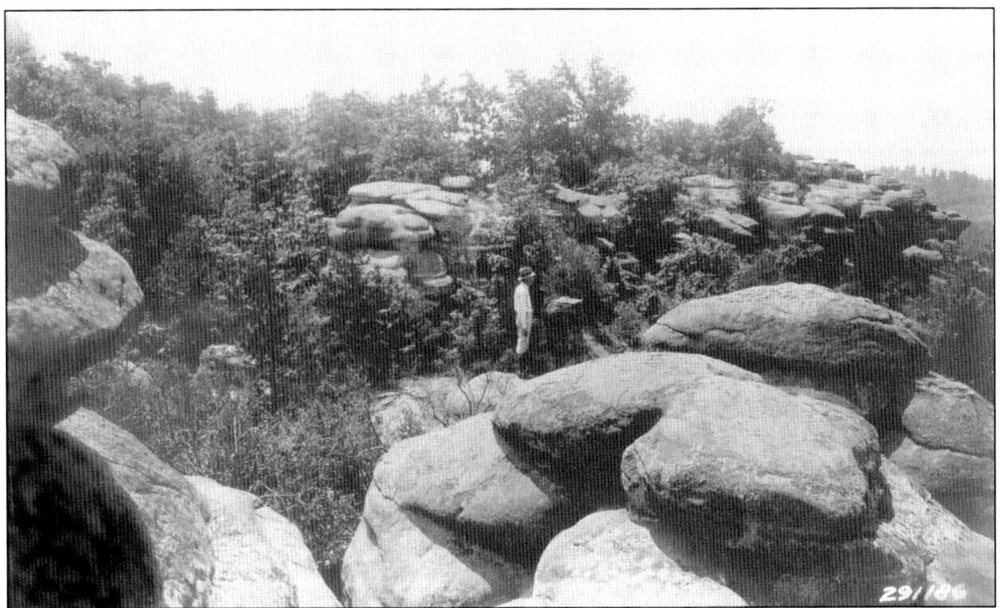

L.O. Trigg stands among the sandstone bluffs of Garden of the Gods on the 1934 Ozark Tour. This was the second Ozark Tour to visit the Anvil Rock area. Though these scenic vistas are currently the most visited area of the forest, they were very difficult to get to by automobile during Trigg's tours. This photograph was taken near the "hump" of Camel Rock.

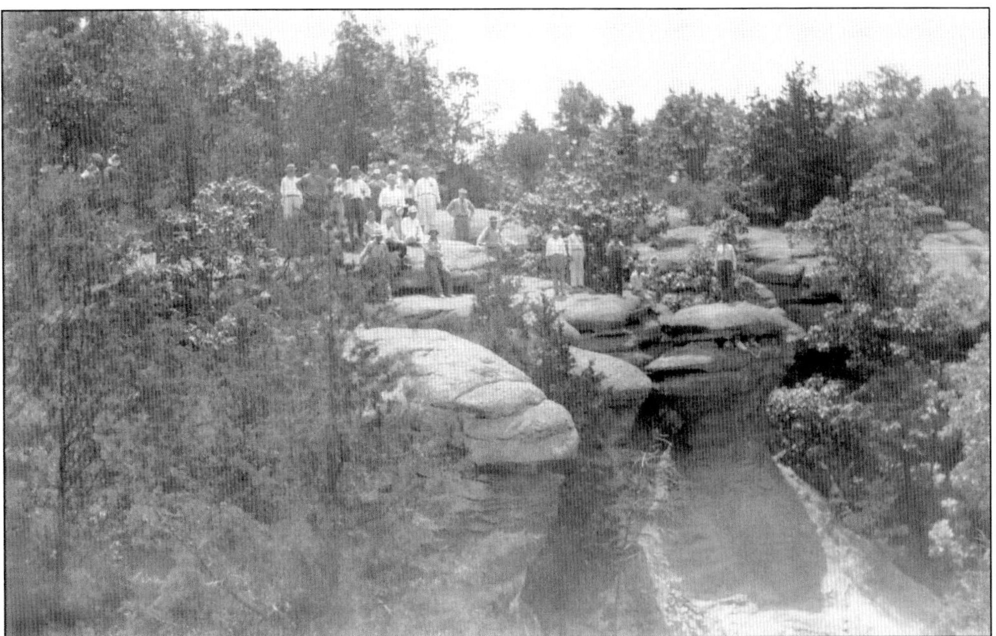

The 1934 Ozark Tour poses at the Garden of the Gods several years before the Shawnee National Forest made improvements at the site. Today, the wooden boardwalk of the observation trail is directly below the sandstone bluff on which the Ozarkers are standing. L.O. Trigg is standing at far right. On this tour, Dr. M.M. Leighton, chief of the Illinois Geological Survey, lectured on the geology of the area.

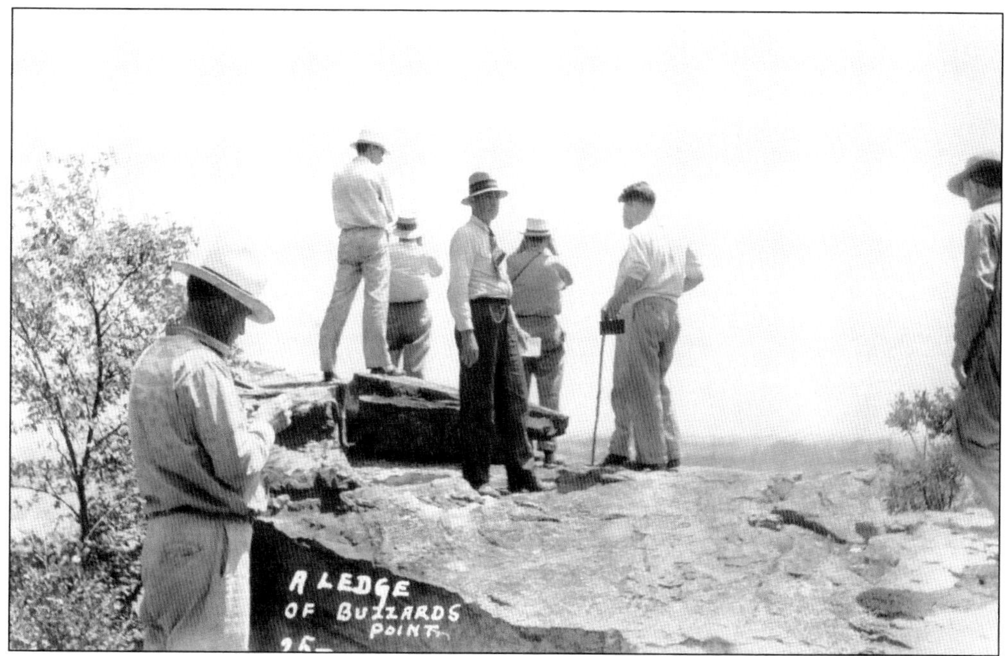

The 1931 Ozark Tour is pictured at Buzzard's Point in the southwest corner of Gallatin County. Hardin, Pope, and Johnson Counties can all be seen from this summit. L.O. Trigg also claimed that the rounded hills of Kentucky could be seen in the distance. Partain's Spring is located in the hollow below the bluff.

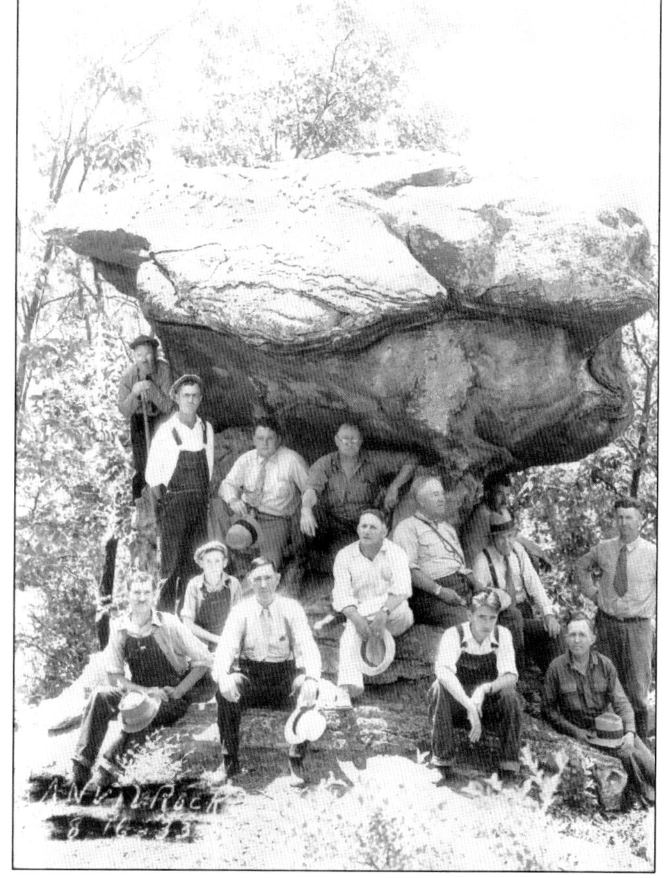

The 1933 Ozark Tour poses at Anvil Rock, which was described in Peck's *Gazetteer of Illinois* in 1837: "Devils Anvil is a singular rock, of considerable elevation, and the top jutting over its base, near the road from Equality to Golconda. The surrounding country is very hilly, with rocky precipices, and exhibiting all the desolation and wilderness of a mountainous region."

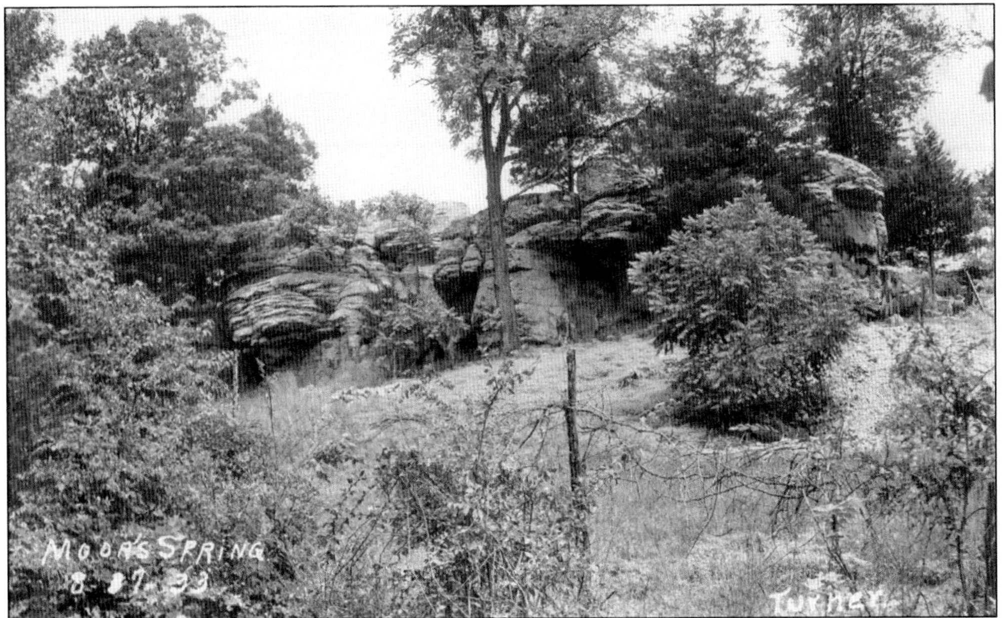

Moore's Spring, near Elizabethtown, was visited by the 1933 Ozark Tour. Iron ore (limonite) was mined on this farm to feed the Hardin County iron furnaces in the 19th century. Moore's Spring is located halfway between the Illinois Iron Furnace and Elizabethtown.

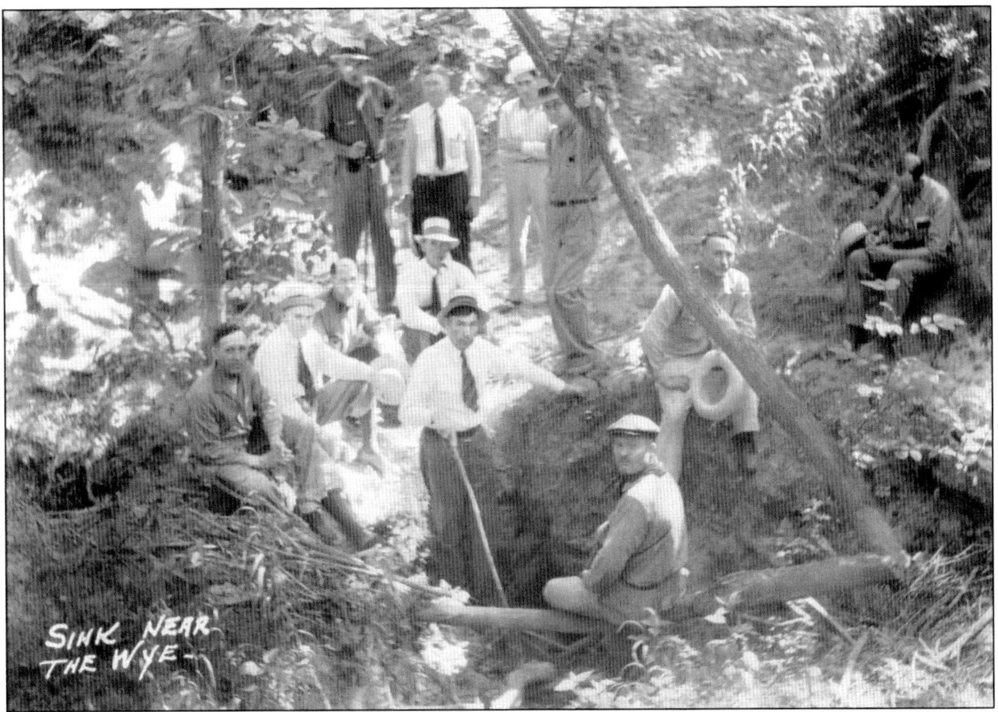

The 1931 Ozark Tour is shown examining a sinkhole near the intersection of Illinois State Routes 34 and 146 in Hardin County. The drainage in this area does not have an outlet to a stream or river; instead, the runoff drains underground through this sinkhole. An "underground river" flowing out of a hill to the east was believed to be the outlet for the sink.

The 1931 Ozark Tour explored the springs, crags, and natural beauty of Jackson Hollow near the Johnson and Pope County line. Ozarkers stand beneath Dripping Rock, a shelter bluff in the hollow, where a constant drip of water falls from the rock above even in dry weather.

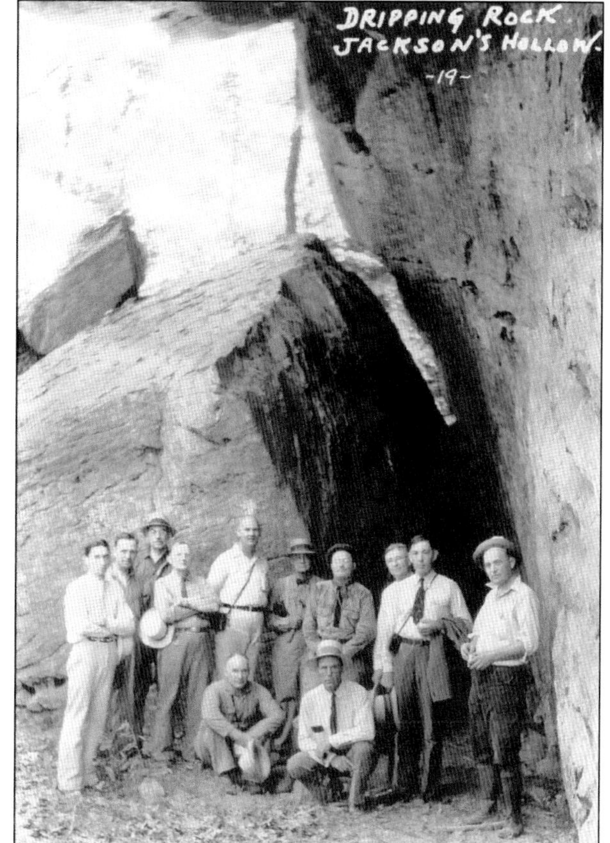

This photograph was taken during the 1931 Ozark Tour at Devil's Backbone in the canyons of Bell Smith Springs. The rock formation looks like a monstrous, jagged backbone poking out of the Hunting Branch stream near where it joins Bay Creek. In wet weather, this is one of several swimming holes in the four creeks that meander through the valley.

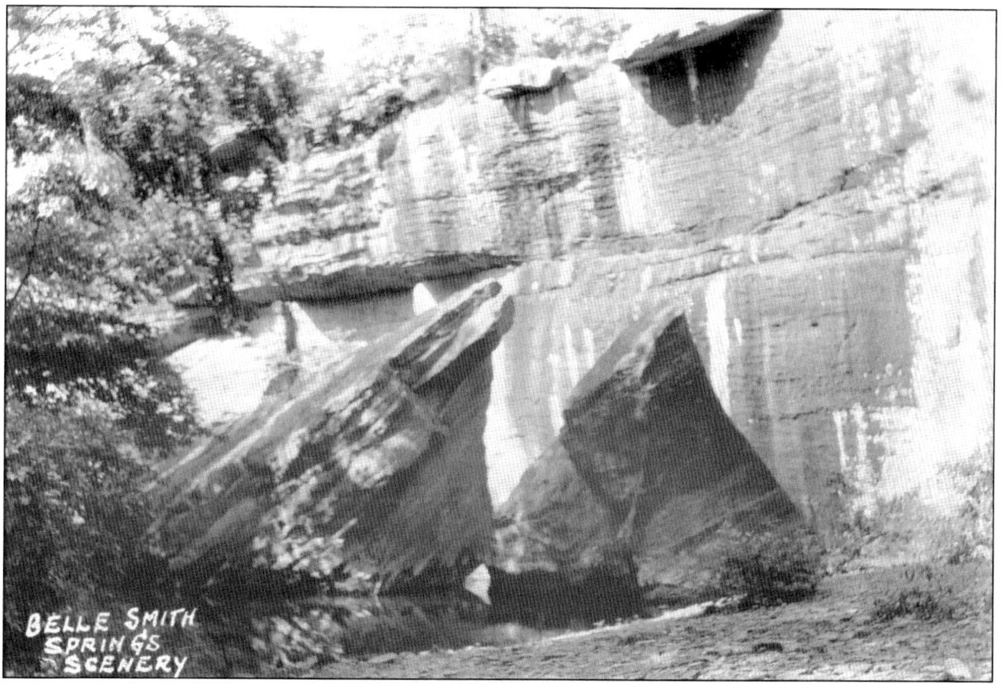

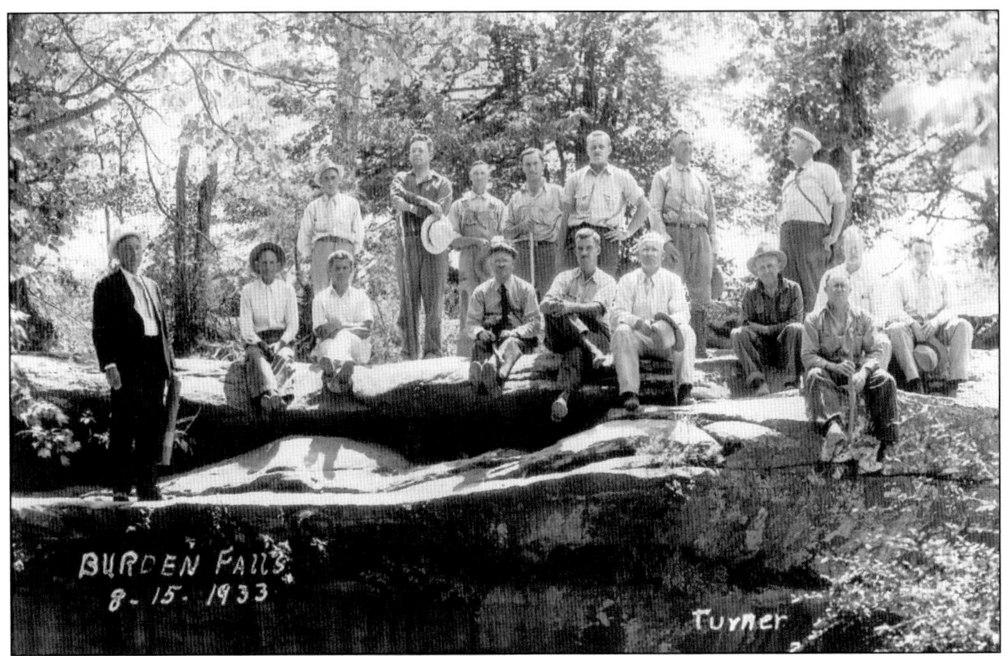

Ozarkers sit on the edge of the upper falls at Burden Falls, located just a few feet from a country road, on the 1933 Ozark Tour. In wet weather, a waterfall 35 feet high plunges over the lower lip of rock to the boulder-strewn canyon below. Burden Creek then continues to cascade several yards from the waterfall down a U-shaped canyon.

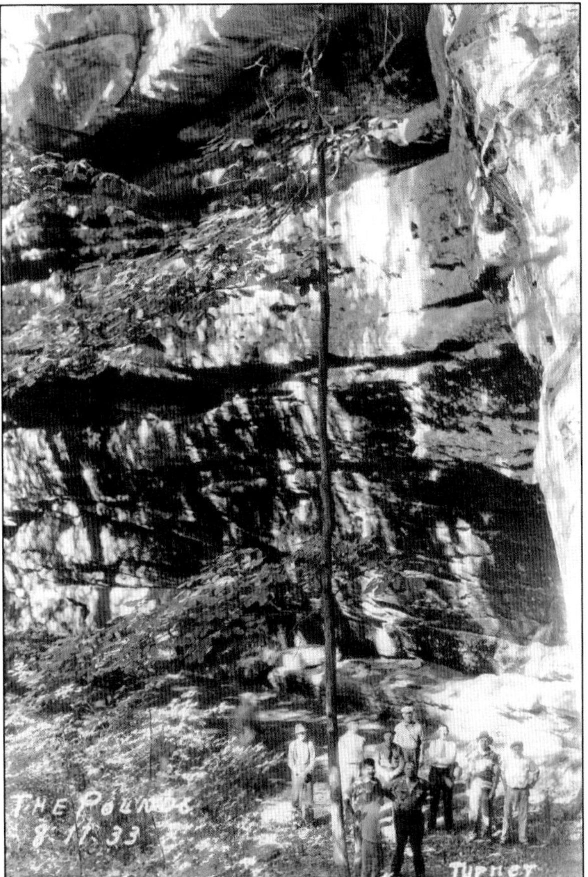

L.O. Trigg leads the 1933 Ozark Tour to the Ox-lot Cave, or "Pound," from which Pounds Hollow gets its name. Today, this is part of the Rim Rock National Recreation Trail. Following the bluff line east leads hikers to the Beaver Trail that connects the Rim Rock parking area and Pounds Hollow Lake. Following the bluff west leads to the "Fat-Man's Squeeze" and stairs to the trail on the upper bluff.

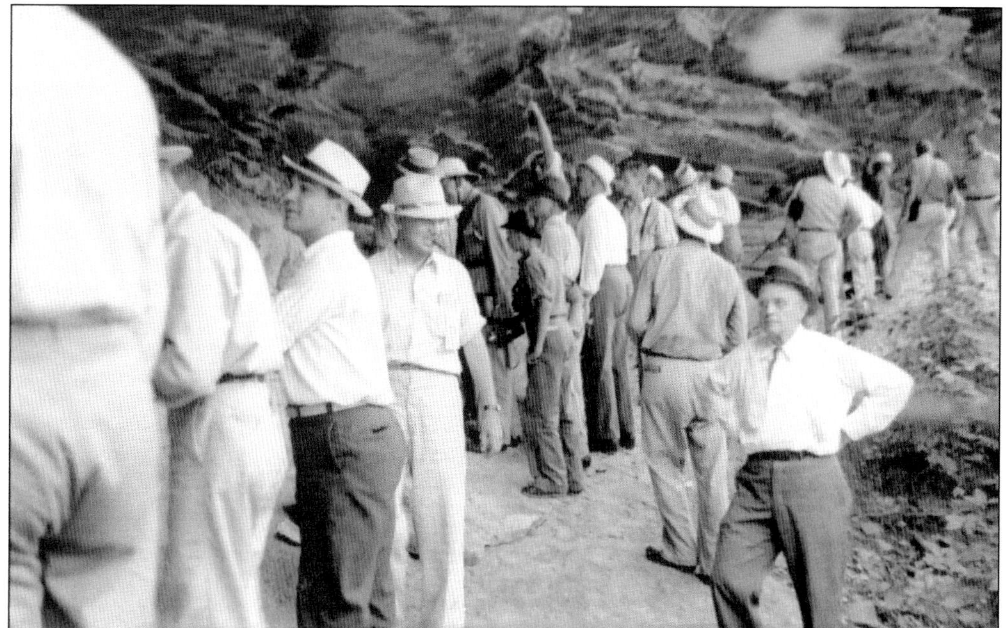

During the 1939 Ozark Tour, Ozarkers visited Alum Cave in Williamson County. L.O. Trigg reported that "Sheriff" Jacob Myers shared "ultra-scientific" information on alum with the Ozarkers. Nearby, a quarry with a rock crusher was installed to prepare road rock.

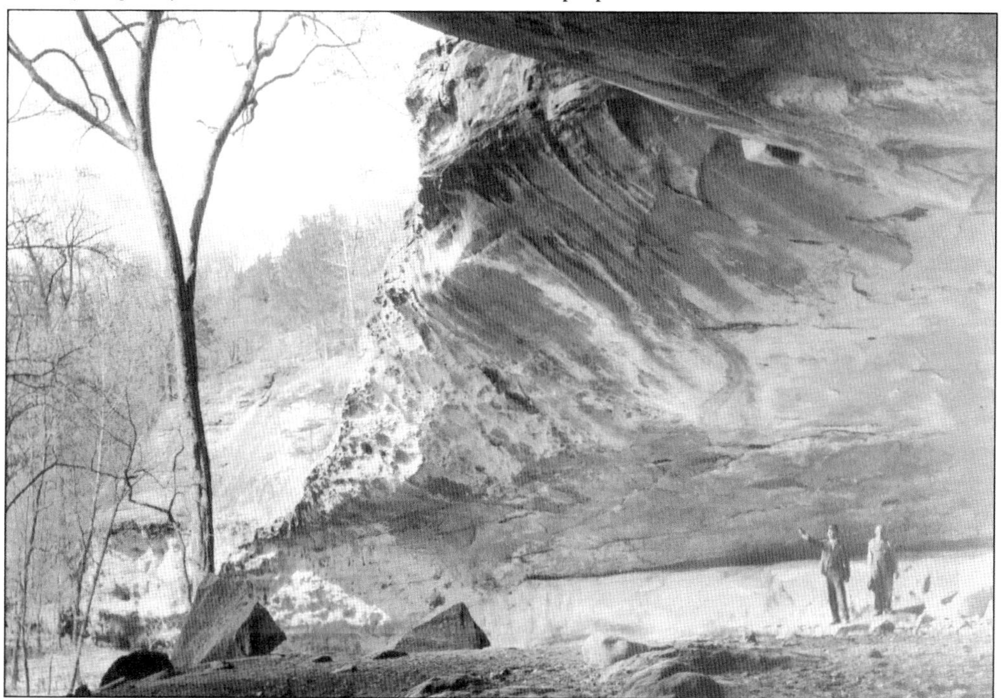

The 1939 Ozark Tour explores Grammer (or Saltpeter) Cave south of Murphysboro, Illinois, on the farm of the late J.W. Grammer. Ozarker Don L. Carroll, of the State Geological Survey, made "an enlightening talk explaining the quirks of nature that bring about such formations of sandstone." Today, this site is a venue for hosting outdoor events. (Kenneth Price.)

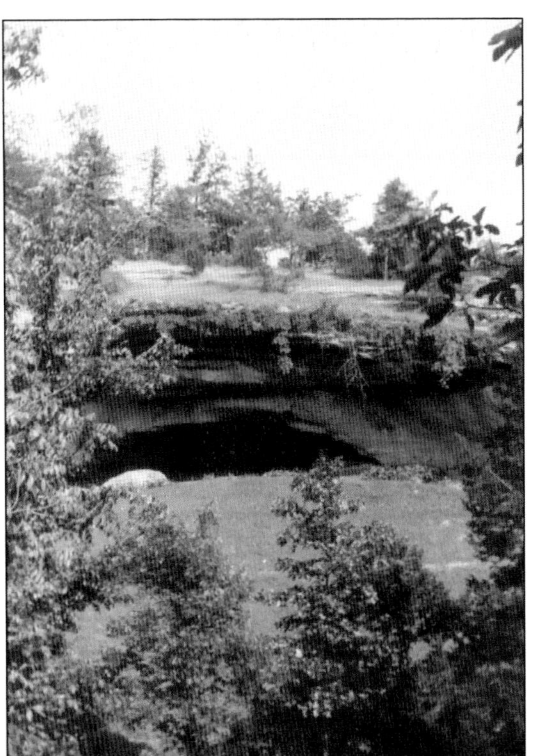

The 1942 Ozark Tour visited Sand Cave on the Miles Farm south of Goreville near Ferne Clyffe Park. After leaving Sand Cave, the Ozarkers visited the site of the Old Elvira Courthouse, which was built in 1814 as the first seat of government in Johnson County. (Kenneth Price.)

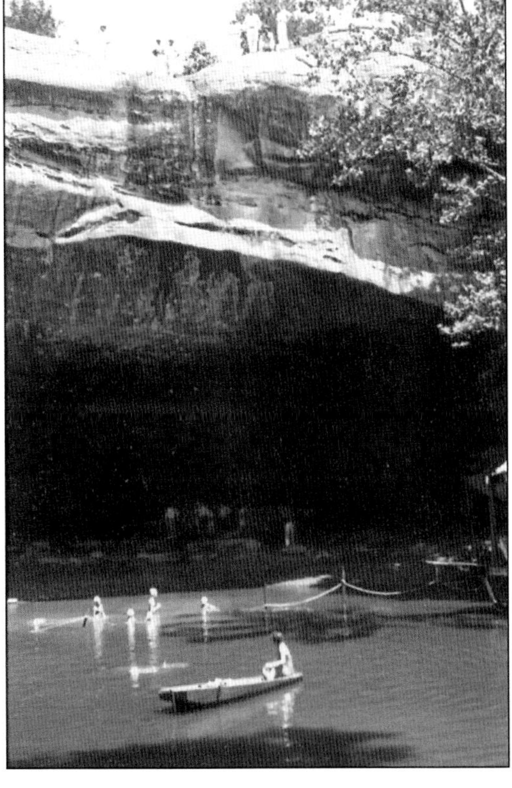

Near L.O. Trigg's birthplace in Ozark, Illinois, the 1936 Ozark Tour visited the Boy Scout Camp Pakentuck to view "Little Niagara" Falls, also called Lay Falls. The Scout camp used the pool below the falls as a swimming hole. This is now Camp Ondessonk, and the waterfall, now known as Pakentuck Falls or Cedar Falls, is reported to be the tallest waterfall in Illinois.

Three

Historic and Man-Made Wonders

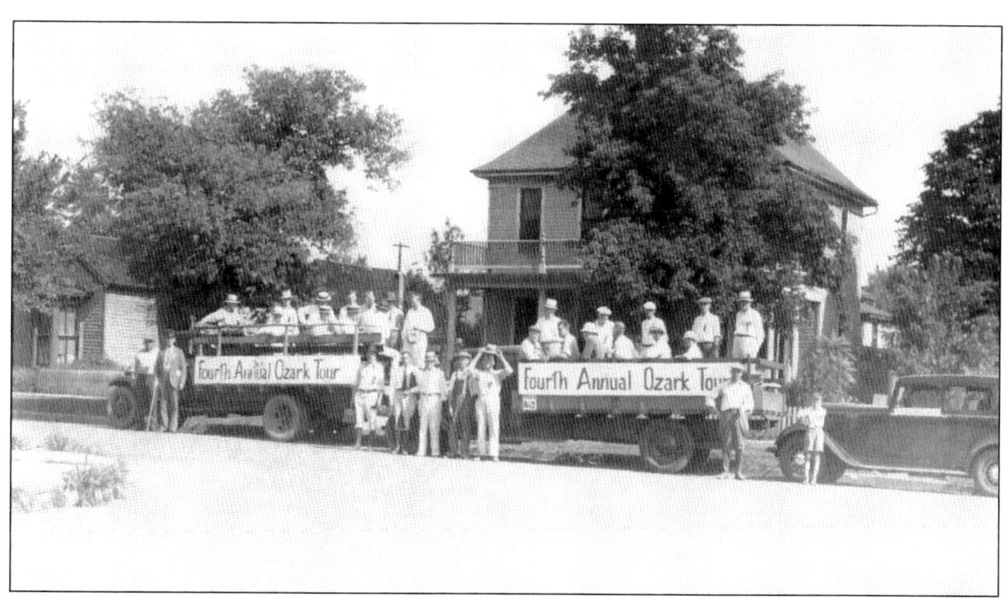

The 1934 Ozark Tour is ready to leave from the Horning Hotel in Harrisburg. That year, 33 Ozarkers registered for the tour. Highlights included fishing and exploring Golconda; Illinois Iron Furnace; the Anvil Rock area; Cave-in-Rock; and, for the second year, a cruise on the Ohio River. On the first day, lunch was served at the new Eddyville CCC camp.

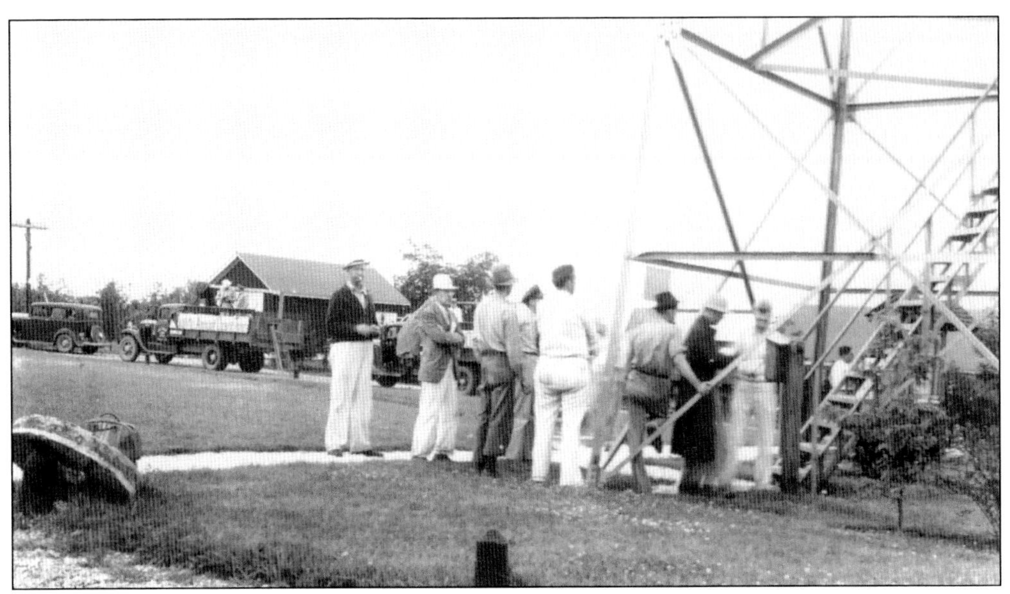

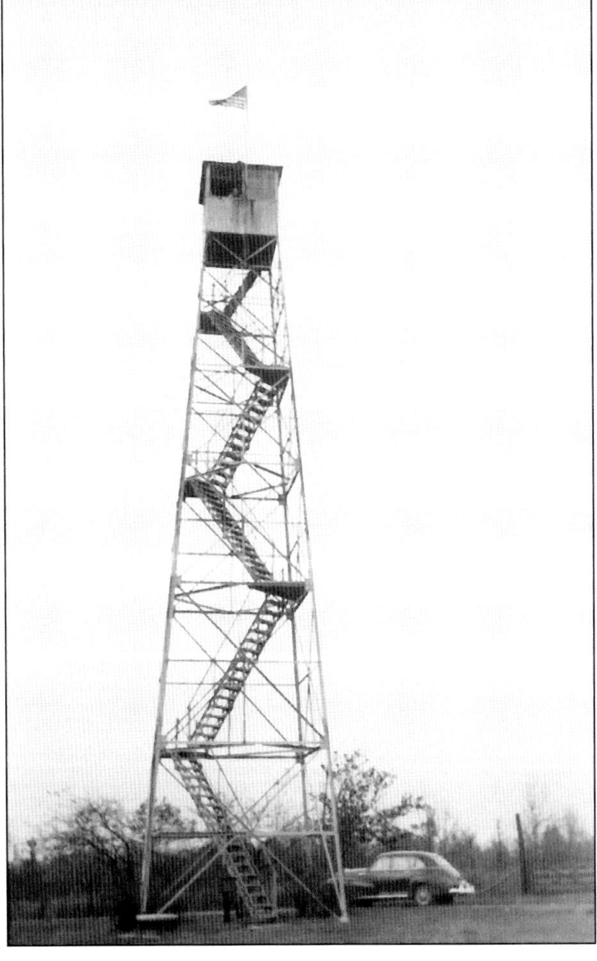

The Ozarkers sign in at the 60-foot steel lookout tower on Williams Hill, near Herod, on the 1938 Ozark Tour. At an elevation of 1,064 feet, Williams Hill is the highest point in southern Illinois and the second-highest point in the entire state. The CCC built the tower and later built tables and grills so that visitors could picnic at the tower site. (Above, Jeff Robinson.)

The historical marker at right was erected in 1935 for the Great Salt Spring. The marker contained racially insensitive language and is no longer on display. Below, L.O. Trigg stirs a salt well near Equality. Native Americans used clay pottery and earthenware to evaporate the salt water, while early pioneers used iron pots and kettles. As fuel near the salt wells became scarce, wooden pipes were constructed to transport the brine closer to sources of wood. The salt industry was an early contributing factor to the deforestation of southeastern Illinois. (Right, Kenneth Price.)

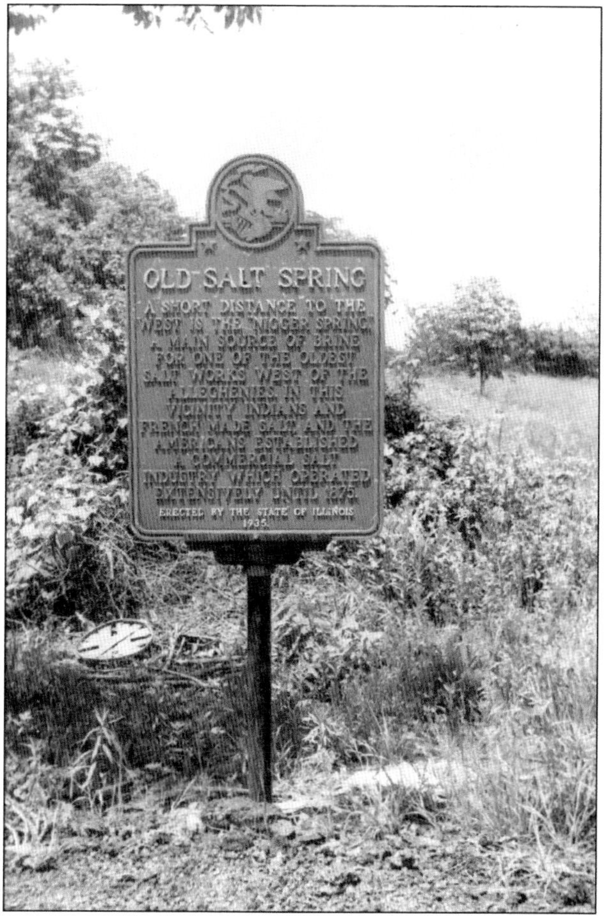

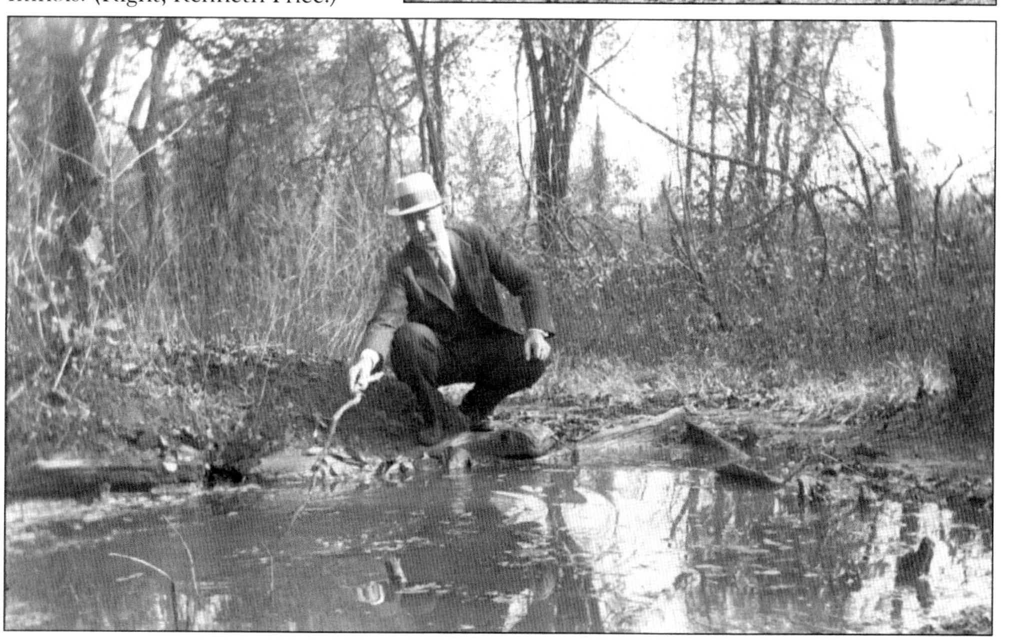

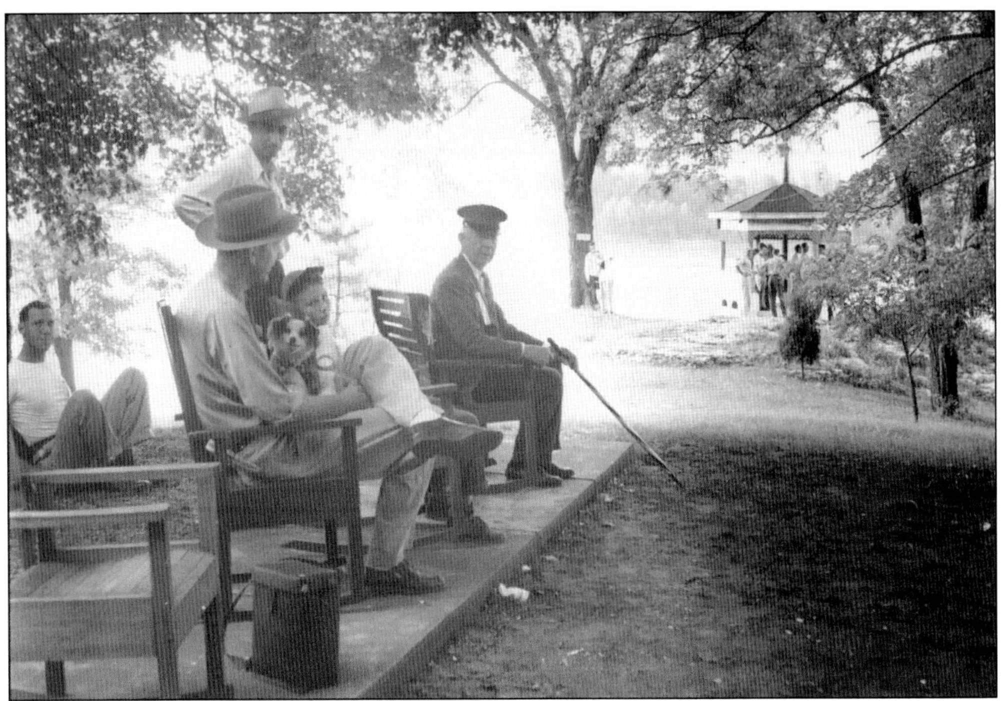

Pictured above are the 1947 Ozarkers stopped at the Rose Hotel in Elizabethtown for breakfast. It is believed that the founder of Elizabethtown built the hotel's original structure as the McFarlan Tavern in 1812. An addition in 1848 expanded the first and second stories on the front of the hotel. A second extension added a dining area and more lodging to the second story on the back side of the hotel in 1865. The "Summer House" on the bluff, constructed in 1882, was the final addition to the property. Below, the 1933 Ozark Tour poses around the Summer House before boarding the mailboat *Katheryne* for a cruise to Cave-in-Rock. In 1916, Rose Hotel owner Sarah Rose sued the Village of Elizabethtown to maintain control of the Summer House after the village tried to assume control of the Summer House and bluff when Rose attempted to repair damage from the 1913 flood; the court found in Rose's favor. (Above, Kenneth Price.)

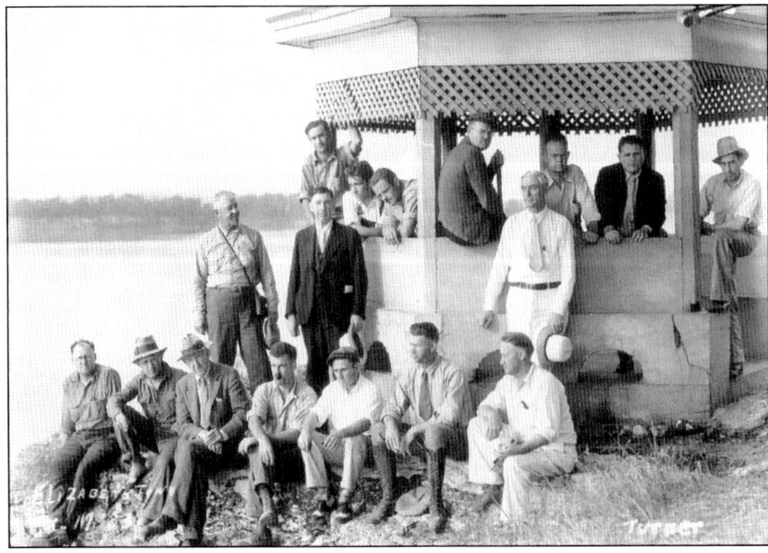

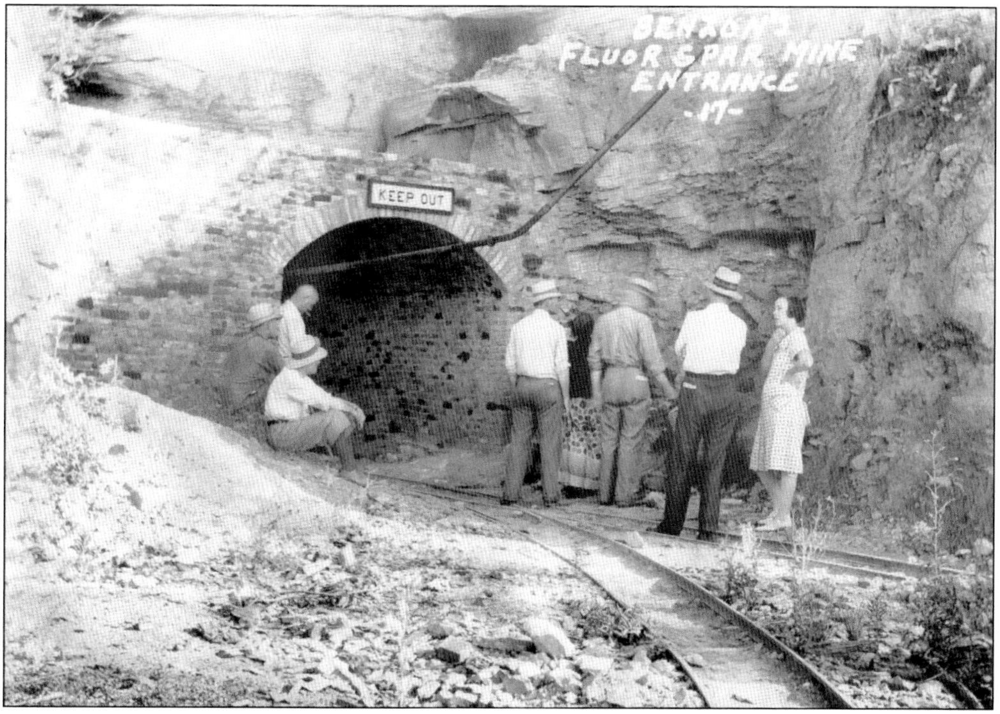

The 1931 Ozark Tour visited the Benzon Mining Company's fluorspar mine located at Spar Mountain between Elizabethtown and Cave-in-Rock. The Benzon mine was unique in that the fluorspar was in a horizontal vein instead of the usual vertical pockets. When the mine sold a few years prior to the tour, a 26-year-old mule named Red was included in the sale; it had been with the mine since its opening. The Benzon Mining Company was a British company.

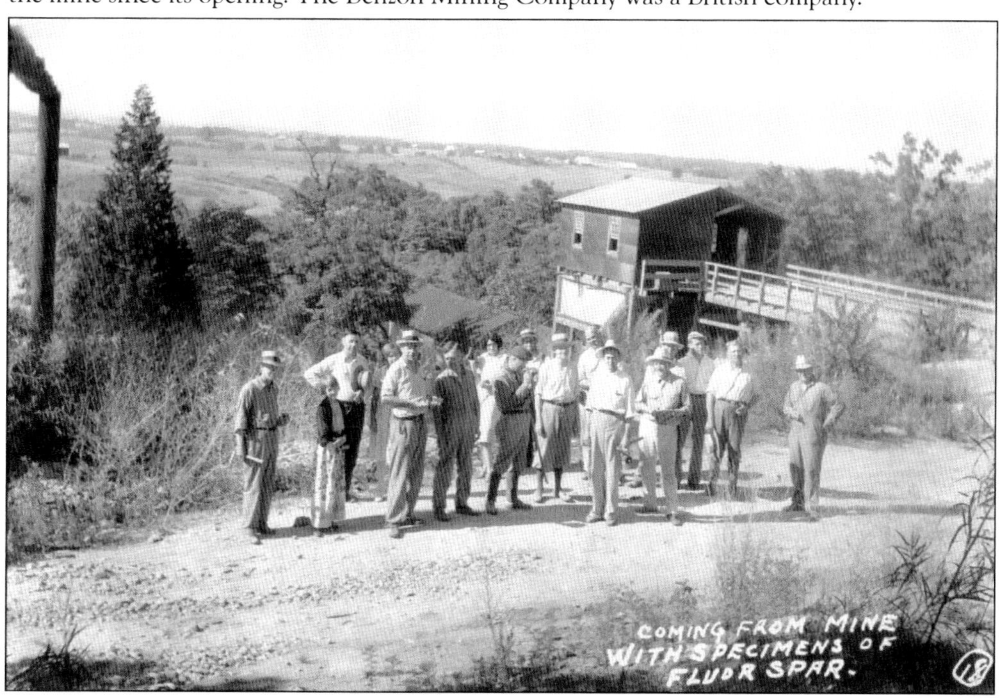

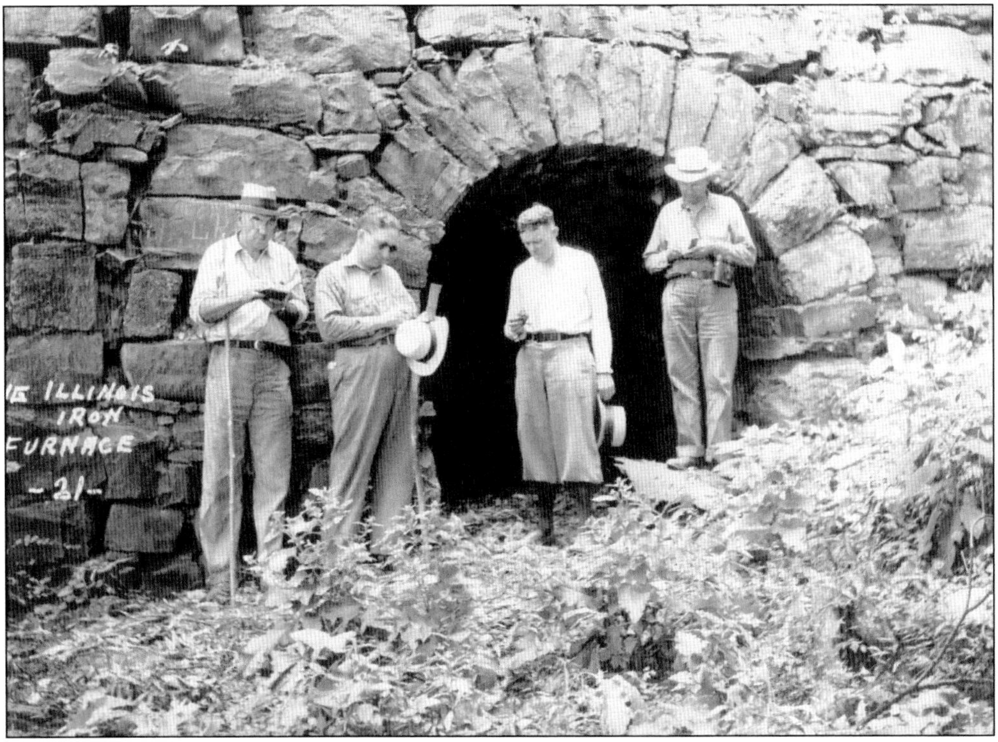

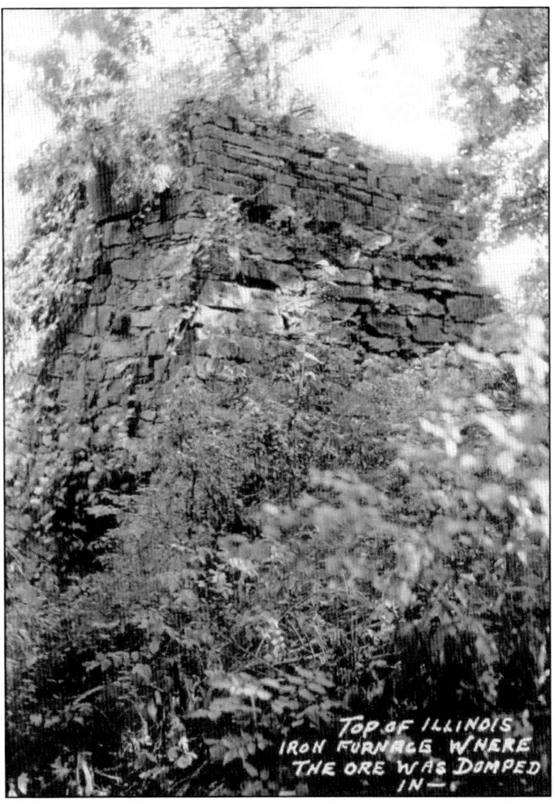

The 1931 Ozark Tour examined the remains of the Illinois Iron Furnace near Elizabethtown. The furnace was built in 1837 by investors from the saltworks in Gallatin County. Pig iron was produced at the site prior to the Civil War, and a community formed around the furnace. Iron production resumed after the Civil War and continued until the early 1880s, when richer deposits elsewhere made competition difficult. Iron ore (in the form of limonite), charcoal, and limestone were loaded at the top of the furnace by way of a bridge from an adjacent hill. After 12 hours of smelting, the furnace was tapped at the lower chamber, and molten iron was allowed to run into channels cut in sand to form the iron pigs. High demand for charcoal to feed the ironworks's furnace helped contribute to the early deforestation of southeastern Illinois.

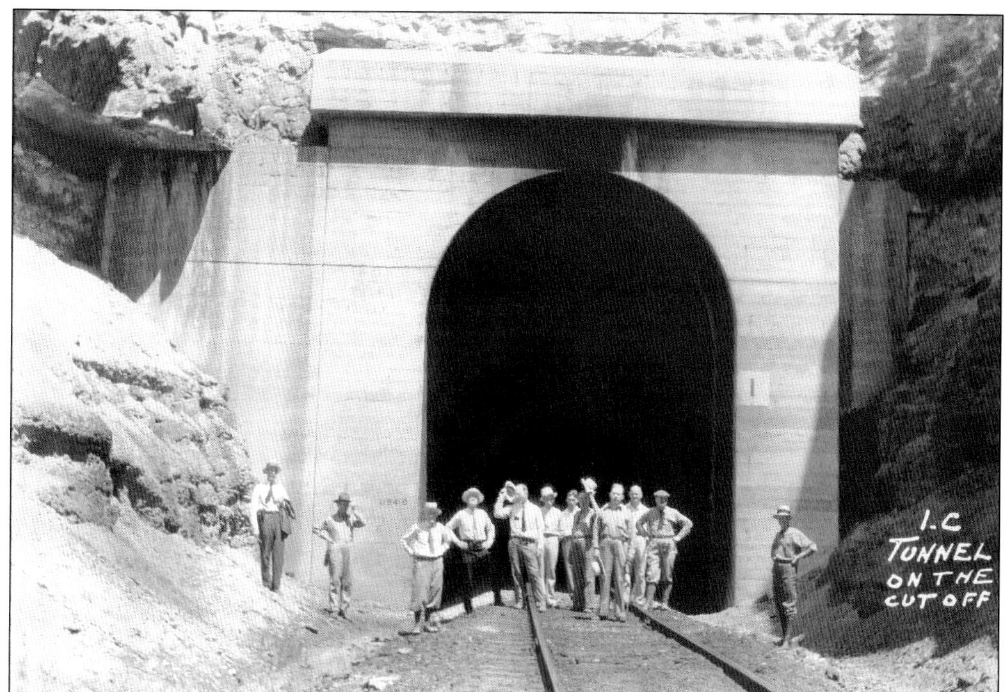

The 1931 Ozark Tour stands at the mouth of Tunnel One on the Edgewood Cutoff of the Illinois Central Railroad. This was the northernmost tunnel and, at 803 feet in length, the shortest of the three tunnels on the cutoff. This tunnel was near the Sidney Sheldon farm in rural Pope County.

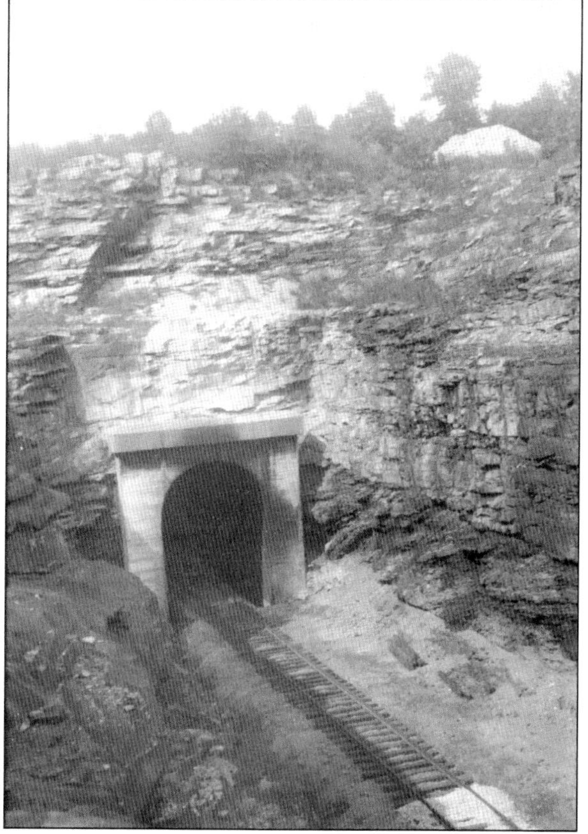

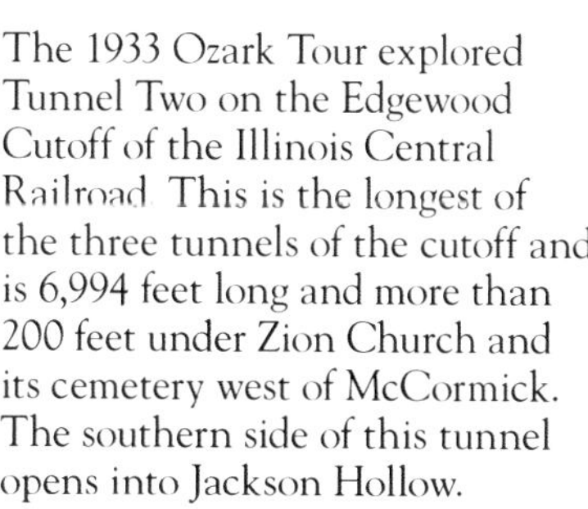

The 1933 Ozark Tour explored Tunnel Two on the Edgewood Cutoff of the Illinois Central Railroad. This is the longest of the three tunnels of the cutoff and is 6,994 feet long and more than 200 feet under Zion Church and its cemetery west of McCormick. The southern side of this tunnel opens into Jackson Hollow.

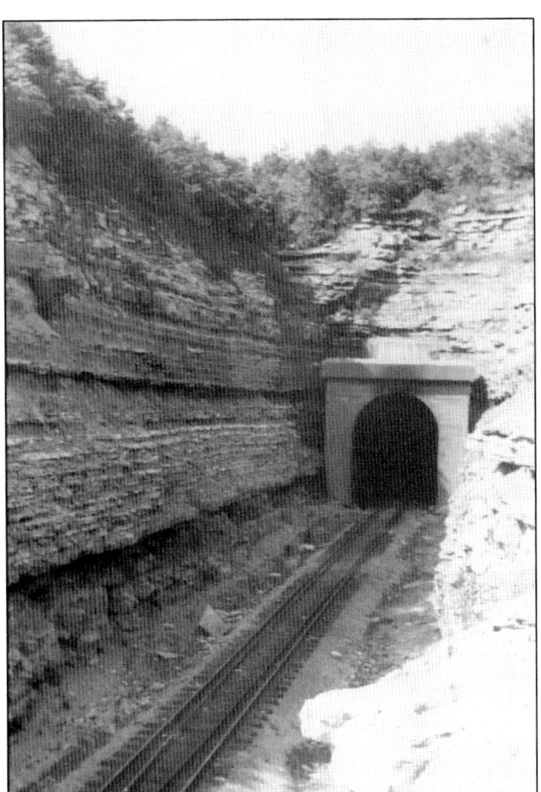

The 1940 Ozark Tour explored Tunnel Three on the Edgewood Cutoff of the Illinois Central Railroad. This southernmost tunnel of the cutoff is 2,623 feet long. The Edgewood Cutoff was built in the 1920s to ease congestion on the main rail line bridge at Cairo, Illinois. The Edgewood Cutoff crosses the Ohio River at Metropolis.

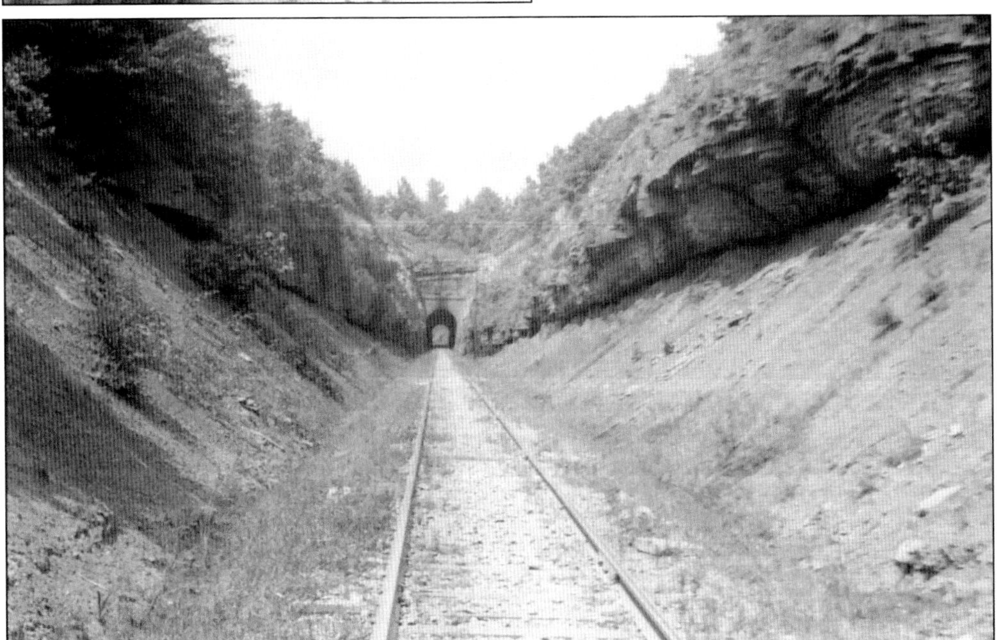

The 1942 Ozark Tour visited the south entrance of Tunnel Hill on the Big Four Railroad at Tunnel Hill. This tunnel is now part of the 45-mile Tunnel Hill Bike Trail from Karnak to Harrisburg, Illinois. At one time, the tunnel was over 800 feet long, but a section of the roof collapsed in 1929, shortening it to 543 feet.

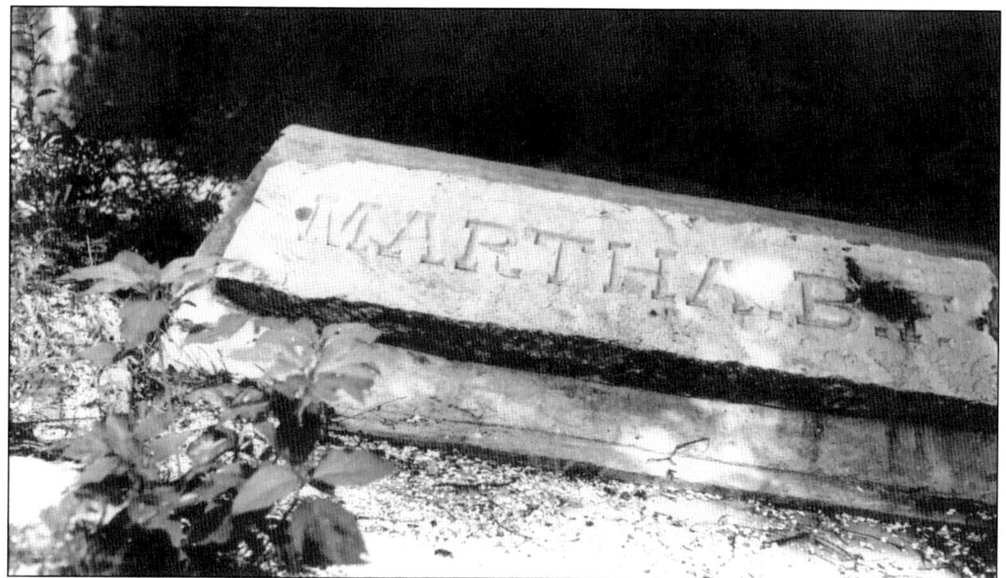

The Martha Blast Furnace operated for about a decade in the mid-19th century. While the output of the nearby Illinois Furnace was nine tons of iron when in full blast, the Martha Furnace produced seven tons. This stone was recovered by the Hicks Camp CCC while crews were doing roadwork in the 1930s. The stone marks the original furnace's location and was believed to have been part of its structure. (Jeff Robinson.)

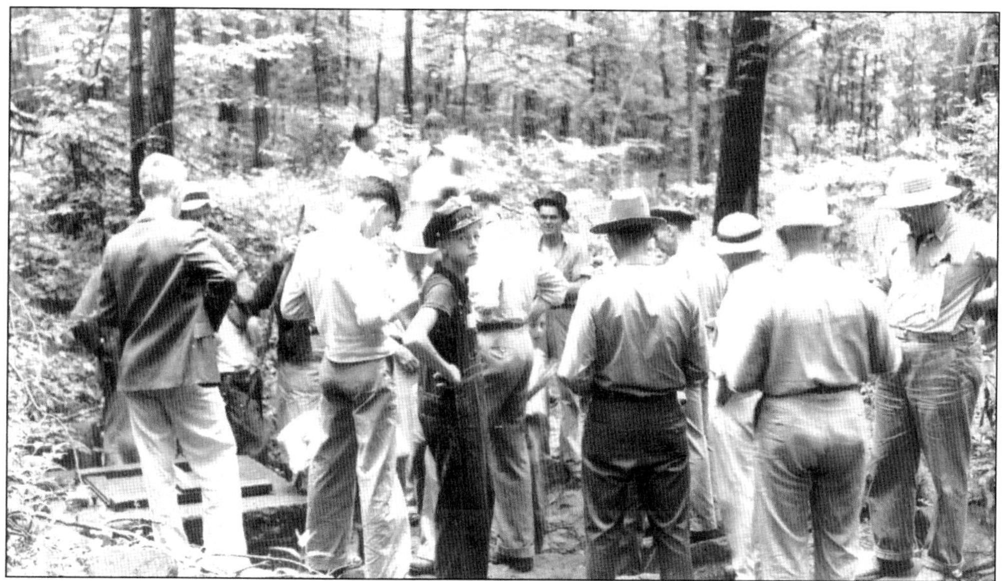

The 1938 Ozark Tour views studies underway at the US Central States Forestry Experiment Station and Plantation in Hardin County. The site was established as the Kaskaskia Experimental Forest in 1942. This forest is the location of one of the few remaining tracts of virgin forest in southern Illinois. (Jeff Robinson.)

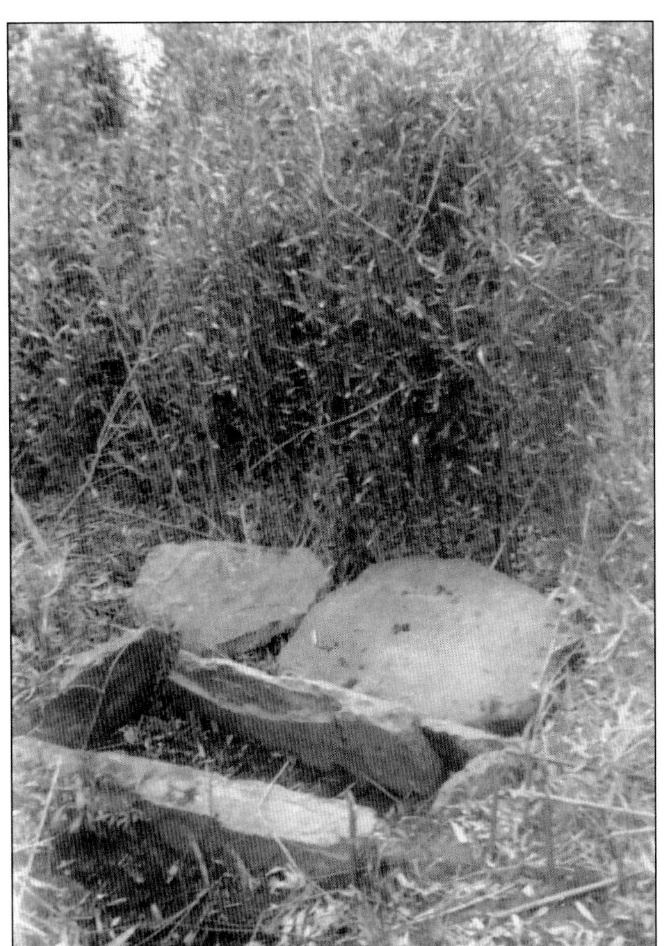

The Ozarkers viewed this Native American stone grave near Rattlesnake Ferry in Jackson County. (Kenneth Price.)

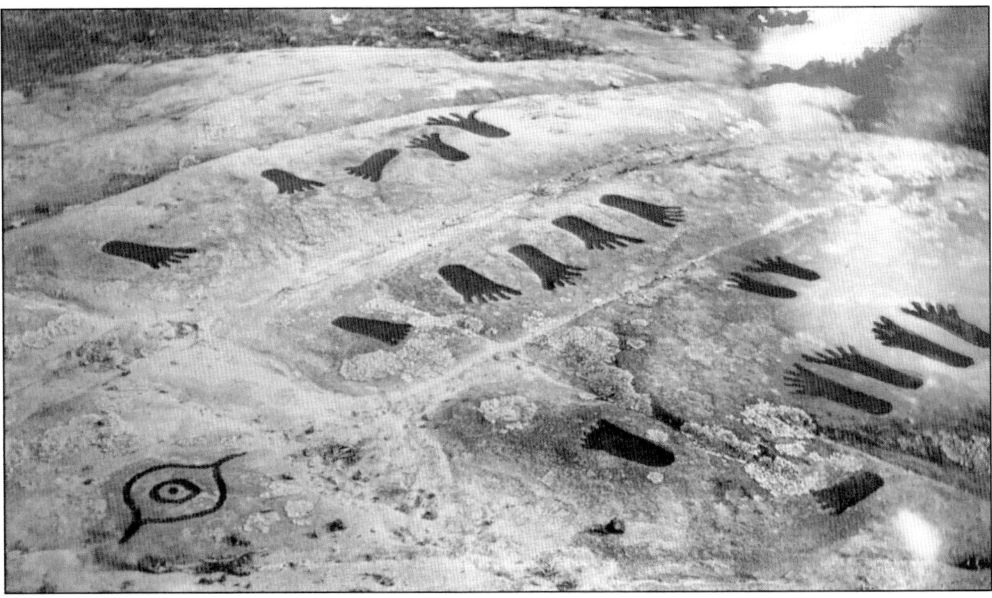

The 1936 Ozark Tour visited "footprint rocks," Native American petroglyphs on the Sherman Evans farm in Johnson County. The Ozarkers were retracing part of George Rogers Clark's 1778 march from Fort Massac to Kaskaskia to take the Illinois Territory from the British. (Kenneth Price.)

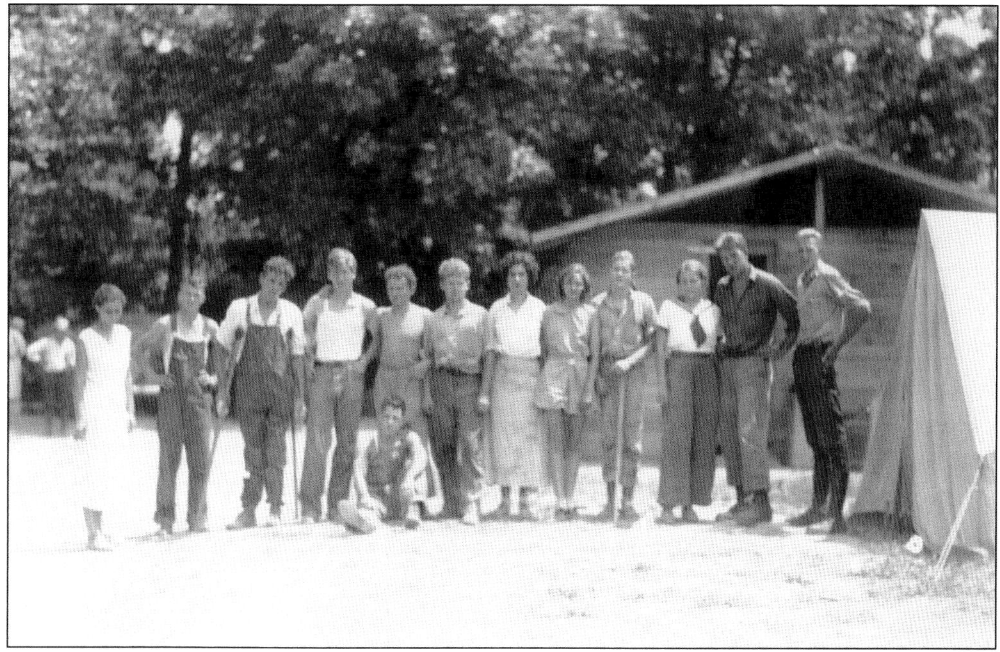

The 1934 Ozark Tour visited the students and faculty at the College in the Hills in Hardin County. College in the Hills was started by graduates of the University of Chicago and Northwestern University and held classes from 1934 to 1936. Their hope was to bring higher education to youth who could otherwise not afford it by allowing students to pay for part of their tuition through working for the college.

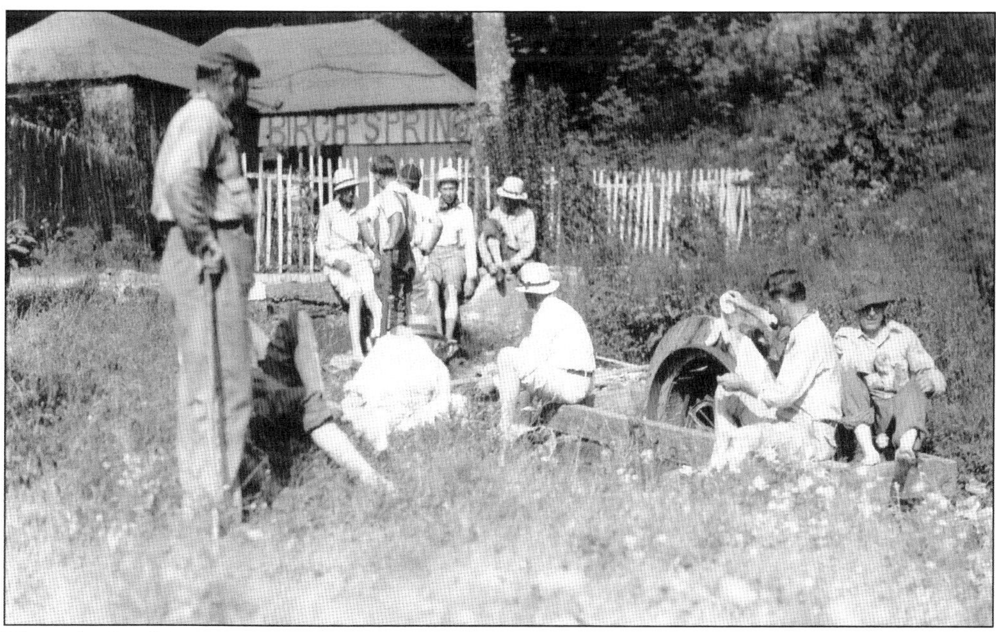

The 1934 Ozark Tour participates in a foot-washing at Birch's Spring, also known as Decker Springs, in rural Hardin County. The stone marker for the Martha Furnace is located nearby. The Ozarkers visited the spring on the first Ozark Tour in 1931 for "mountain dew" (probably moonshine).

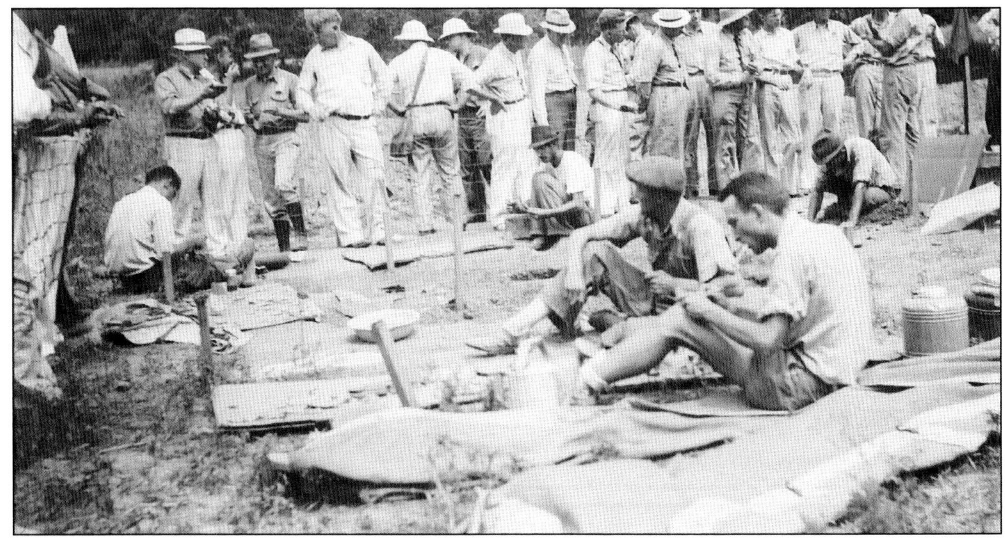

At the Kincaid Mounds near Brookport, the 1936 Ozark Tour examines archeological digs conducted by scientists from the University of Chicago. The university held active digs at this site from 1934 through 1944. More recently, the site was studied by researchers at Southern Illinois University. At least 19 large mounds and several smaller platforms and walls have been found at the site, which was occupied from approximately AD 1050 to AD 1400.

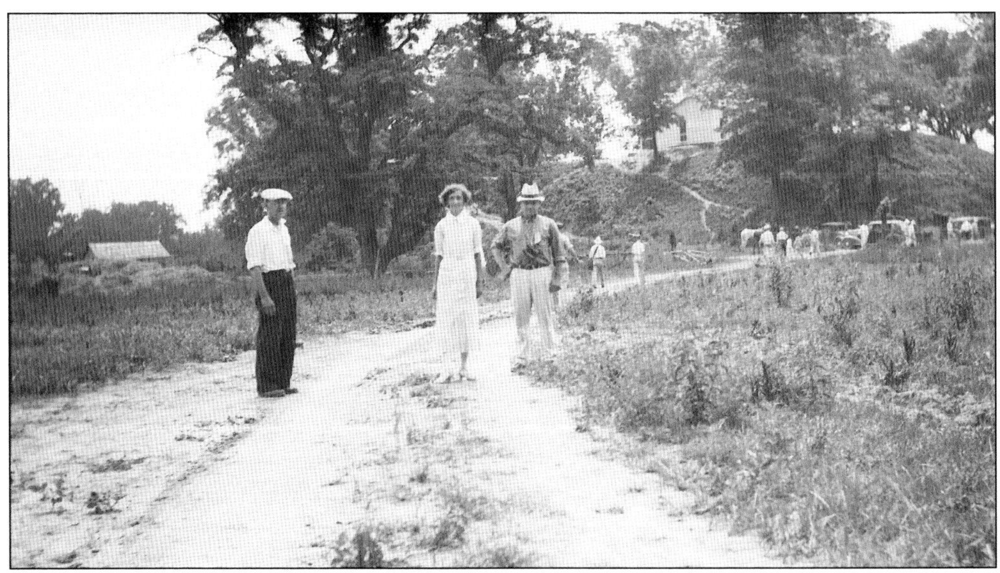

In this photograph taken when the 1936 Ozark Tour stopped at Kincaid Mounds, the woman pictured at center is Julia Kincaid, whose family owned the property for many years. At the previous night's program in Metropolis, Illinois, Kincaid shared her family's private collection of Native American artifacts from the site. Note the modern house built on the 30-foot-tall American Indian mound in the background.

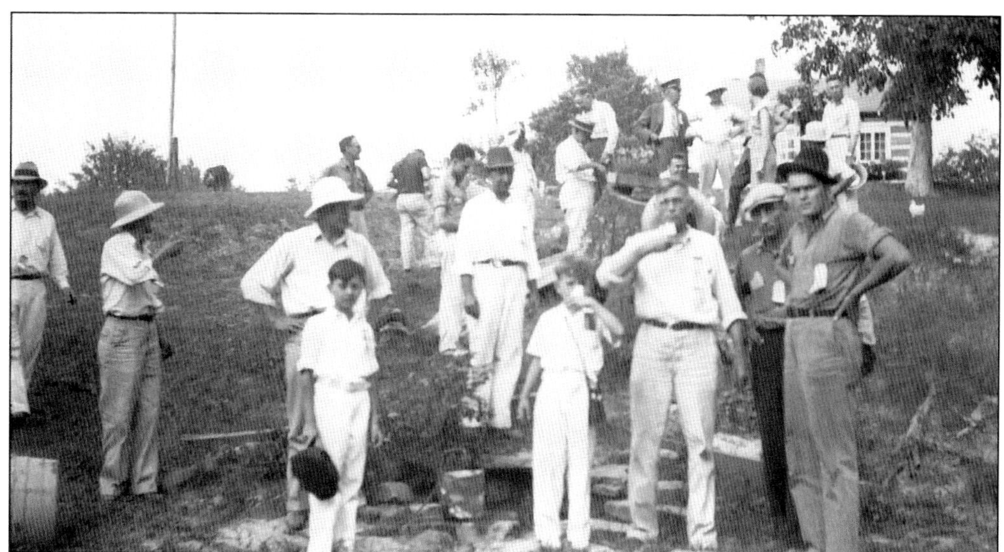

Members of the 1936 Ozark Tour drink from Nutty Spring, located 12 miles north of Metropolis, Illinois. L.O. Trigg stated that this is where George Rogers Clark's expedition stopped to fill their canteens on the first day of their march from Fort Massac to Kaskaskia to take the Illinois Territory from the British during the Revolutionary War.

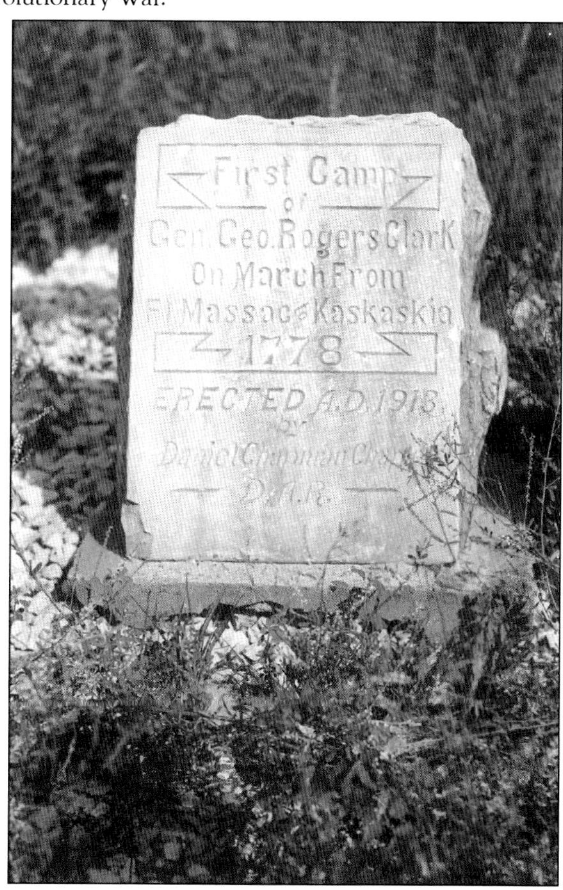

The 1936 Ozark Tour stopped at the Daughters of the American Revolution marker showing the location of the first night's camp of George Rogers Clark's 1778 expedition to take the Illinois Territory from the British. The marker was located south of Vienna, Illinois, near Forman, between the country road and the Chicago, Burlington & Quincy Railroad tracks.

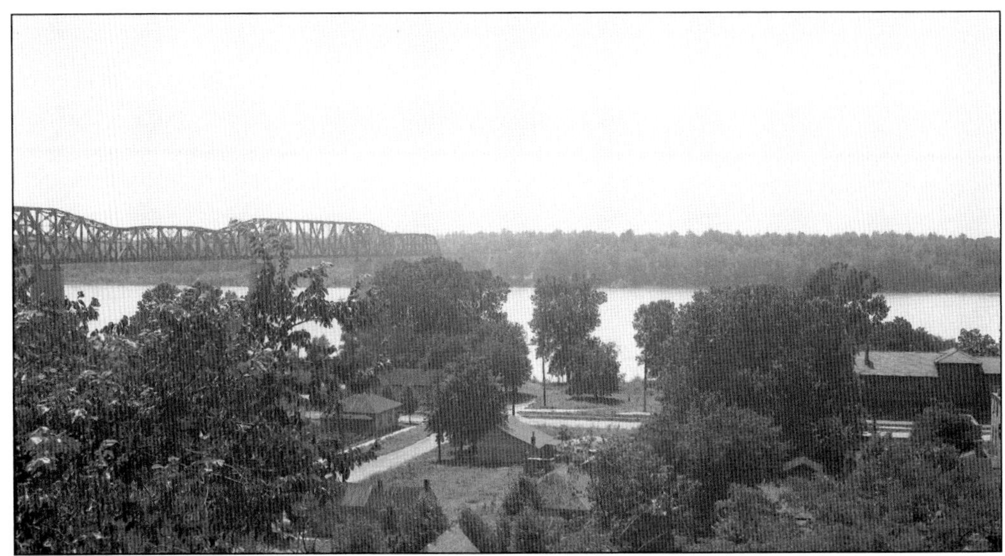

This is a view Ozarkers had of downtown Thebes and the Mississippi River on the 1937 Ozark Tour. At left is the Thebes railroad bridge, built in 1905, which connects Illinois and Missouri. Thebes was founded as "Sparhawk's Landing" in the early 1800s by the Sparhawk brothers, who were traveling up the Mississippi River from New Orleans looking for a port to use for trade.

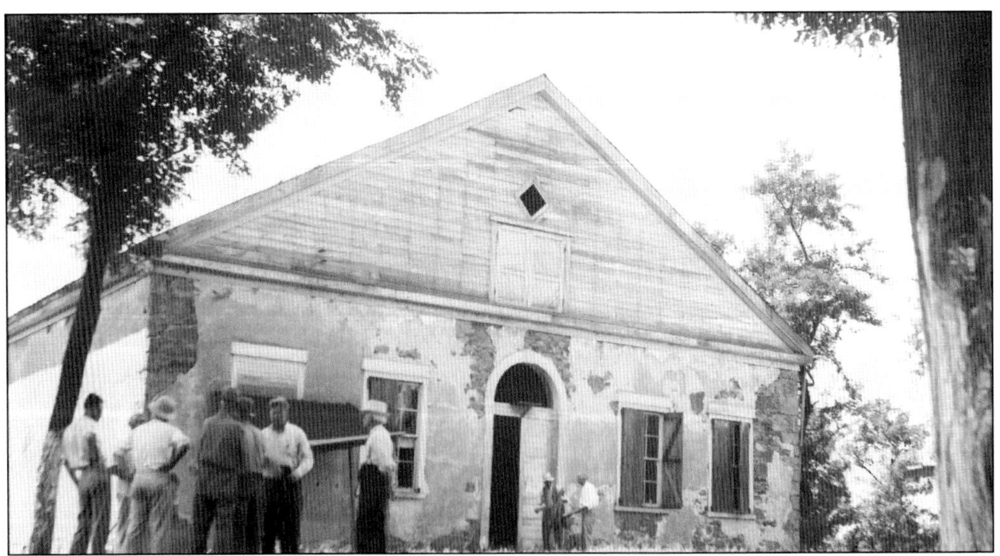

The 1937 Ozark Tour explores the Thebes Courthouse, which served as the seat of Alexander County from 1846 to 1859. The courthouse was built in 1848 at a cost of $4,400. Supposedly, both Abraham Lincoln and Stephen Douglas visited the courthouse—Lincoln appeared there between 1854 and 1858, when he was a frontier lawyer, and a rally was held there for Douglas in 1858. Civil War hero Gen. John A. Logan argued cases here in the years before the war.

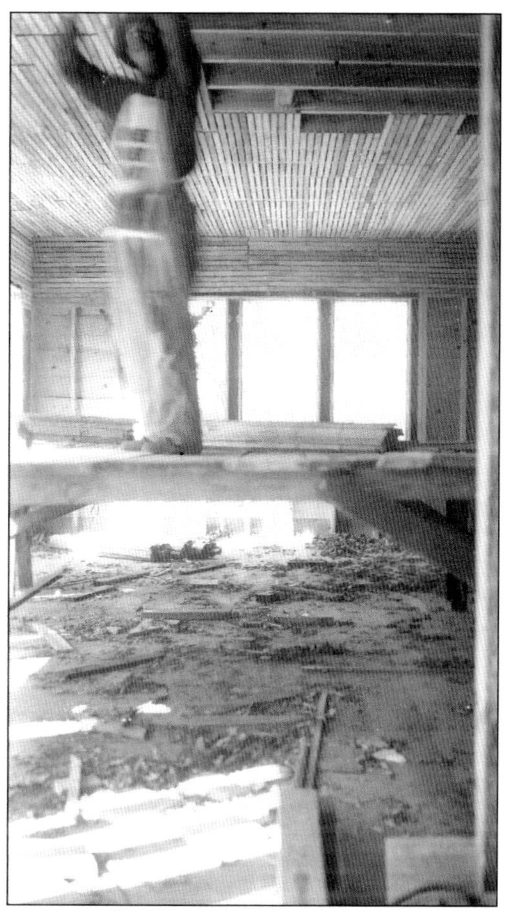

Ozarkers viewed ongoing renovation work at the courthouse at Thebes during the 1937 Ozark Tour. When voters moved the county seat from Thebes to Cairo in 1859, the courthouse was remodeled and used as a Baptist church. At various times over the years, it was used as a boardinghouse, school, library, public hall, and polling place. L.O. Trigg reported that when the tour visited in 1937, the building had recently been used as a refuge for flood victims. The courthouse was built in 1848, with local materials extensively used in the construction. The sandstone walls and foundation were acquired locally. Trees in the area were felled, hand-hewn, and whipsawed for the walls and roof. Even the mortar and plaster stucco were manufactured locally.

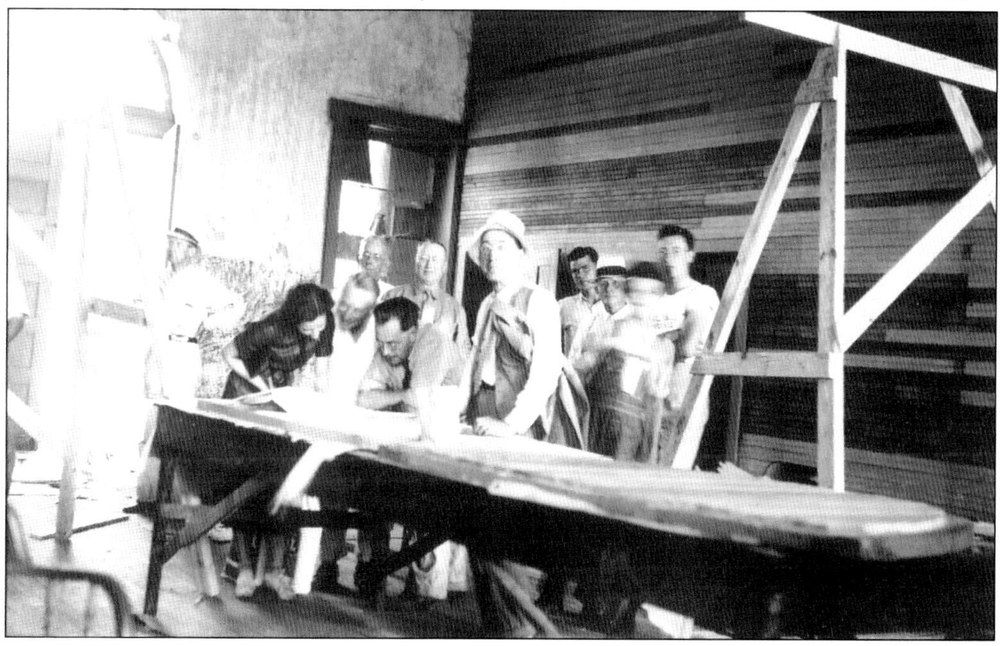

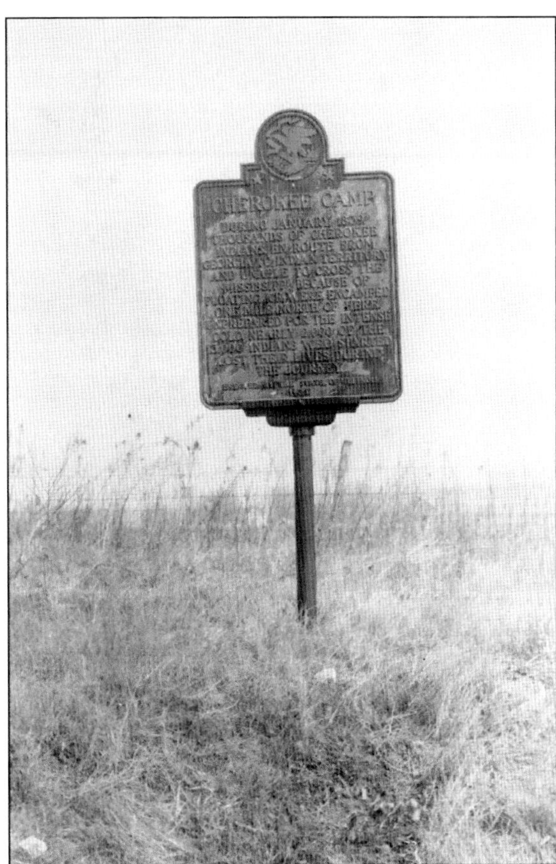

Southern Illinois was a crossing on the Northern Route of the federal Trail of Tears campaigns that forced thousands of Cherokee Indians to relocate from their homelands to areas west of the Mississippi. This historical marker notes that ice prevented the crossing of the Mississippi River in 1839, forcing the Native Americans to camp near the river, where they were unprepared for the extreme cold. The Trail of Tears entered Illinois at Golconda on the Ohio River. (Kenneth Price.)

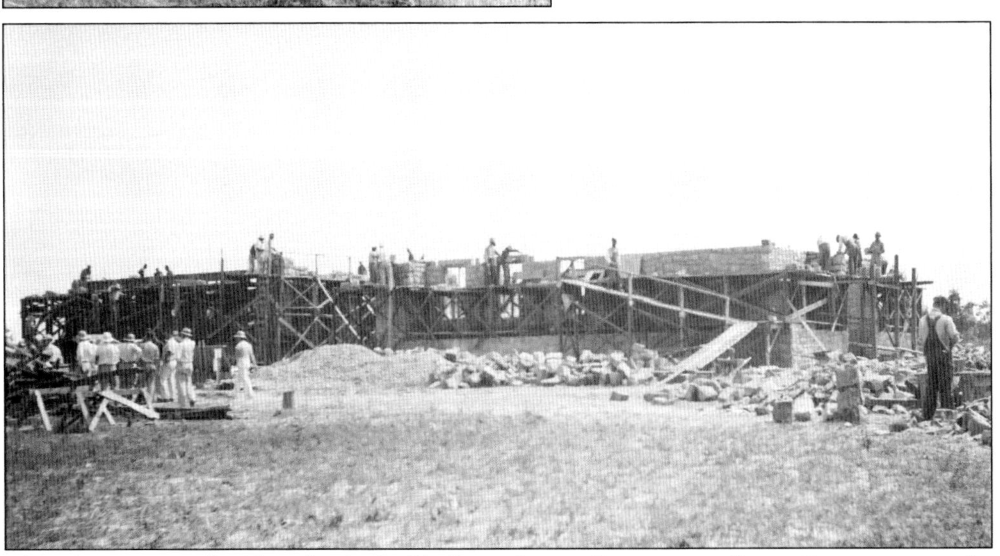

The administrative building for the Robbs Resettlement Project near Dixon Springs was under construction when the 1936 Ozark Tour visited. The Ozarkers learned about ongoing research on the best grasses to grow in southern Illinois, and the construction included barns for cattle, horses, and sheep. Today, this is the Dixon Springs Agricultural Center, which includes about 5,100 acres.

The 1936 Ozark Tour visited the carved inscription in the rock near Eddyville that gives Bell Smith Springs its name. The inscription reads "Bell Smith 1890" and is near the cleft in the rock where the namesake spring is located. Bell Smith was the name of an early settler in the area.

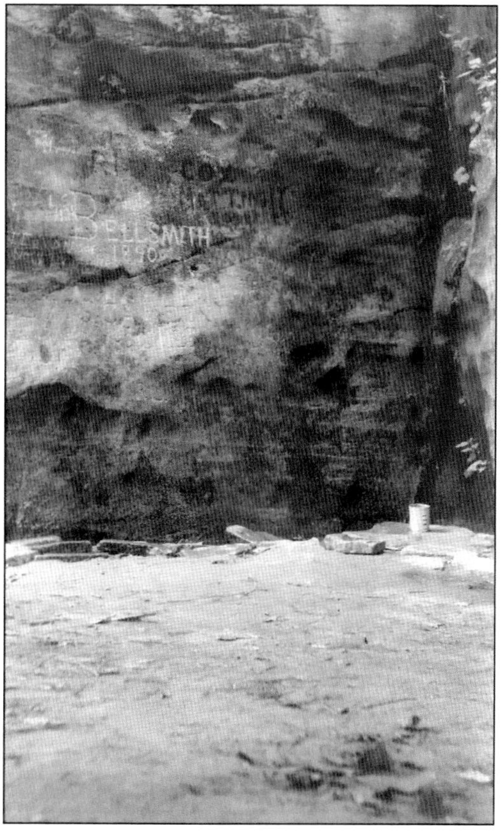

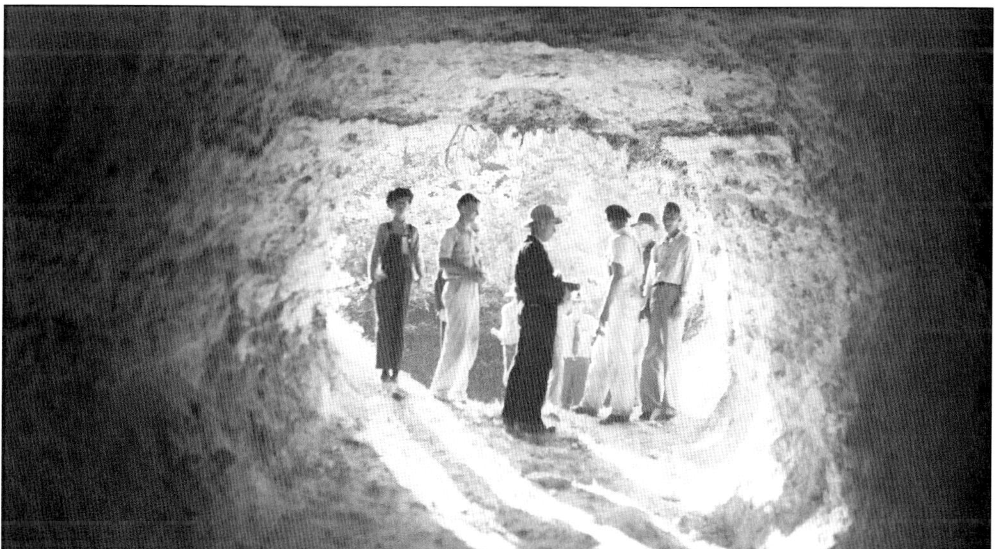

The 1937 Ozark Tour is shown exploring silica mines at Elco. The white-walled tunnels did not require roof props as in coal mines. The walls were drilled with compressed air and then dynamited. Workers loaded silica ore by hand into dump cars for transportation to a plant in Elco for milling. L.O. Trigg reported that at the time of the tour, the Elco plant had been in business for 22 years, while the mine had operated since 1928.

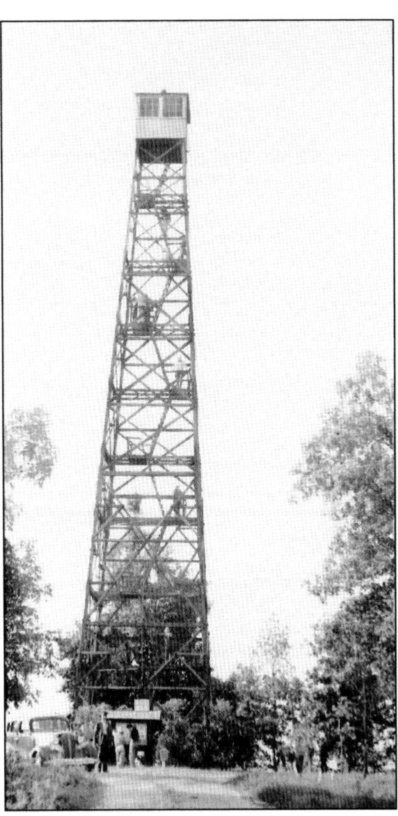

The 1937 Ozark Tour visited the Bass Hill lookout tower. This lookout tower was 90 feet aboveground and 870 feet above sea level. Ozarkers who climbed the tower learned how to sight fires through the fire finder in the tower room. A detailed map held stationary under the fire finder was used to determine the location of the sites.

The 1940 Ozark Tour visited the site of the 1858 Lincoln-Douglas debate held on the old Jonesboro Fairgrounds. This was the third of seven debates between the two men. Ninety-year-old Monroe Sensmeier of Union County, Illinois, stands left of the stone marker; as a boy, he attended the debate with his father.

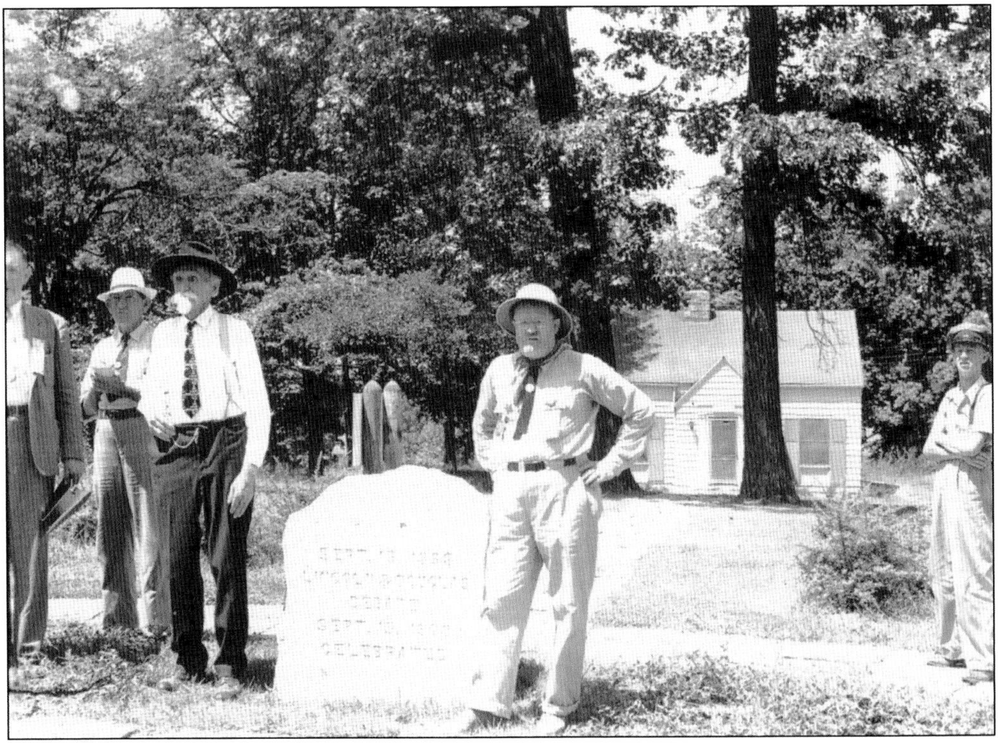

The 1937 Ozark Tour visits the Mound City National Cemetery near Mound City, Illinois. This large monument, the Illinois State Soldiers and Sailors Monument, was erected in 1874. The cemetery was established for the interment of Union and Confederate troops who succumbed to their wounds at the nearby Civil War naval hospital. This became a national cemetery in 1864 and was listed in the National Register of Historic Places in 1997.

The 1937 Ozark Tour views the marine ways on the Ohio River at Mound City. During the Civil War, the federal government leased the marine ways where James Eads oversaw the building and refitting of ships for service in the war. In 1863, the Mississippi River Squadron made Mound City its base of operations. More than 1,500 people were employed at the marine ways during the war.

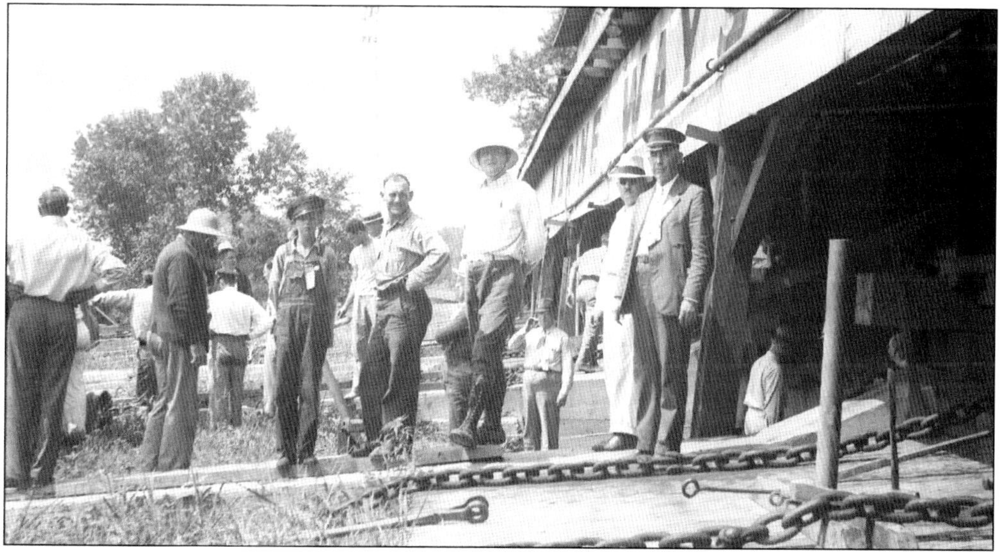

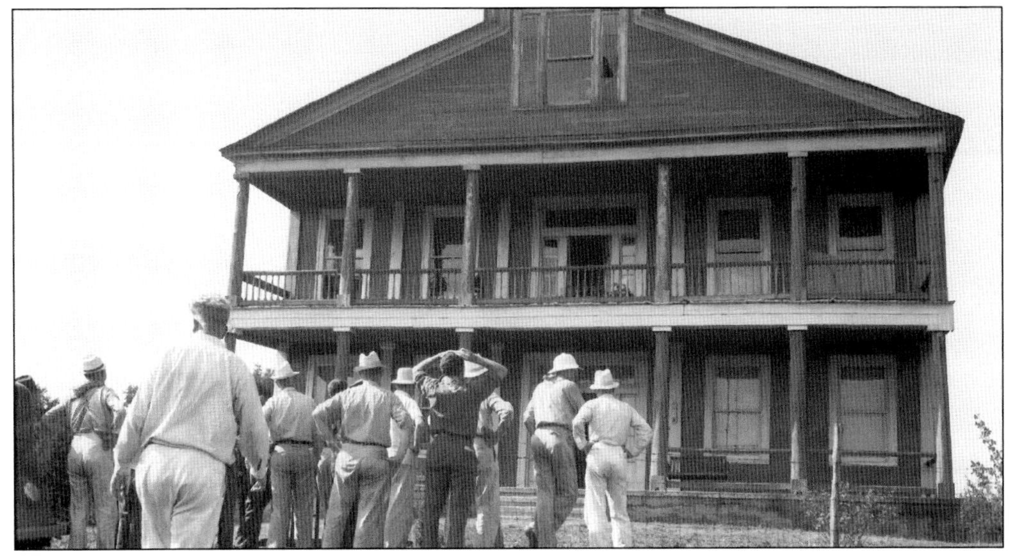

The 1938 Ozark Tour visits Crenshaw House near Equality, which was billed to tourists as the Old Slave House. According to folklore, John Crenshaw operated a reverse Underground Railroad here, bringing African Americans into a form of indentured servitude or slavery working the nearby salt wells and caging them in the infamous third-story attic. Some more recent speculation claims that the third-story rooms may have been used for lodging for overnight guests from the nearby railroad.

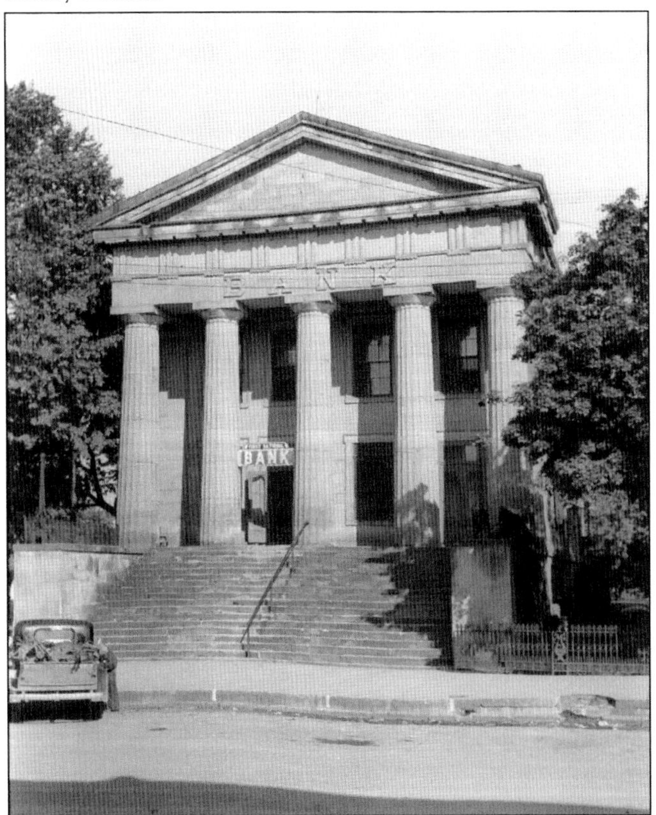

The Bank of Illinois built this Greek Revival structure to replace the bank in the John Marshall House in Shawneetown, Illinois. After being under construction from 1839 to 1941, it was open for a year before an economic downturn caused it to suspend operations. It reopened in 1854 as the State Bank of Illinois. Following the disastrous 1937 flood and the town's move to New Shawneetown, the bank closed its doors in 1942.

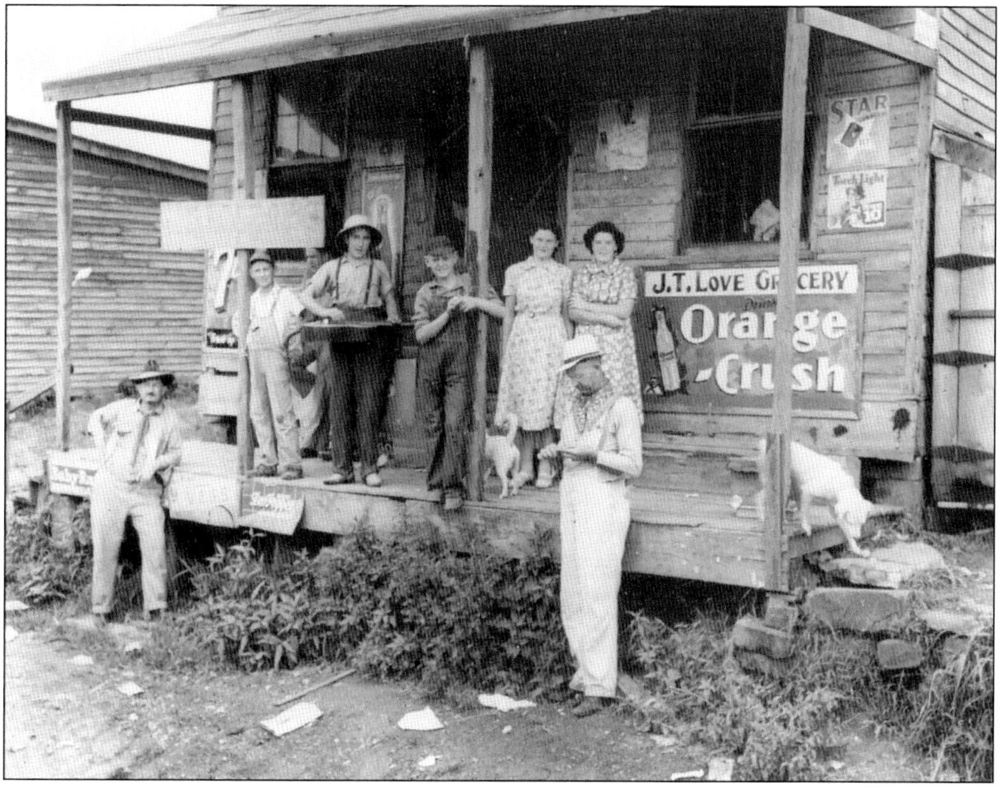

The 1938 Ozark Tour stopped for refreshments at J.T. Love's grocery store in the Sparks Hill community in Hardin County. Ozarker Hugh Baumgardner of Milwaukee, Wisconsin, bought out the store's supply of handkerchiefs, which he then proceeded to auction off to the highest bidders among his fellow explorers.

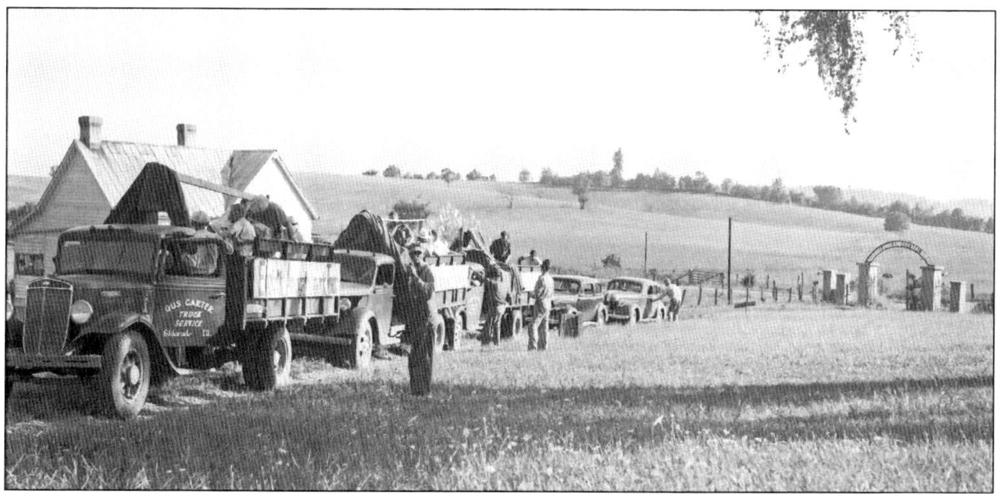

The 1938 Ozark Tour also stopped at the historic Westwood Cemetery near Shawneetown. Westwood was the home of Gen. Joseph M. Street and Eliza Maria Street, the daughter of Gen. Thomas Posey. While General Posey was visiting his daughter in March 1818, he caught a cold that developed into a fatal case of typhus fever. General Posey was buried in the home's rose garden, which eventually became Westwood Cemetery.

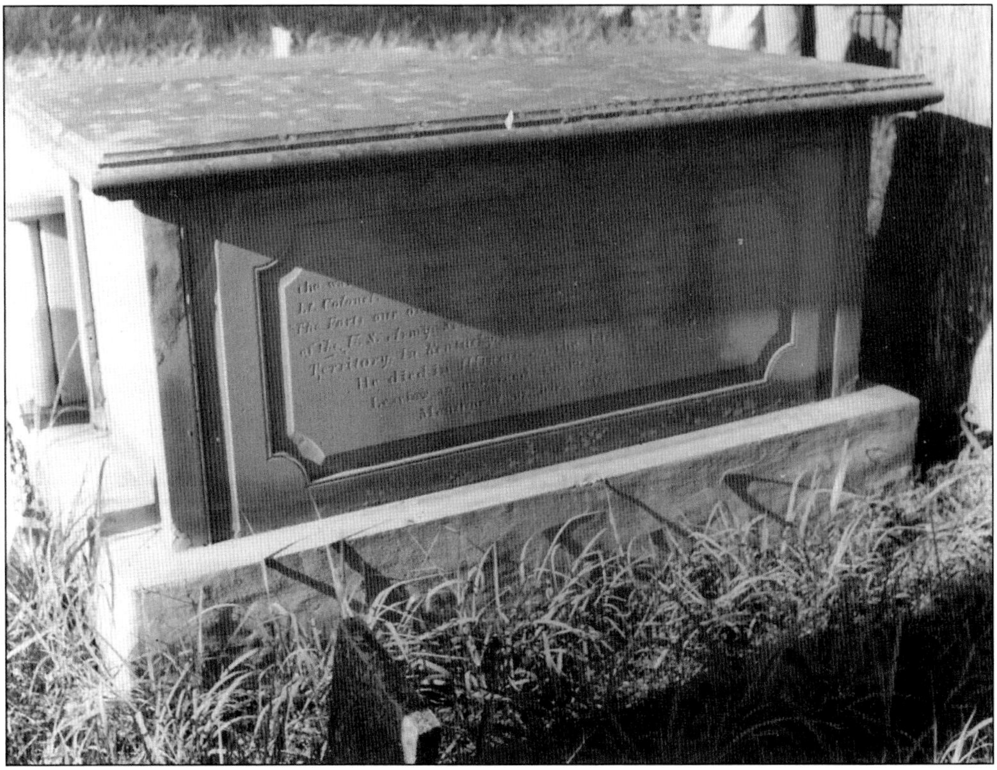

This is the gravesite of Gen. Thomas Posey (1750–1818), an officer during the American Revolution and aide-de-camp to Gen. George Washington. Posey was a lieutenant governor of Kentucky, a US senator from Louisiana, and governor of the Indiana Territory from 1813 until Indiana gained statehood in 1816. The 1938 Ozark Tour visited General Posey's grave in Westwood Cemetery.

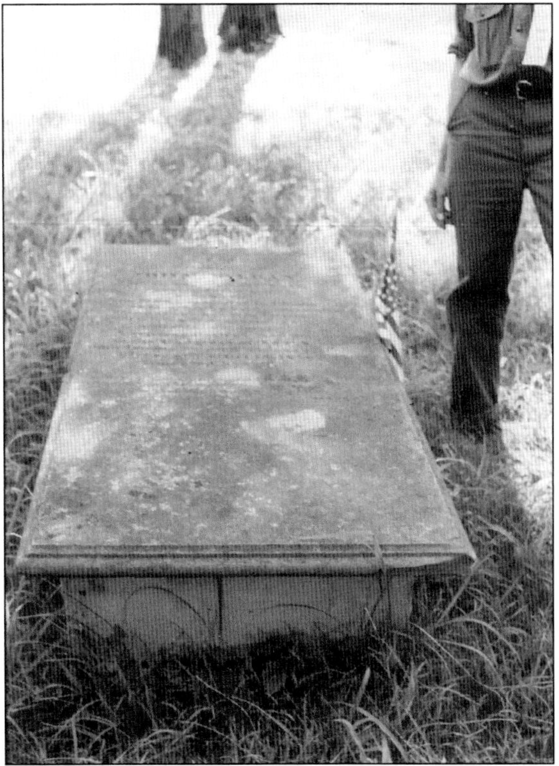

The 1938 Ozark Tour visited the gravesite of John McClean (1791–1830) at Westwood Cemetery near Shawneetown. McLean, an attorney from Shawneetown, was elected as a US congressman when Illinois entered statehood in 1818. He was later elected to the Illinois General Assembly and served as speaker. He died while serving in the US Senate.

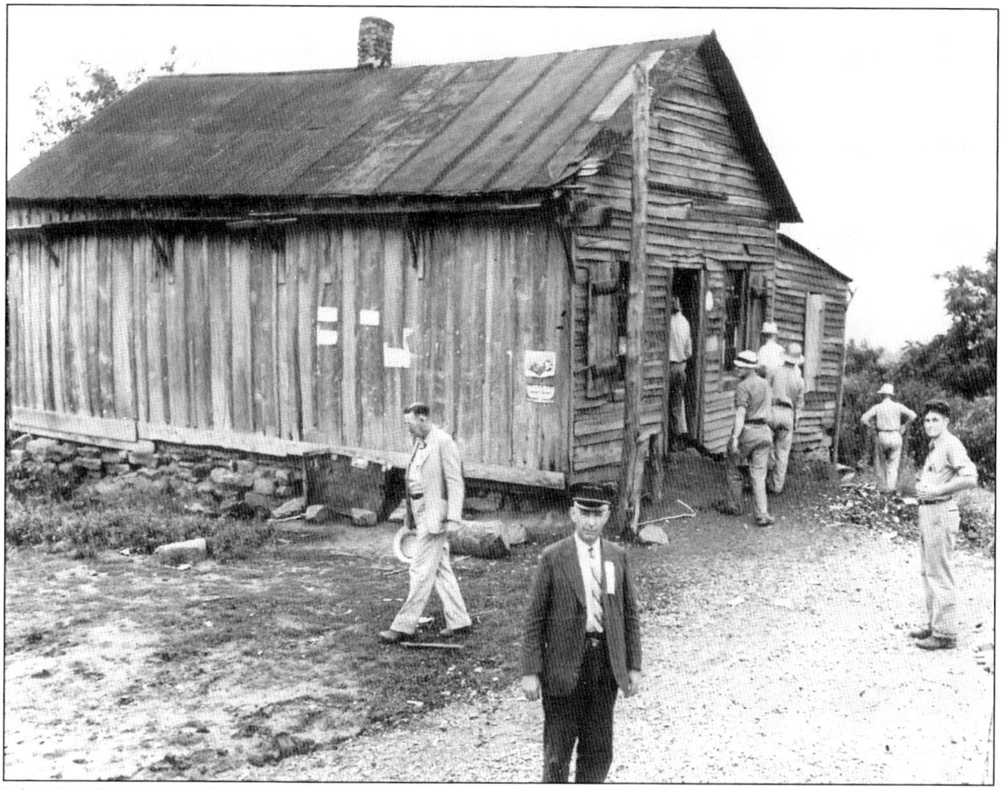

The Ozarkers came through Johnson's Store in rural Hardin County, near the CCC's Camp Cadiz, during the 1938 Ozark Tour. J.L. Johnson, who had run the grocery store for 25 years at the time the Ozarkers visited, was blind. According to L.O. Trigg, the Ozarkers marveled at Johnson's knowledge of his entire inventory and how he kept track of prices of items via notches he made in the packaging with his thumbnail. Johnson was also a Victrola repairman. Trigg reported that before radios became popular, there were always five or six Graphophones in Johnson's store in various stages of repair. The 1938 Ozarkers were entertained by several old-time tunes played on a cylinder-type Edison Victrola. Pictured below are Trigg (left) and Mr. and Mrs. Johnson.

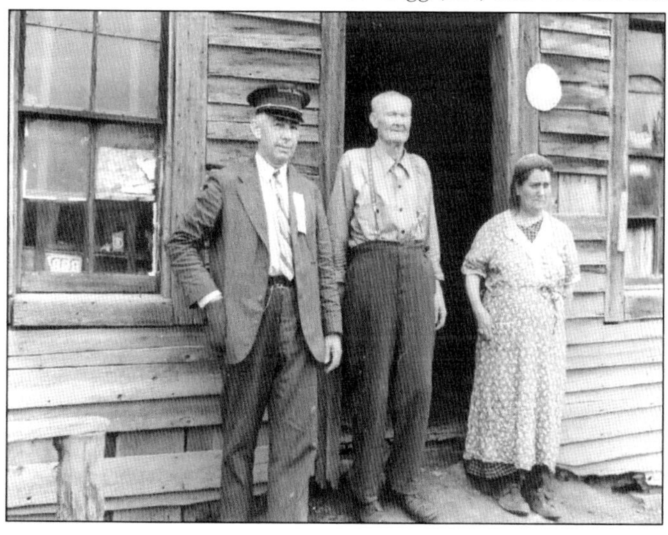

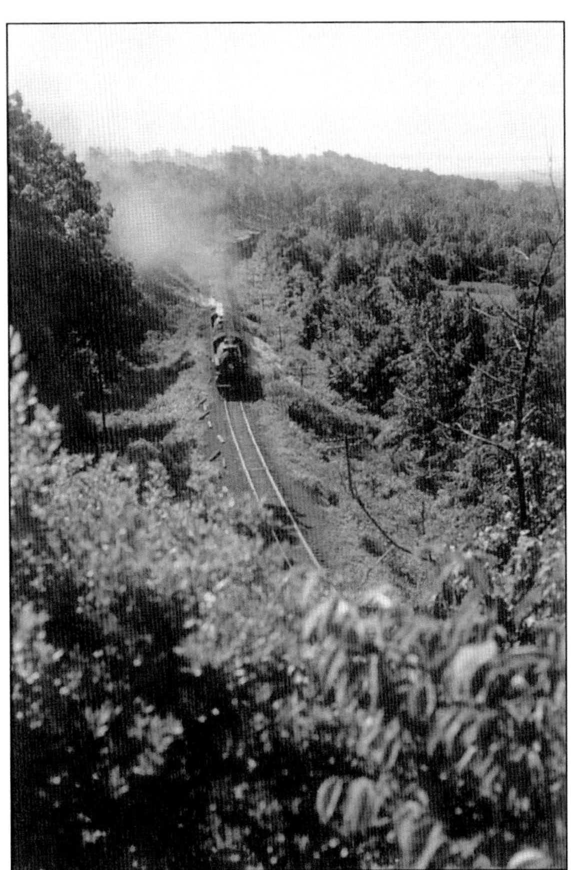

The 1939 Ozark Tour watches a northbound Mobile & Ohio Railroad train pull freight up the steep grade from the scenic overlook near Alto Pass, Illinois. When the community was settled in 1860, it was known as Quetil Gap, named for Charles Julius Quetil. The rail line was abandoned in 1981 for the more gentle grades of the Illinois Central rail line to the east. The abandoned roadbed is now a hiking trail called the Quetil Trail.

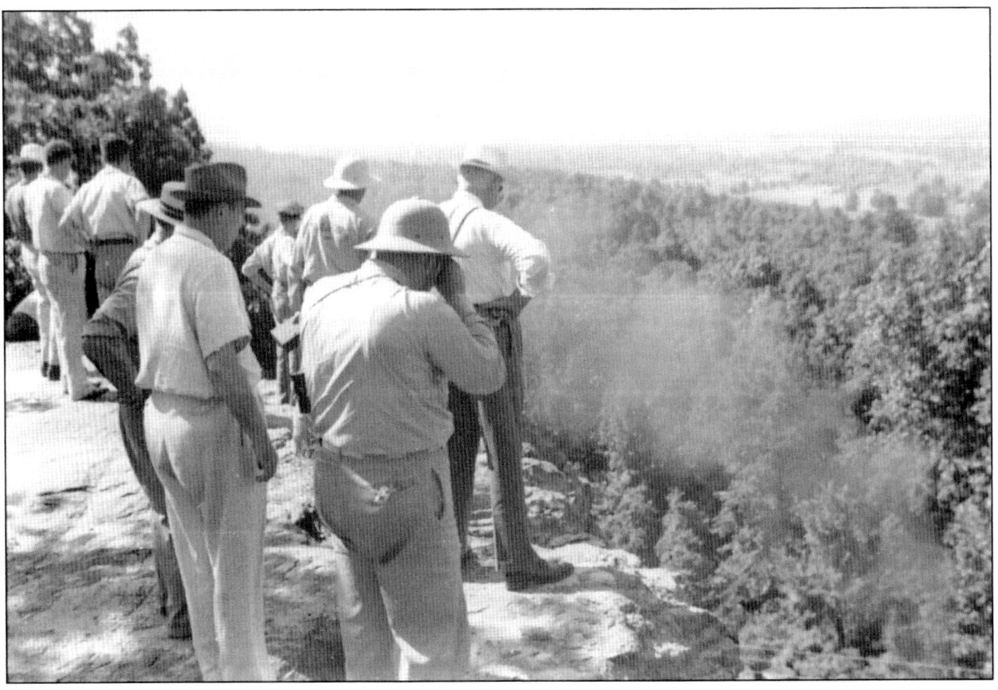

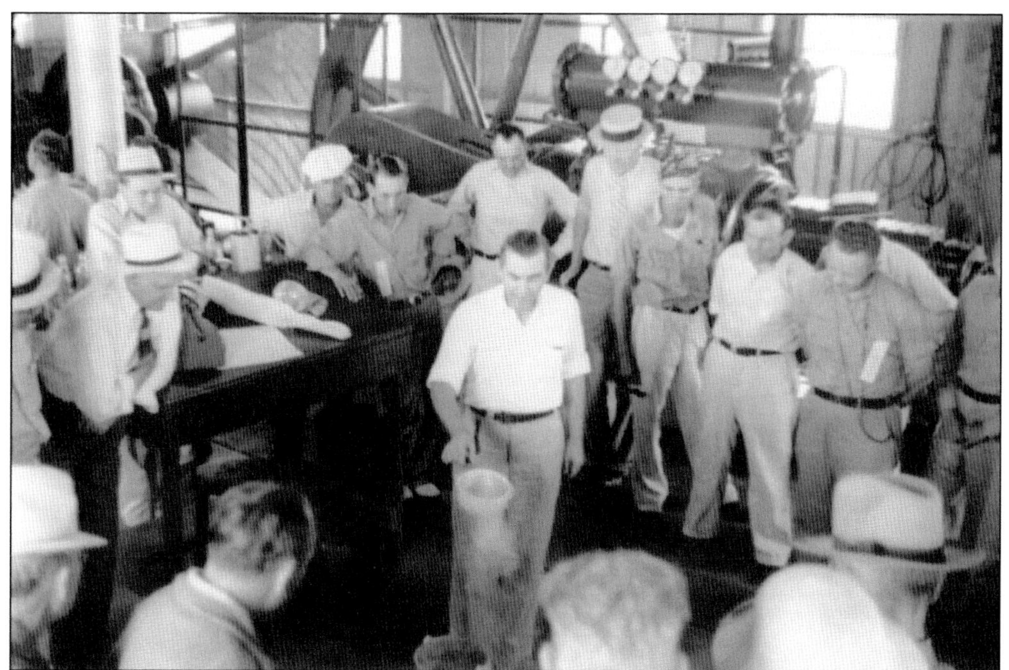

The 1939 Ozark Tour visits the Bankston Creek Colleries Company's liquid air plant near Harrisburg, Illinois. In the photograph, a Mr. McLoud is shown giving a lecture to the Ozarkers and demonstrating how liquid air is used for blasting or crushing the rock overlaying coal seams.

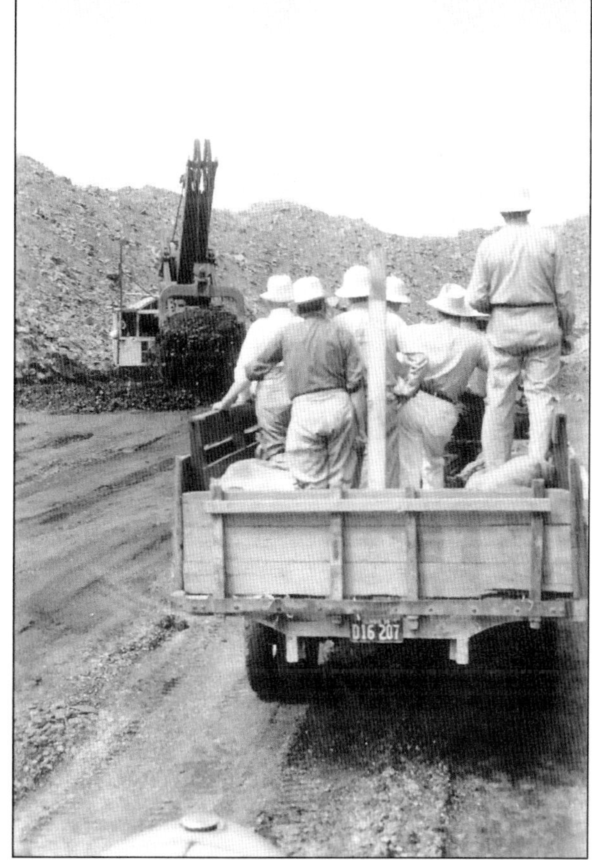

After leaving the Horning Hotel in Harrisburg, the first stop for the 1939 Ozarkers was viewing the Sahara Coal Company's strip mine west of town.

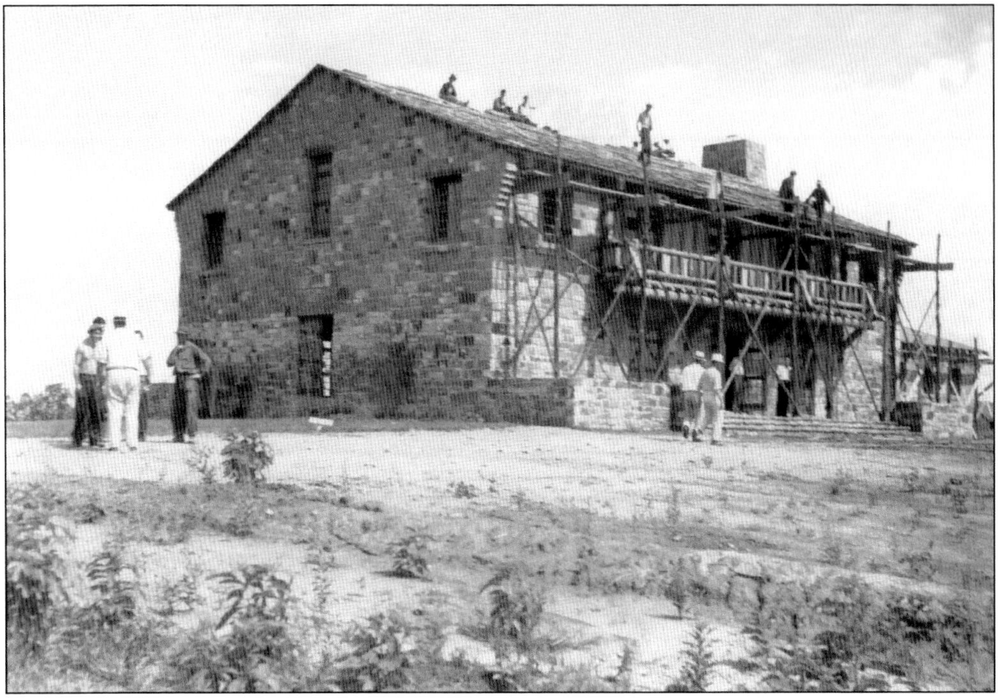

In the above photograph, the 1935 Ozark Tour views Giant City State Park Lodge when it was under construction by the CCC, which had a camp on the site. Building the lodge and making improvements to the state park was such a large project that an additional camp was installed. On the first night of the tour, the 1939 Ozark Tour ate dinner and camped on the grounds of the completed lodge, pictured below. The State of Illinois purchased 916 acres for Giant City State Park in 1927. Today, the park has over 4,000 acres of nature trails for hikers and equestrians.

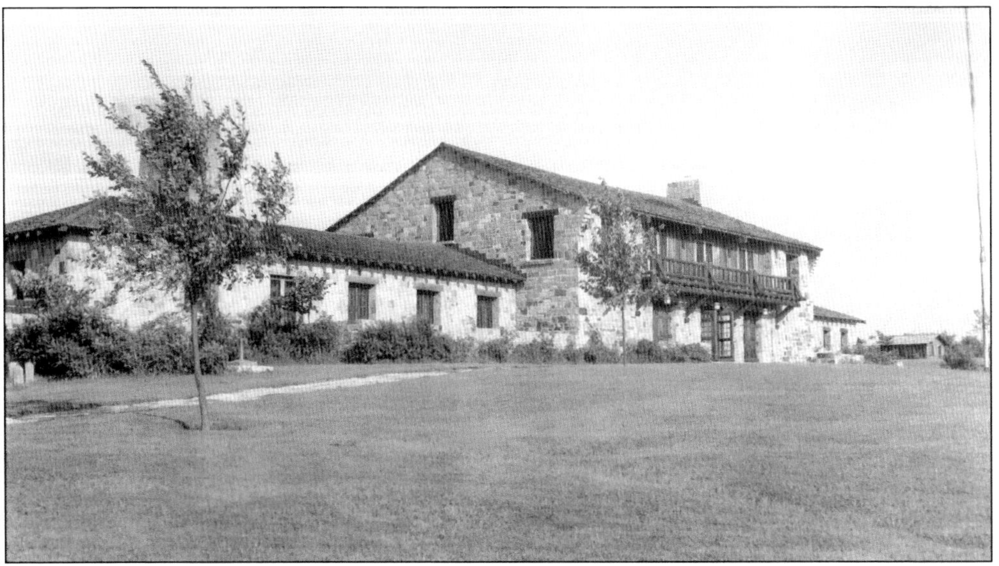

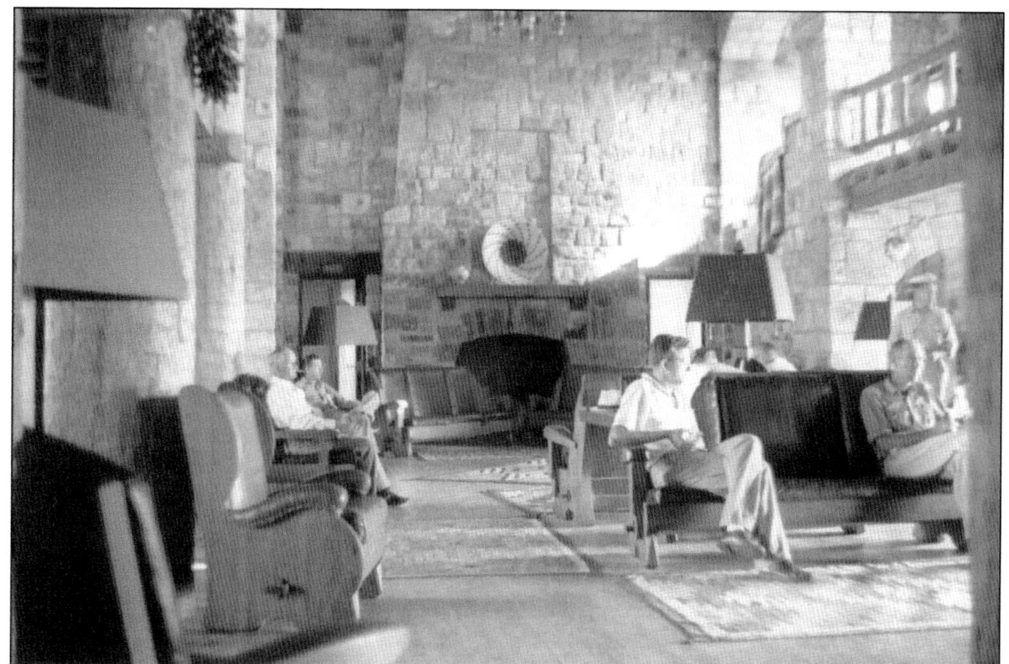

The 1939 Ozark Tour relaxes in the lobby of Giant City State Park Lodge. The Ozarkers visited the state park on tours in 1935, 1939, 1942, and on the final Ozark Tour under L.O. Trigg in 1949.

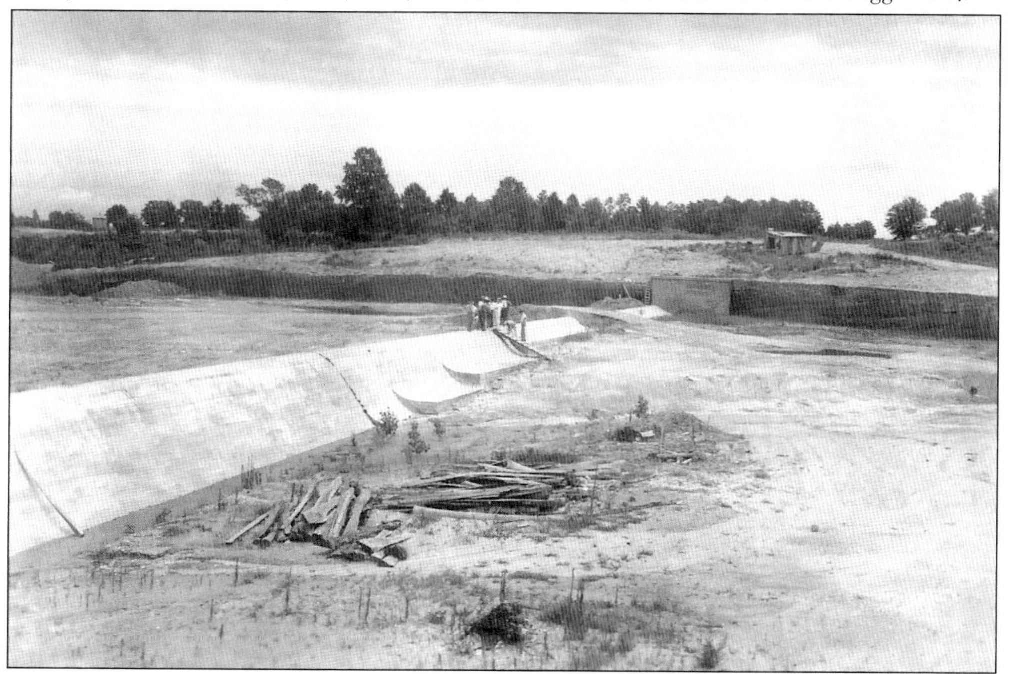

The 1939 Ozark Tour saw the Crab Orchard Lake dam and spillway under construction near Carbondale. When completed, Crab Orchard Lake and its feeder lakes, Little Grassy and Devil's Kitchen, contained much of the 9,000 acres of water of the Crab Orchard National Wildlife Refuge. The Ozarkers returned in 1942 to enjoy boating and the final meal of the tour—a fish fry—at the lake.

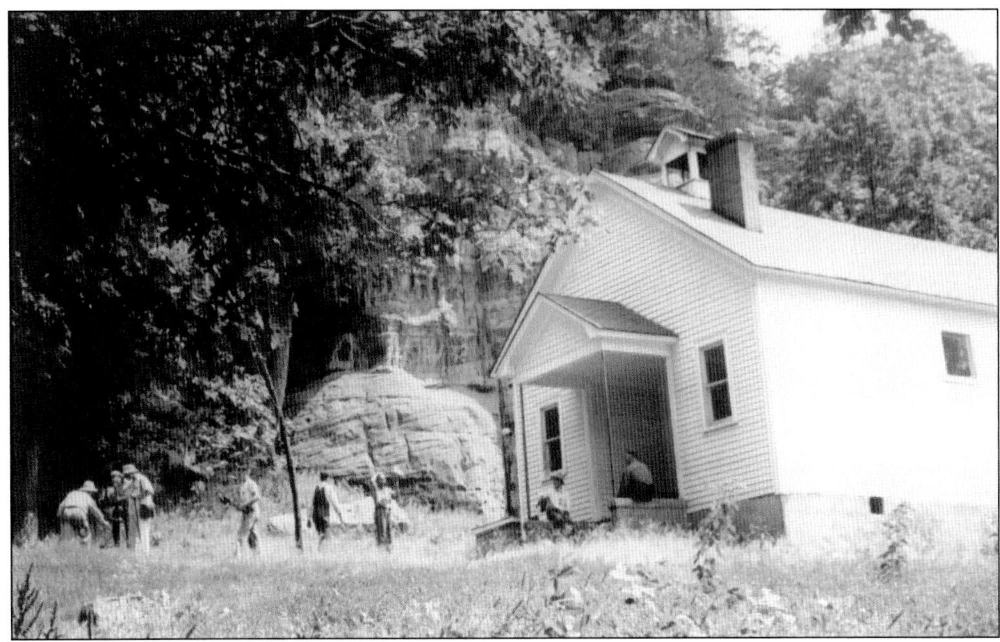

Cedar Bluff School in rural Johnson County could only be reached by climbing 185 steps, since there was no road up from the base of the hill. A shelter bluff next to the school was used as a barn to house students' horses during the school day. This photograph is from the 1942 Ozark Tour. The Ozarkers also visited the school on the 1948 tour.

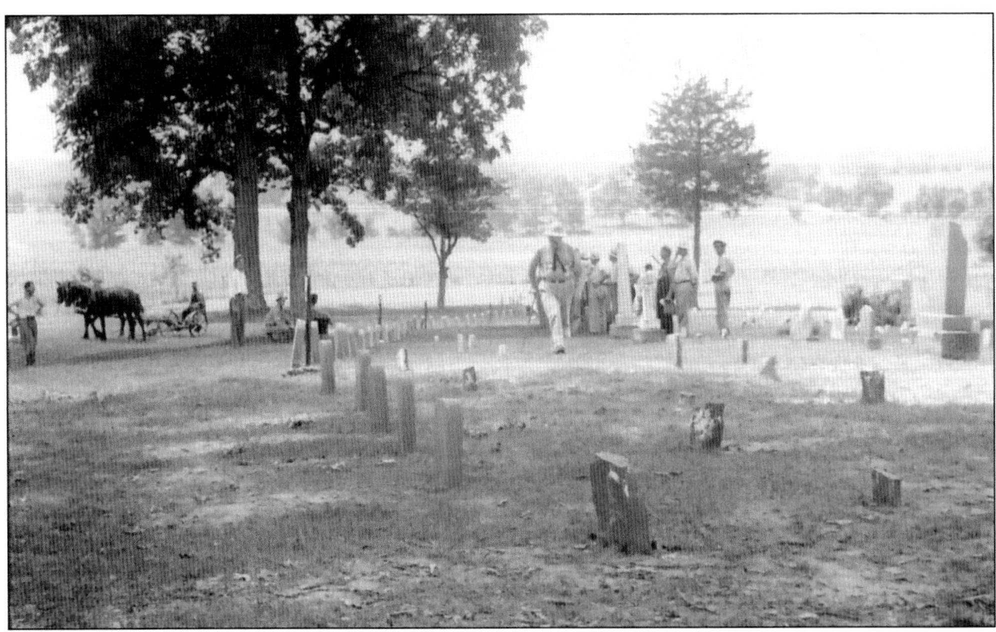

L.O. Trigg called this row of 35 headstones the "Phantom Graves." All 35 headstones are inscribed with "In God I Trust." The 1942 Ozark Tour visited this cemetery east of Cedar Grove Church in Johnson County. Road conditions after a rain shower prevented the 1940 Ozark Tour from visiting the Phantom Graves. The Ozarkers returned on the 1948 Ozark Tour.

Four

Meals, Recreation, and Overnights

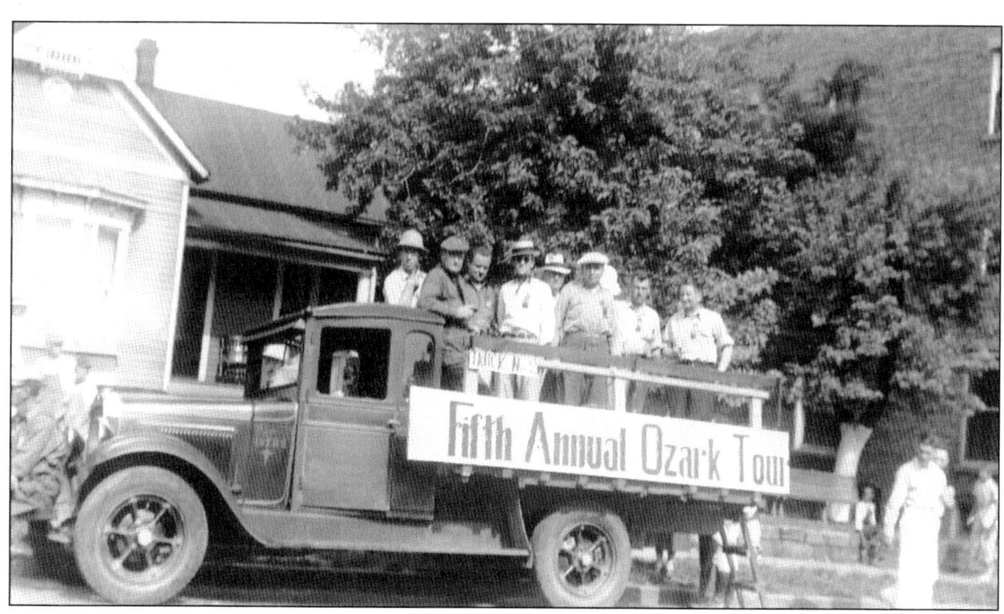

The 1935 Ozark Tour prepares to leave the Horning Hotel in Harrisburg on July 22, 1935. These Ozarkers visited the following CCC camps: Hutchins Creek, Giant City, Riverside Park, and an abandoned camp in Union County. A highlight was touring Emma Rebman's Ferne Clyffe Park near Goreville.

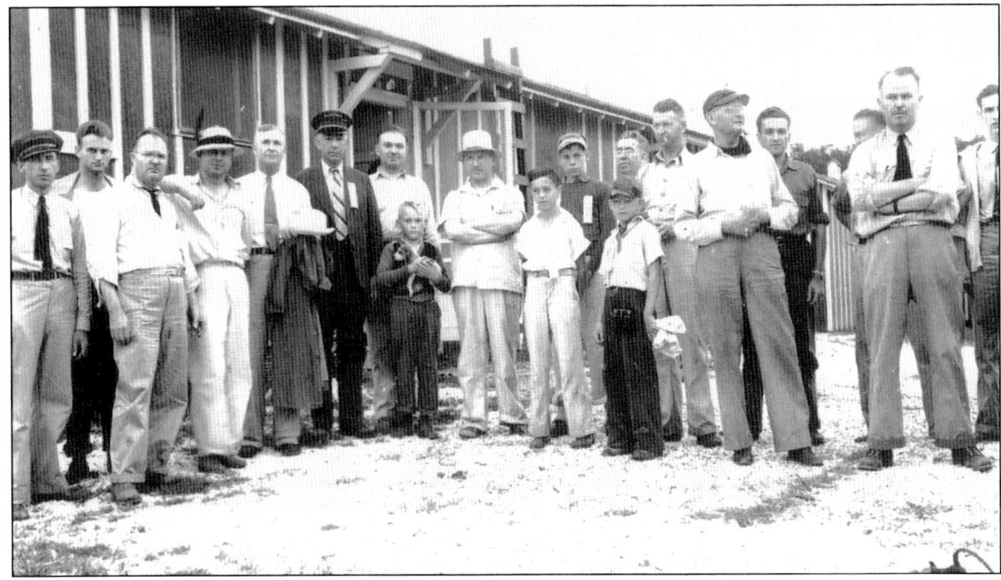

The 1938 Ozark Tour had dinner at the CCC Camp Hicks on the first evening of the tour. The Ozarkers arrived after visiting the highest point in southern Illinois, the Williams Hill Lookout Tower. The evening meal was prepared by some of the camp's recreation leaders. (Jeff Robinson.)

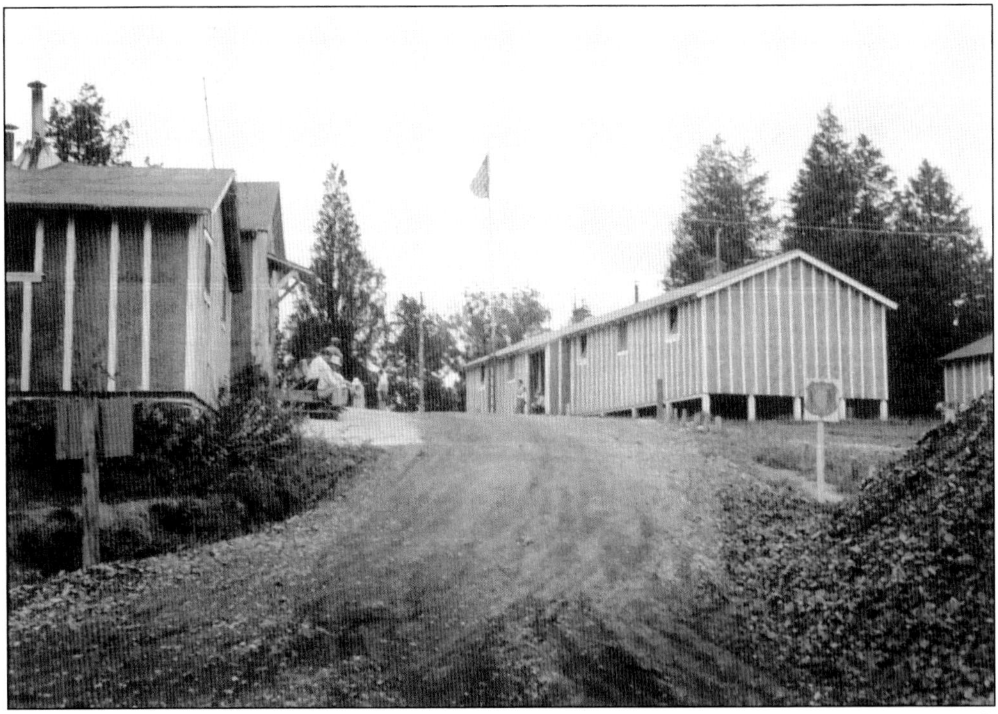

This is the Giant City CCC camp, where lunch was served on the second day of the 1935 Ozark Tour. Here, the Ozarkers abandoned the trucks provided for the tour and climbed into CCC trucks for a driving tour of the sites in Giant City State Park. The CCC was responsible for many improvements in the park, including building the Giant City Lodge.

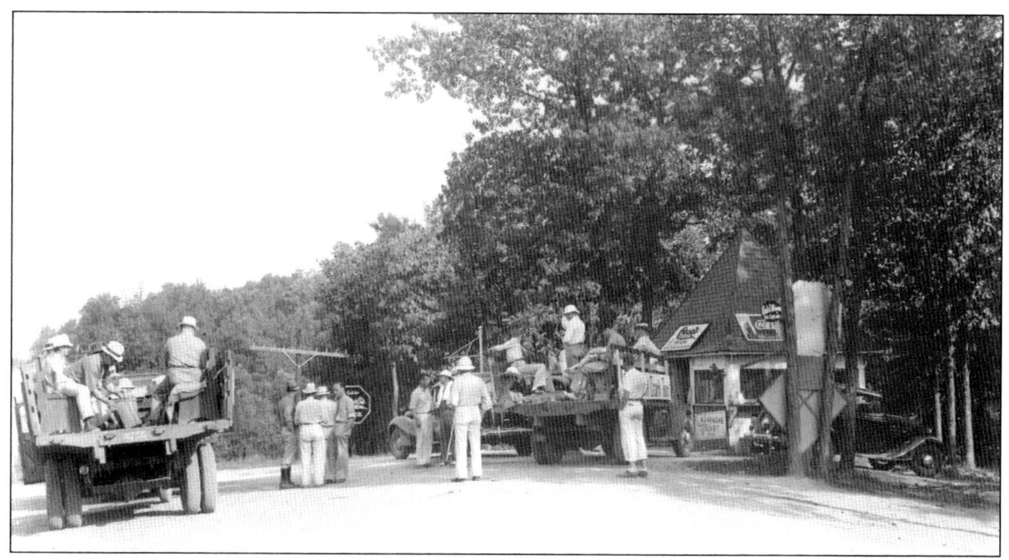

The 1936 Ozark Tour stops at the refreshment stand at Dixon Springs. The stand was located above the park on the pull-out near the bridge on the north side of Illinois State Route 146. The entrance to the Dixon Springs Civilian Conservation Corp camp was across the road.

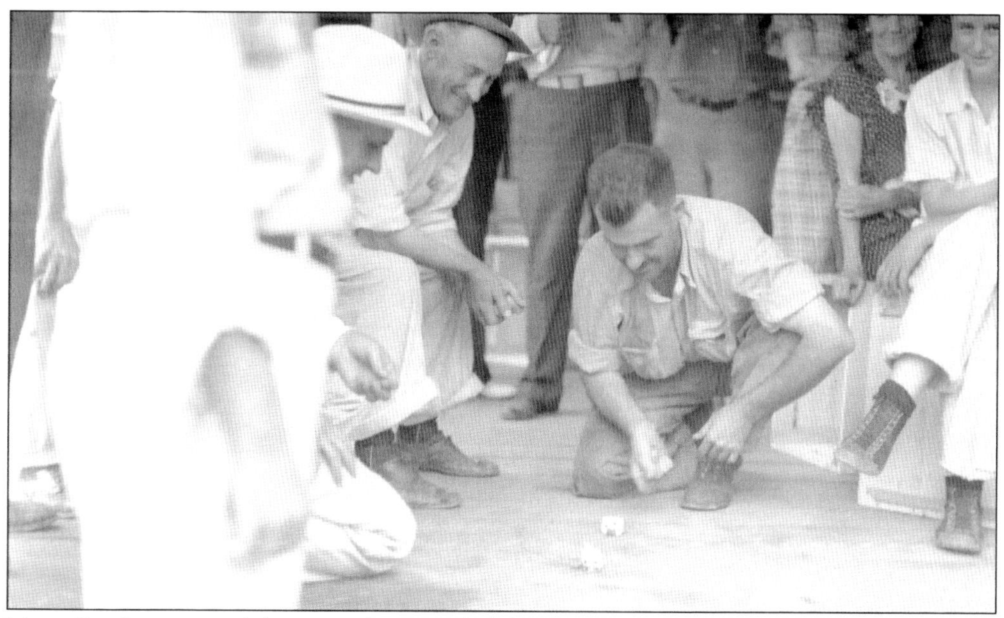

Many Ozarkers enjoyed throwing the "six-sided dominoes." In a 1935 edition of the *Ozark News*, L.O. Trigg reports that a reward was being offered by Ozark Tour "sheriff" Jacob Myers for identifying the persons involved in the gambling. Truck Two champion "Buck" Sawyer is pictured here rolling the dice on the 1935 Ozark Tour.

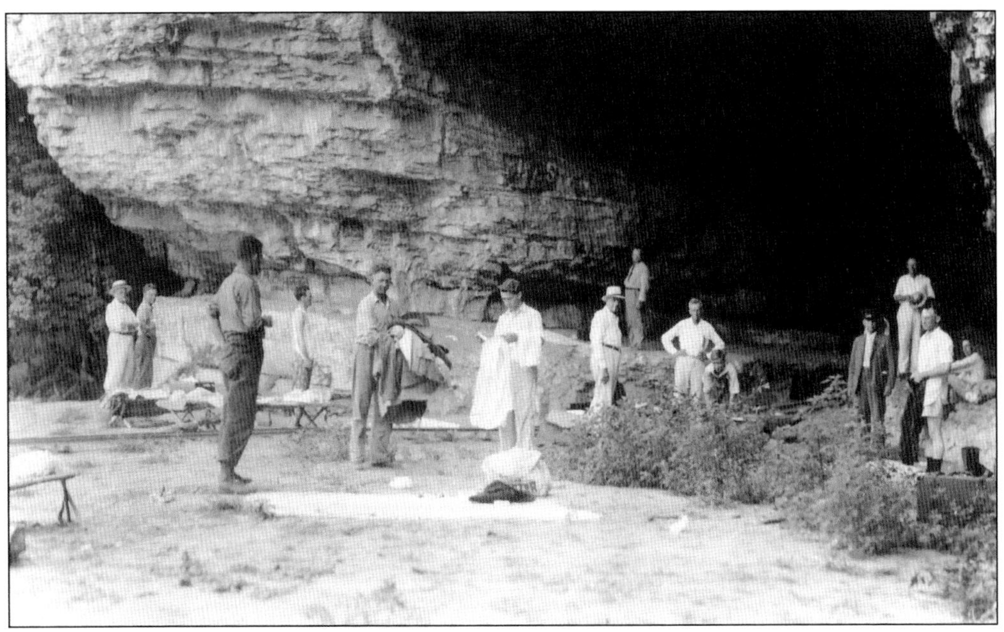

On the second night of their tour, the 1934 Ozarkers camped in the mouth of the Pirate Cave at Cave-in-Rock State Park. Civil Works Administration workers took dirt and debris that had filled the back of the cave and dumped it outside the cave's entrance, creating the large level area on which the Ozarkers camped. The workers kept a wheelbarrow full of bones and elk antlers found during the excavations.

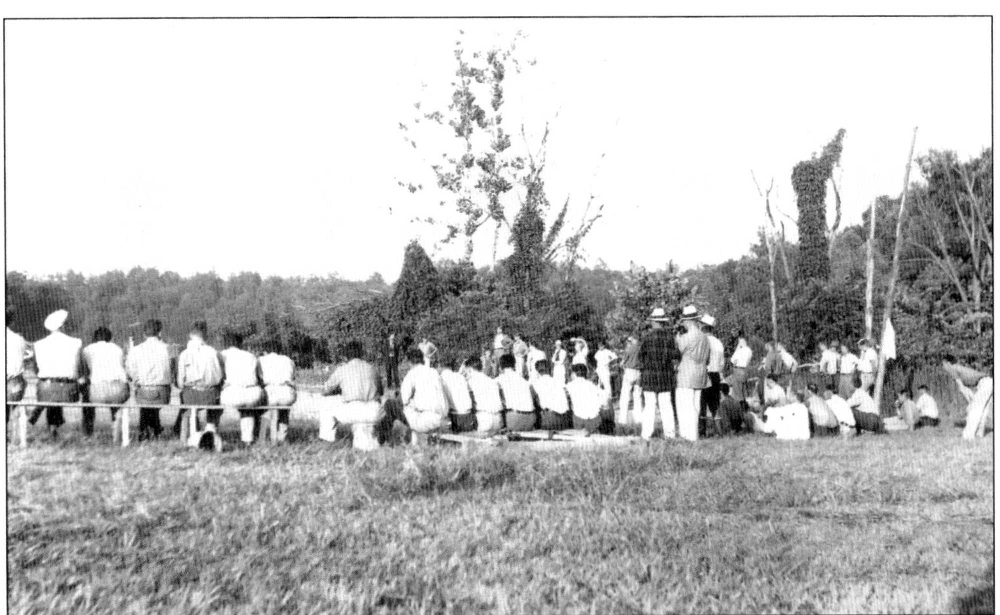

The 1937 Ozark Tour played this baseball game with the men of the CCC's Camp Delta near McClure. The Ozarkers had traveled more than 100 miles before arriving at Camp Delta on the first evening of the tour. (Jeff Robinson.)

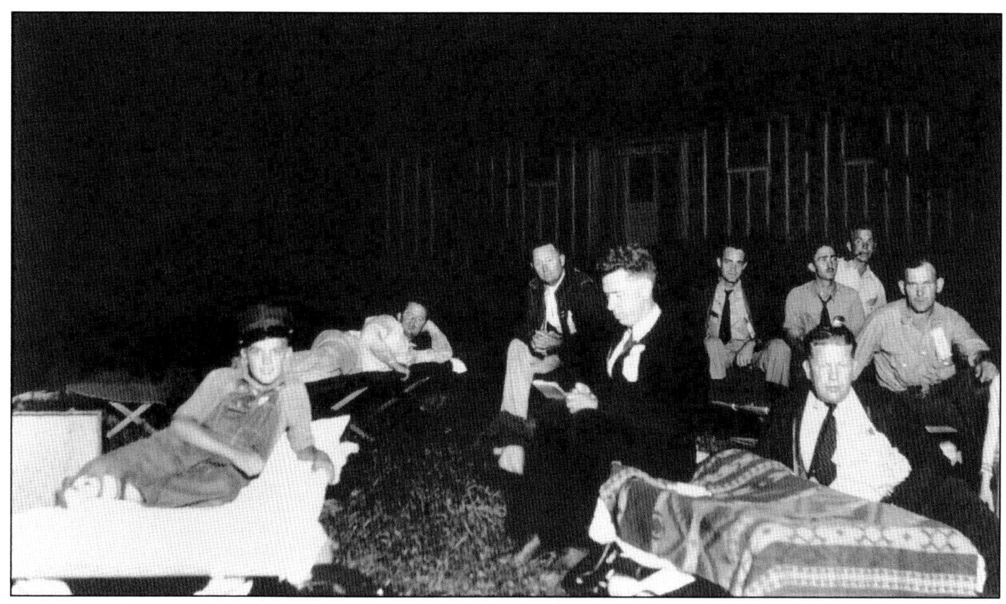

The 1937 Ozark Tour bedded down at the CCC's Camp Delta near McClure. As shown above, most of the Ozarkers slept on cots under the stars outside the camp barracks. Pictured below are W.E. Johnson (in the background at left), Judge D.F. Rumsey (in the foreground at left), and Judge B.F. Anderson, who all preferred "camping" indoors in one of the buildings.

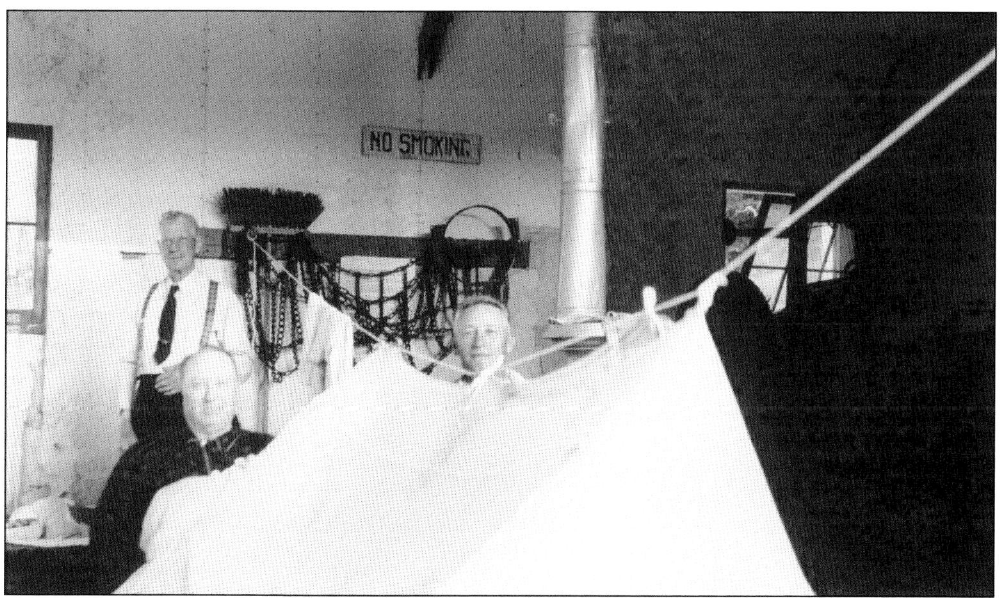

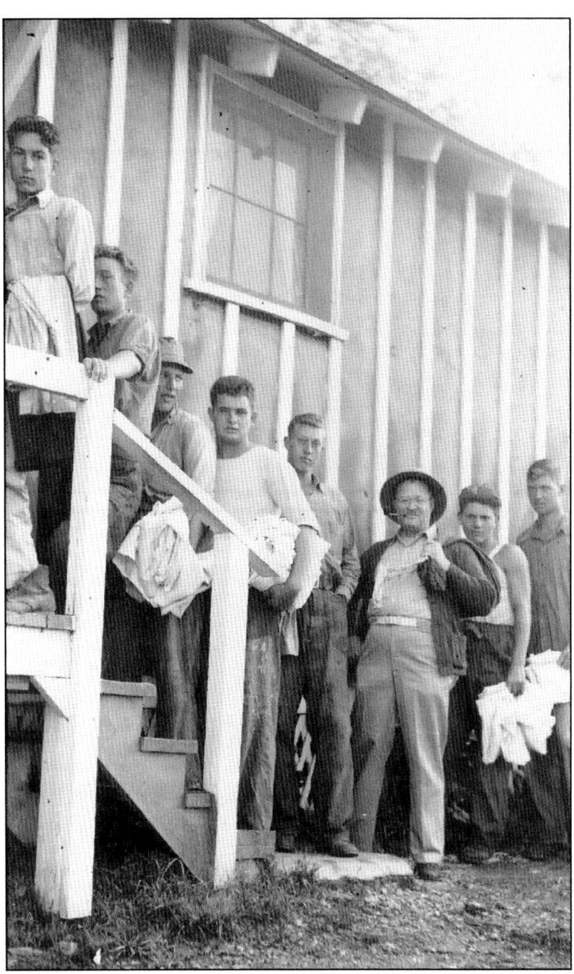

Jokester "Sheriff" Jacob Myers (with pipe and glasses) joined the laundry line with the men of CCC Camp Delta on the 1937 Ozark Tour. (Jeff Robinson.)

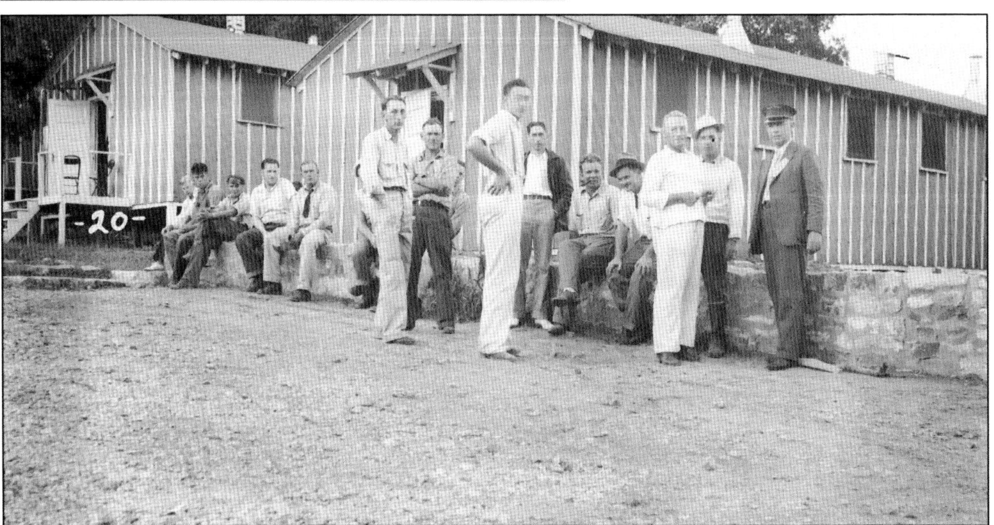

Ozarkers wait for breakfast at CCC's Camp Delta near McClure on the morning of the second day of the 1937 Ozark Tour.

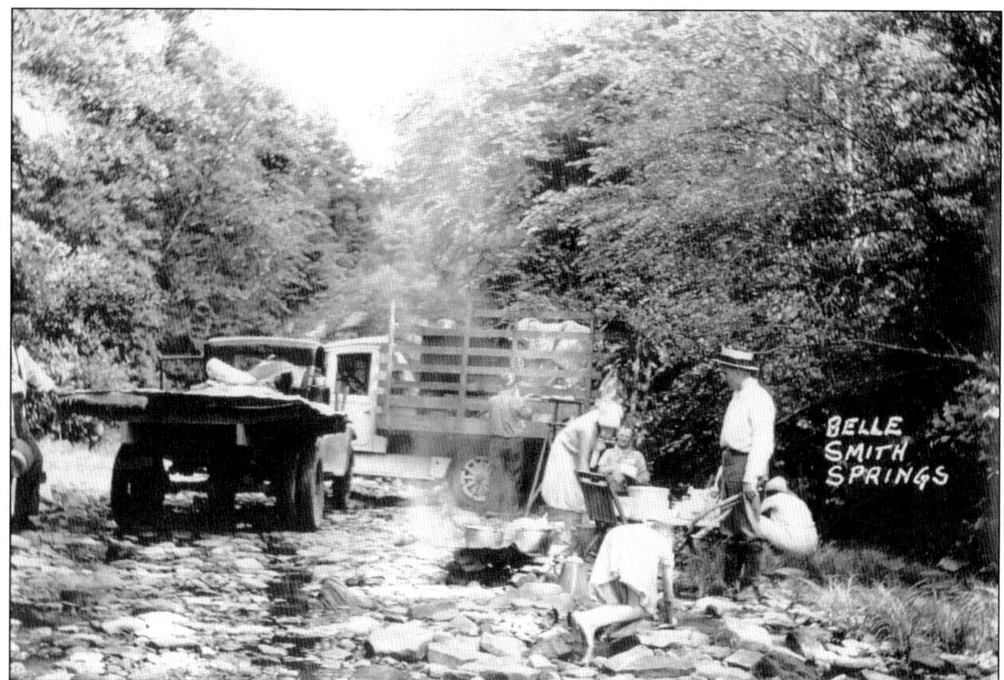

Above, Cal Wiedemann and family, from Harrisburg, are pictured in the dry creek bed of Bell Smith Springs preparing lunch for the 1931 Ozark Tour with equipment Wiedemann brought by station wagon. Below, Ozarkers eat the first meal of the tour atop the back of the flatbed truck that transported them there. After lunch, they toured the many scenic attractions in the canyons of Bell Smith Springs. The truck had difficulty driving out of the canyon, and the Ozarkers spent two and a half hours getting back to the "hard road" and another hour driving to their next overnight stay at a cabin near Golconda.

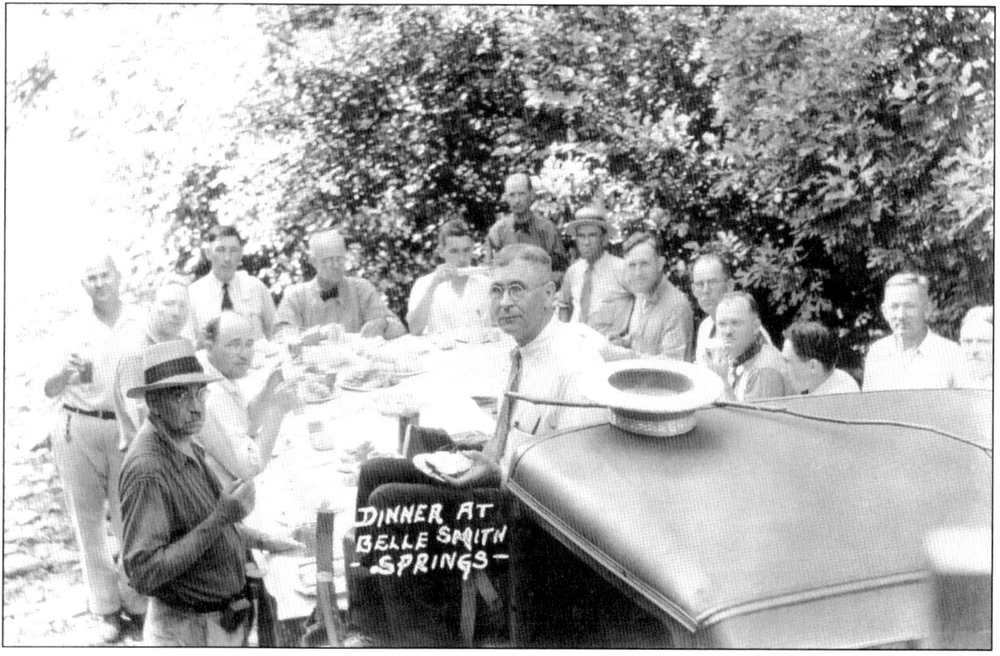

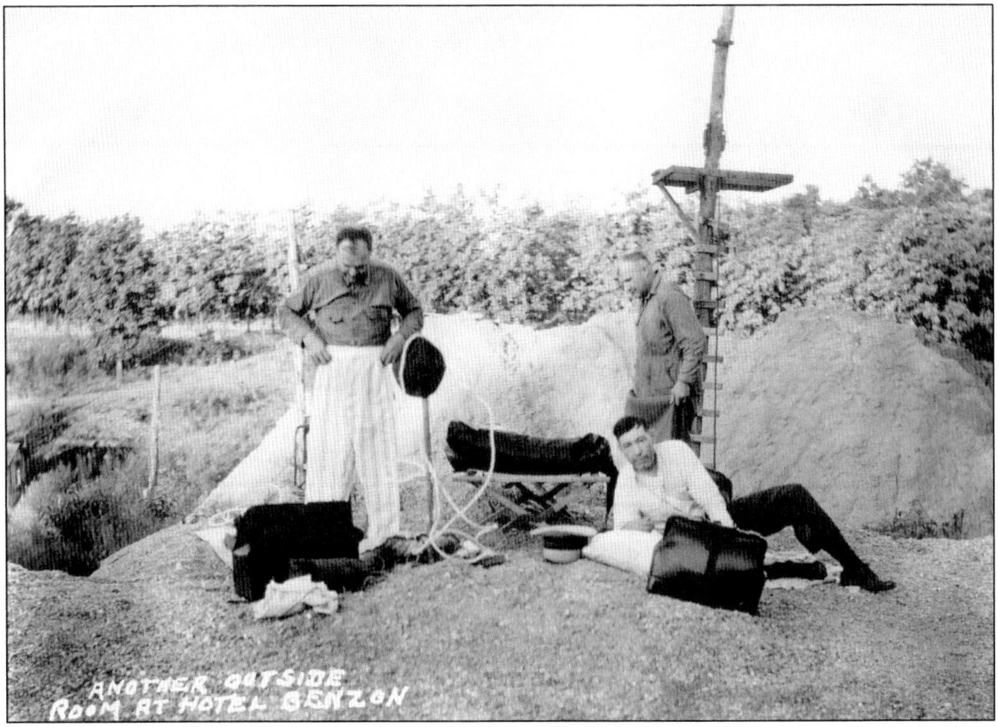

The second night of the 1931 Ozark Tour was spent sleeping on spoil piles at the Benzon Fluorspar Mine in Hardin County. The Ozarkers left the mine to tour the "House of Nature" cave at Cave-in-Rock before heading to Birch Spring and the Volcanic Plug at Sparks Hill. They had a 25¢ chicken dinner at an unidentified location before ending the tour at Harrisburg.

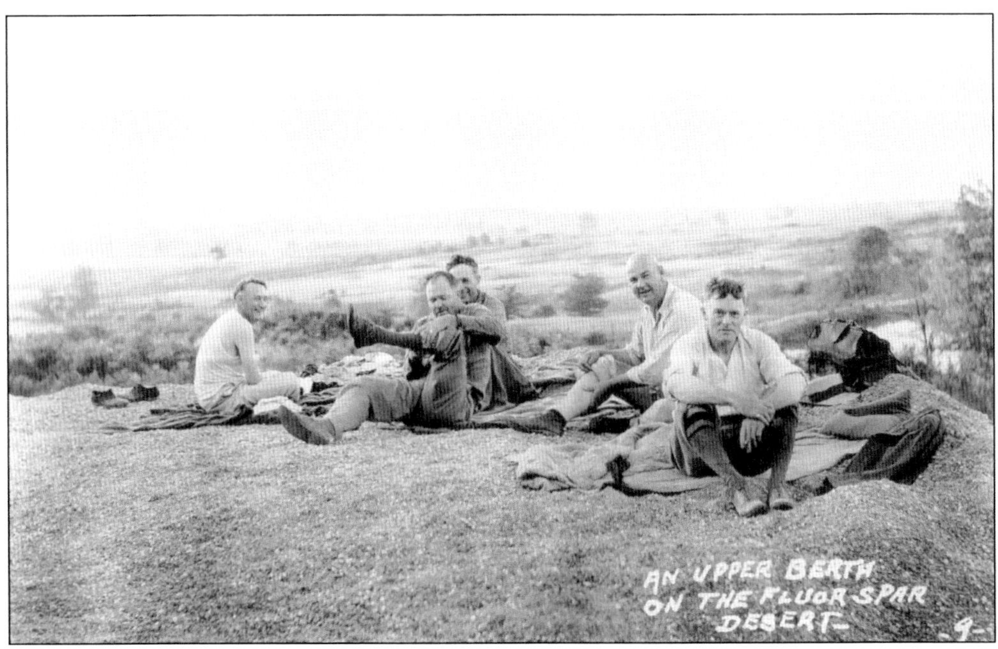

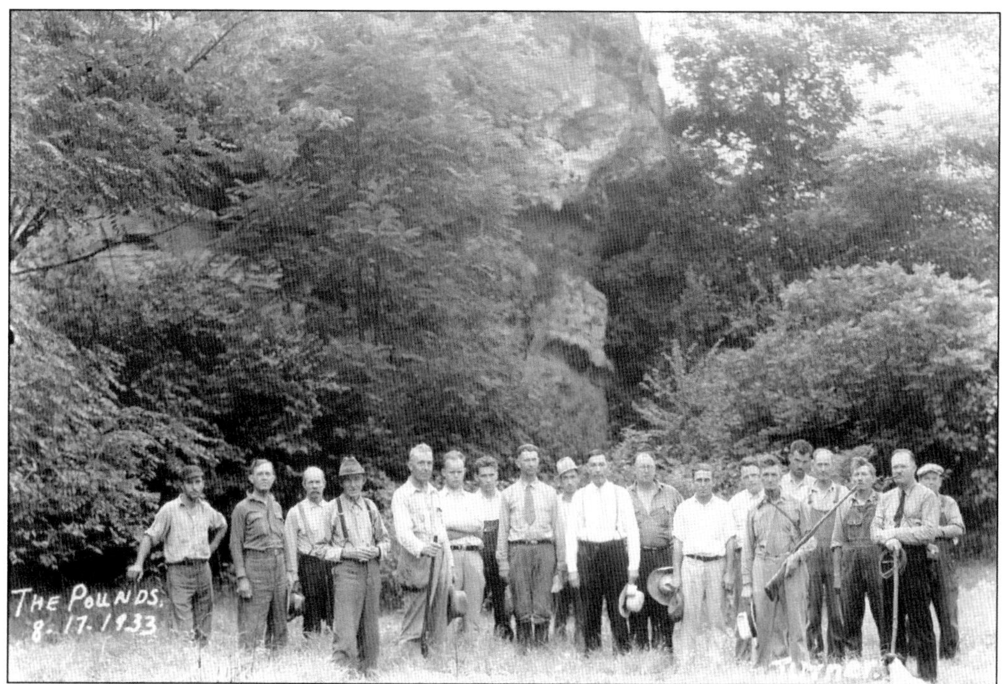

The 1933 Ozark Tour went on a hunting expedition at The Pounds in southern Gallatin County. This area is now part of the Rim Rock National Recreation Trail. Pioneers recognized the area as being similar to the impoundments used for keeping livestock in the eastern United States. An area below the Rim Rock escarpment is called the Ox-lot Cave due to early loggers keeping their oxen penned at the shelter bluff.

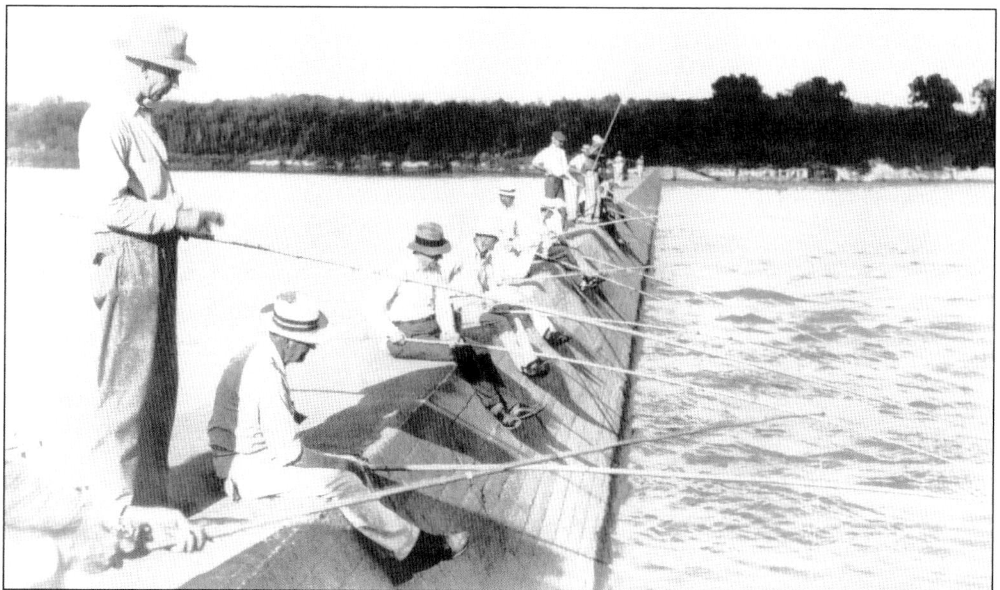

L.O. Trigg hired a local Golconda man to ferry the Ozarkers around the locks and onto Dam 51 to fish during the 1934 Ozark Tour. Later that evening, the Golconda Rotary Club provided entertainment and dinner at the Riverside Hotel. The Ozarkers spent the night in Golconda by camping either on the grounds of the hotel or near the riverfront.

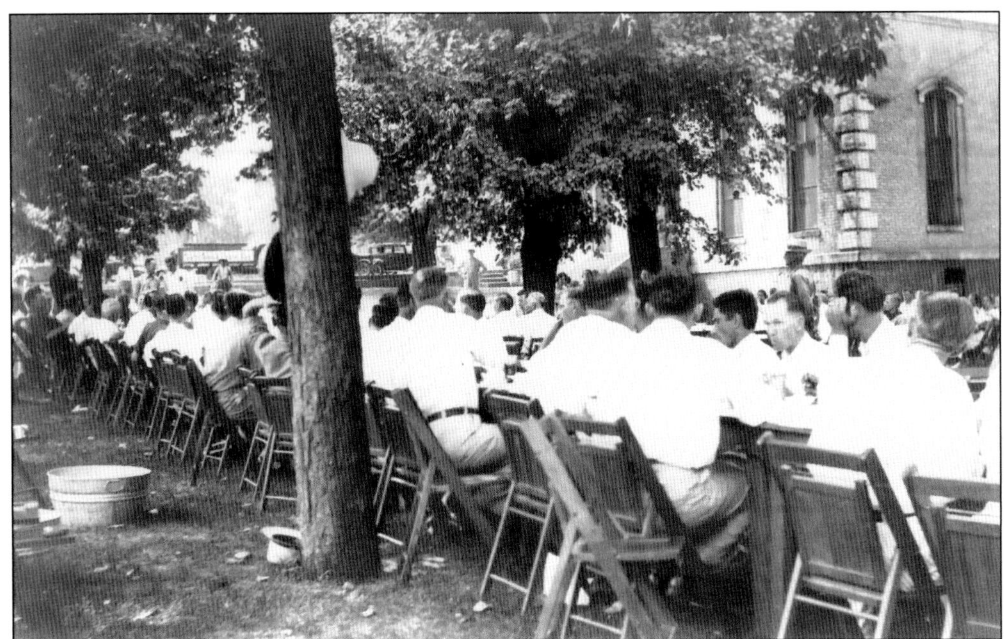

The 1936 Ozark Tour joined a four-county Kiwanis Club meeting on the courthouse lawn in Vienna. The Vienna Kiwanis Club hosted the meeting and provided a fried chicken dinner. Trigg reported that when the Ozarkers left for Metropolis, they circled the courthouse square three to four times while whooping and hollering before heading out of town.

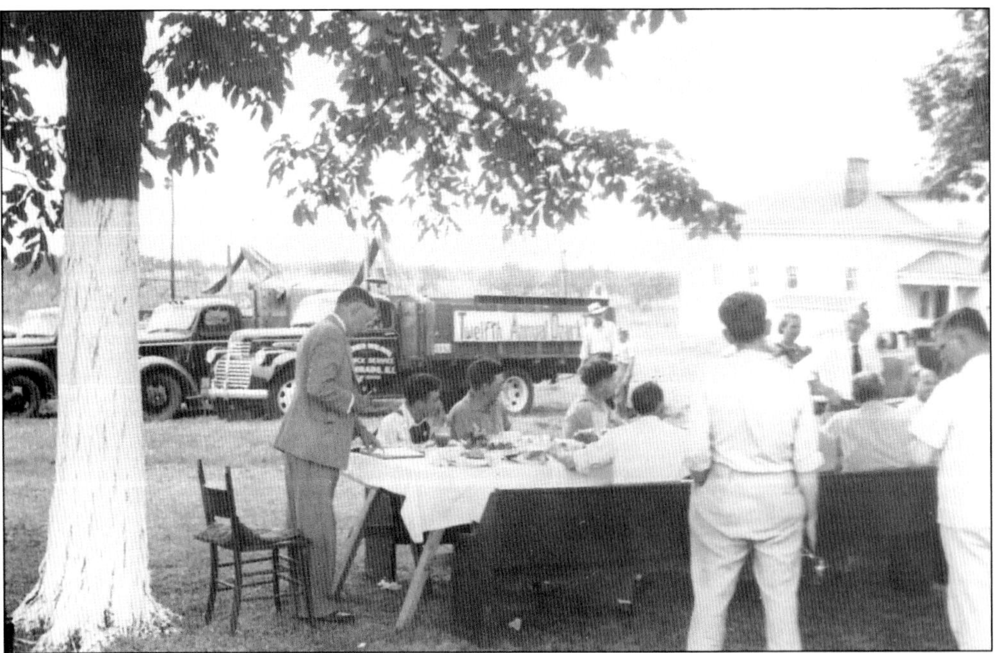

The 1942 Ozarkers ate lunch at the Mormon Temple Church in rural Johnson County. The meal was provided by the ladies of the church. At the luncheon, L.O. Trigg read the names of 11 former members of the tour that were deceased. After lunch, the tour visited Tunnel Hill on the Big Four Railroad (the Cleveland, Cincinnati, Chicago and St. Louis Railway).

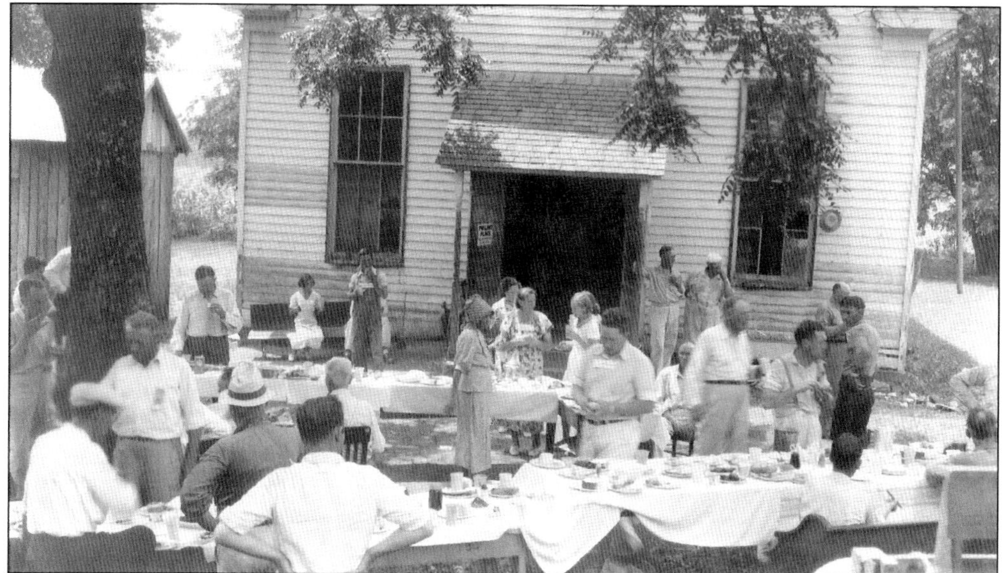

The 1936 Ozark Tour enjoys a feast on the grounds of the New Liberty Schoolhouse in rural Pope County. The Ozarkers had spent the morning touring the University of Chicago archaeological digs at the nearby Kincaid Mounds.

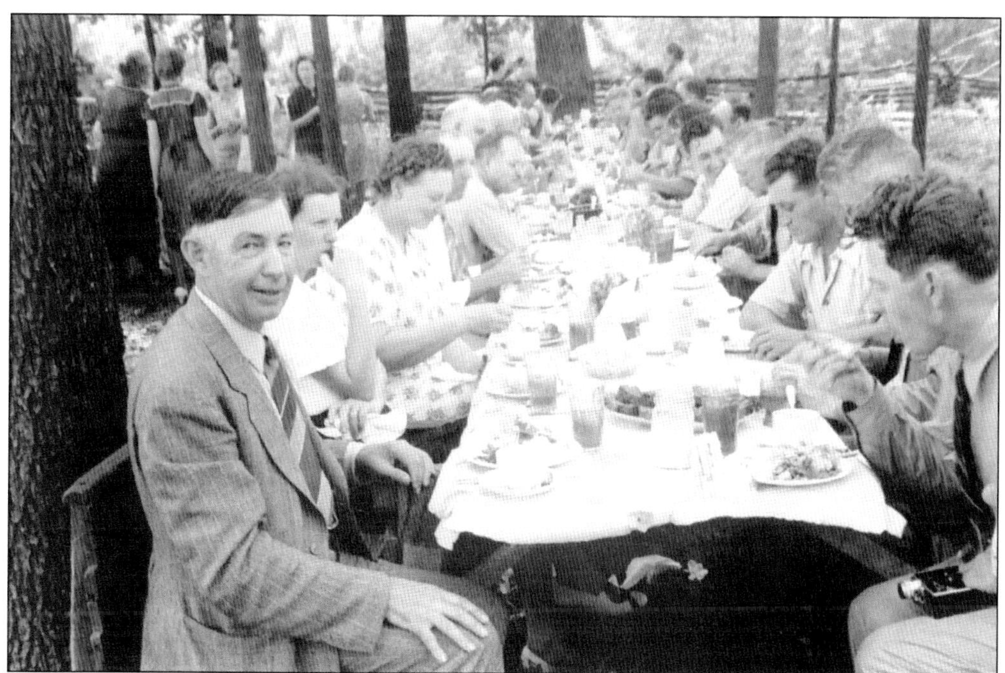

The first day's lunch of the 1939 Ozark Tour was at Hickory Grove Church in Williamson County. The meal was prepared by Flossie Schaubert and the church's Ladies Aid. That morning, the Ozarkers had visited Steve Garris's home near Stonefort to look over his collection of 2,000 Indian relics.

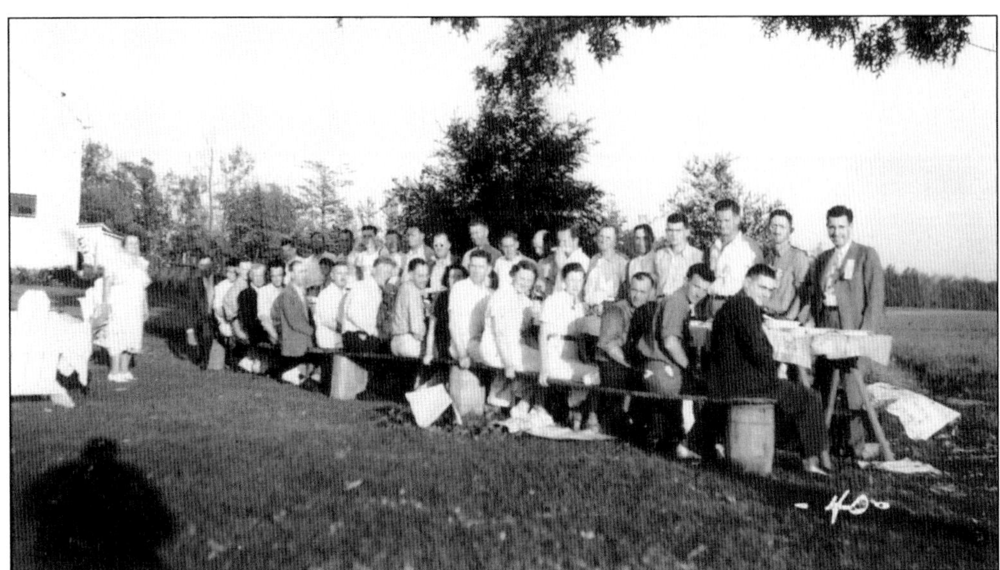

The 1937 Ozark Tour explorers enjoy a fish fry and turtle supper on the lawn of the custodian's house on the island of the Horseshoe Lake State Game Preserve. At farthest right in the photograph is state forester A.J. Thomasek, who had joined the tour for dinner. Horseshoe Lake became a National Natural Landmark in 1972.

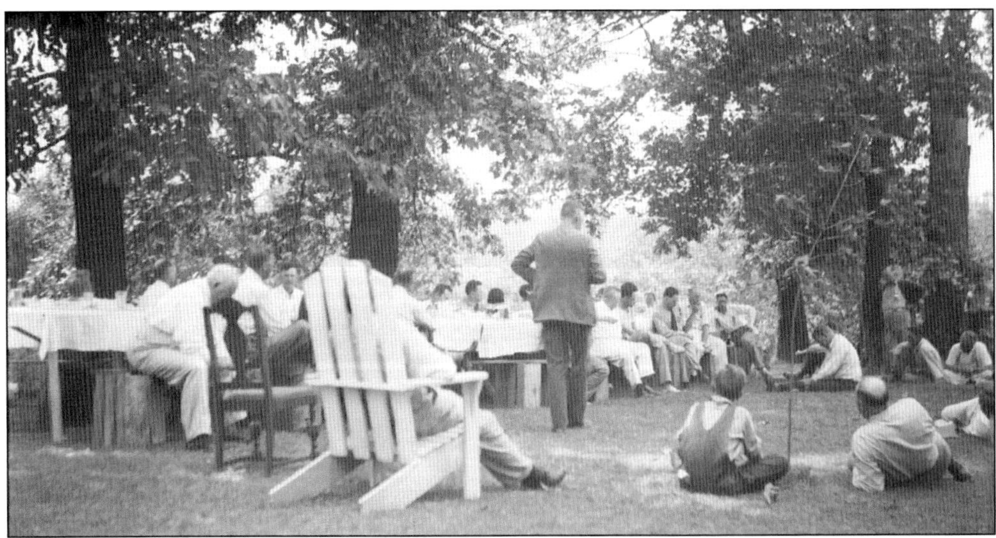

The 1937 Ozark Tour members relax after dinner at Horseshoe Lake. J.C. Conaha, club organizer for the Illinois Department of Conservation, showed a film about the conservation department's work at the state preserves. Much of the presentation concerned quail preservation and the winter wheat provided for wild geese flying to the lake.

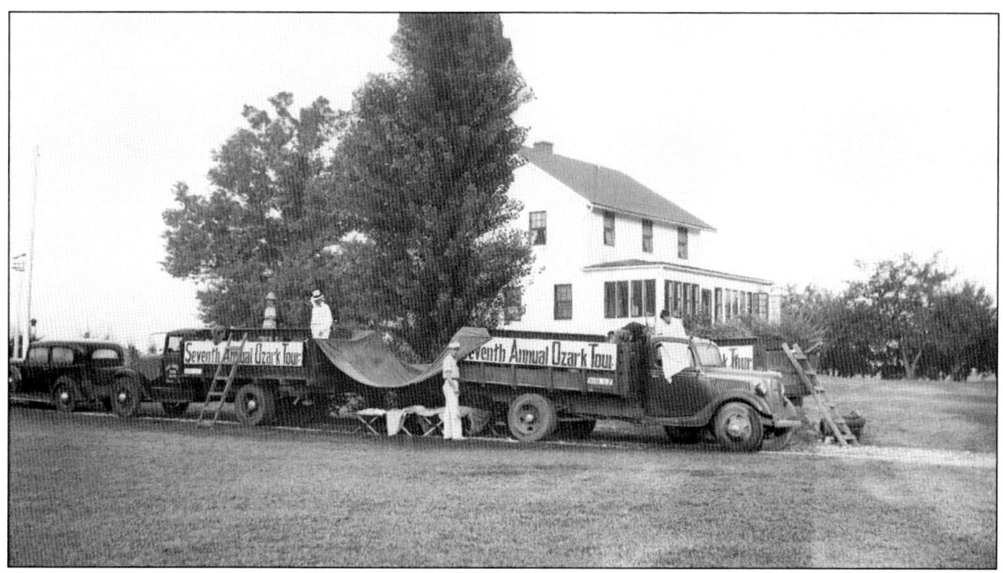

Ozarkers on the seventh annual tour camped on Horseshoe Lake under tarpaulins stretched between the trucks. Later, they took the ferry back across the lake and into Mounds, where breakfast was served by the Mounds First Methodist Church to tour participants and several local businessmen.

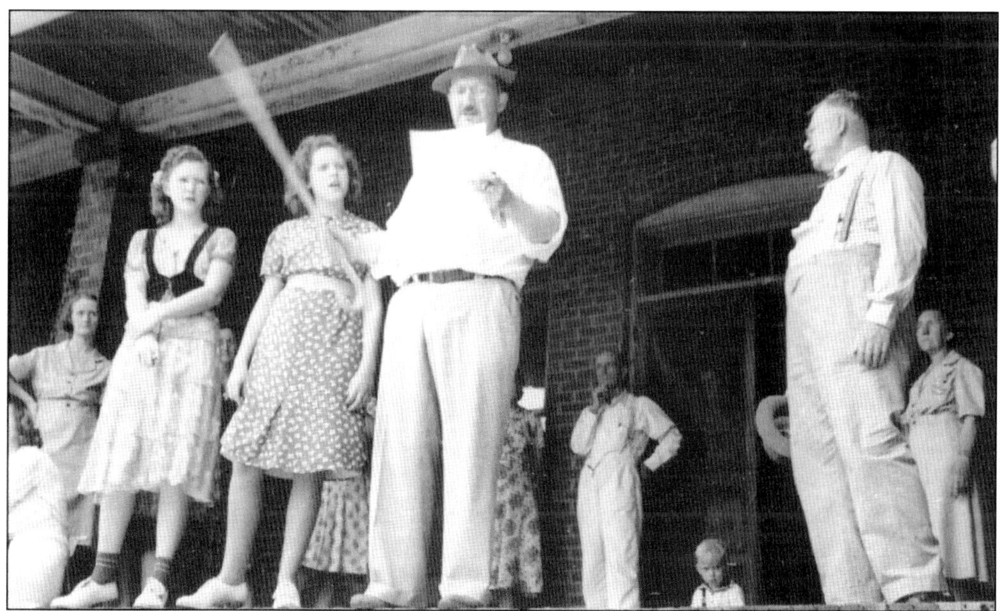

The 1939 Ozark Tour stopped at the former Ozark Hotel in Creal Springs for refreshments of cake and lemonade served by girls of the National Youth Administration. Dr. J.V. Ferrell of Eldorado led a sing-along from the front porch of the brick hotel.

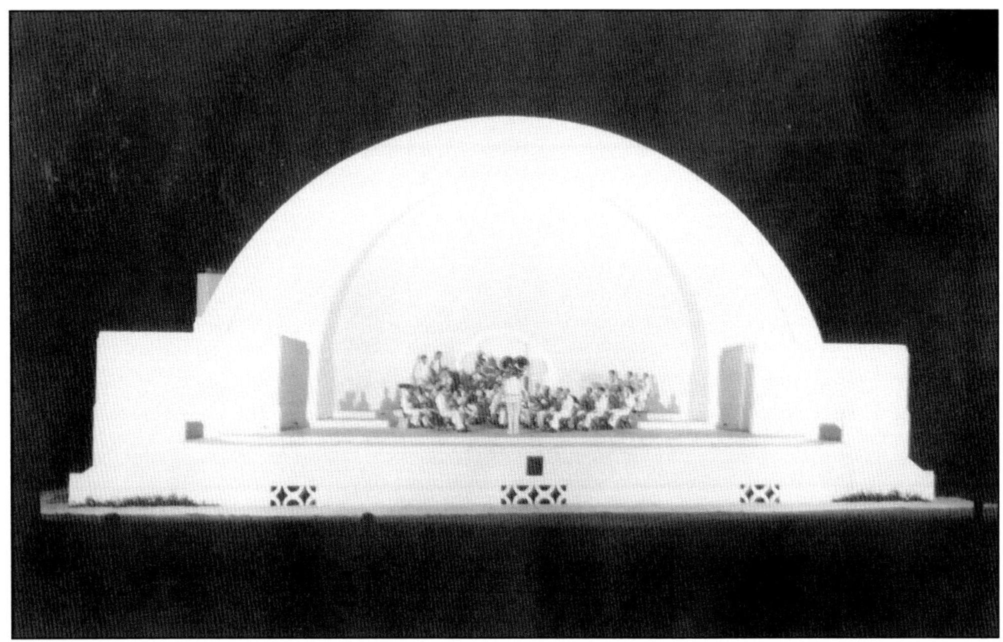

The 1939 Ozark Tour enjoyed an evening concert by the municipal band in its newly built band shell at Riverside Park in Murphysboro. Dinner that evening was provided by the ladies of the Murphysboro Lutheran Church. Many of the Ozarkers slept in the band shell that evening.

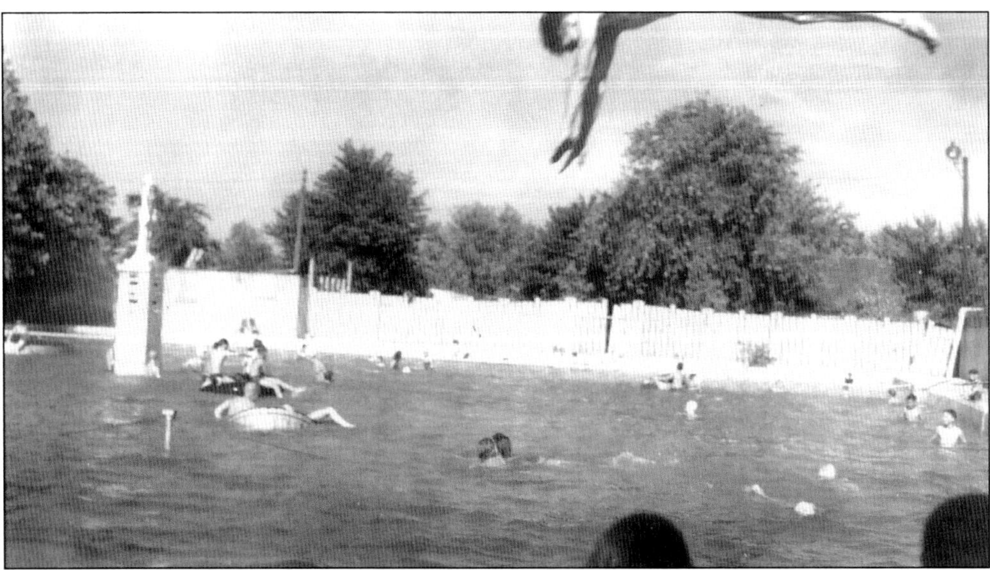

Pictured is the municipal pool at Riverside Park in Murphysboro. Ozarkers who had brought bathing suits enjoyed a swim before dinner and the evening concert on the 1939 Ozark Tour.

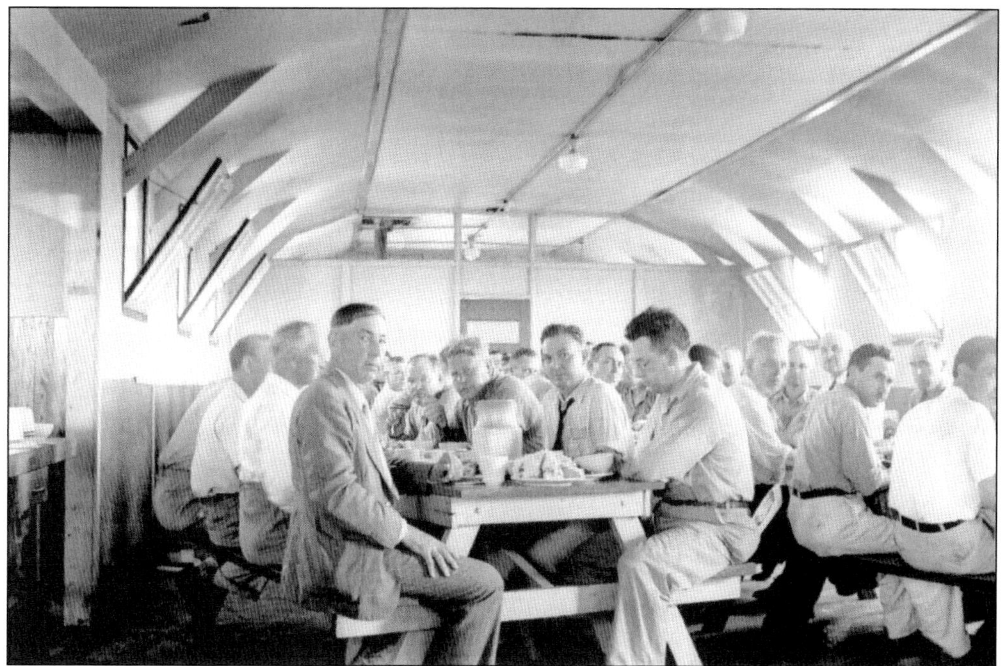

The 1939 Ozark Tour ate lunch at the Pomona CCC camp, the only African American camp in southern Illinois. The hat was passed after lunch to tip the waiters and cooking staff. The Ozarkers spent the morning hiking over the hill to the nearby natural bridge, as wet weather had made the road to the natural bridge impassable by truck.

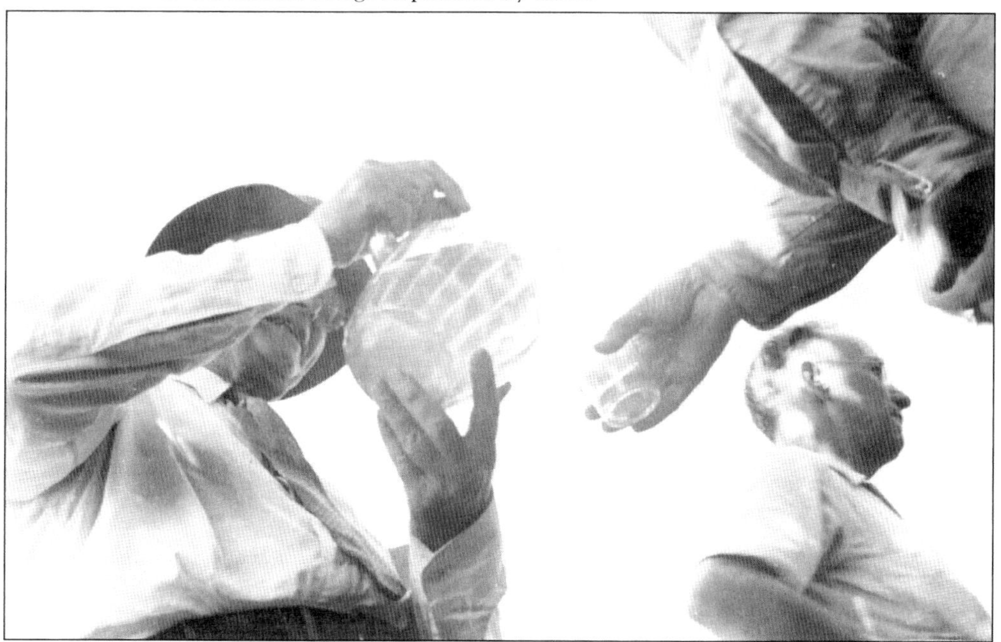

Less than a mile from Giant City Lodge, on their way to breakfast at Midland Hills Country Club, the 1939 Ozark Tour was halted by Ed Roberts (holding pitcher). Roberts had just milked his herd of goats and insisted all the Ozarkers enjoy a snack of graham crackers and a glass of fresh goat's milk.

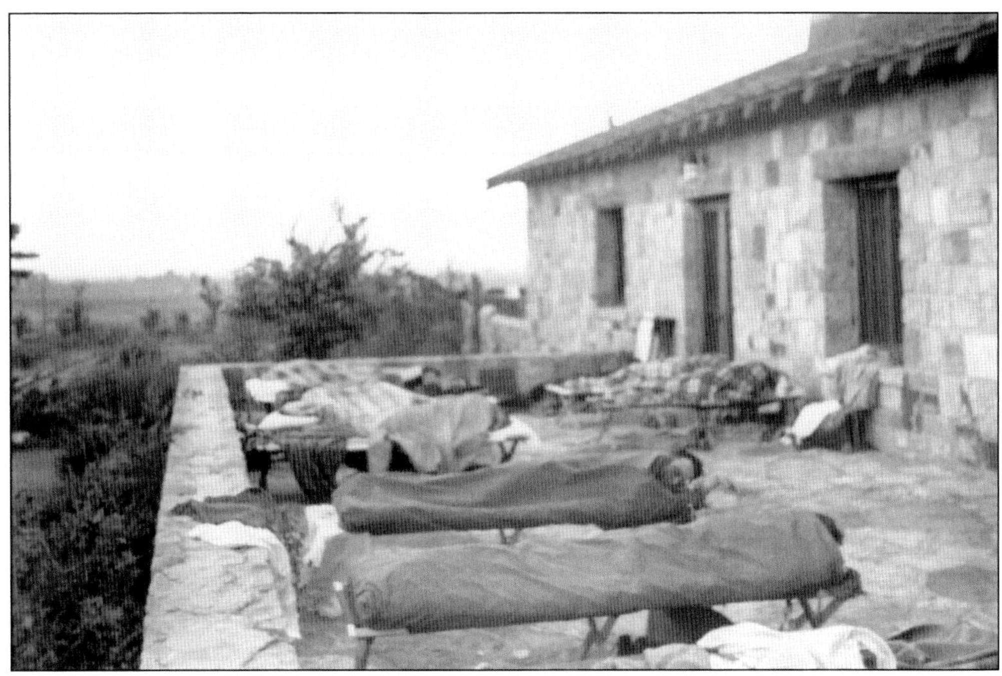

These Ozarkers are sleeping outside Giant City Lodge in 1939 before L.O. Trigg's 6:00 a.m. morning whistle. Trigg reported that some participants were less hardy and slept in cabins. Films of former tours were shown the previous evening before everyone bedded down for the night. Several visitors from Carbondale and the surrounding area were present for the program.

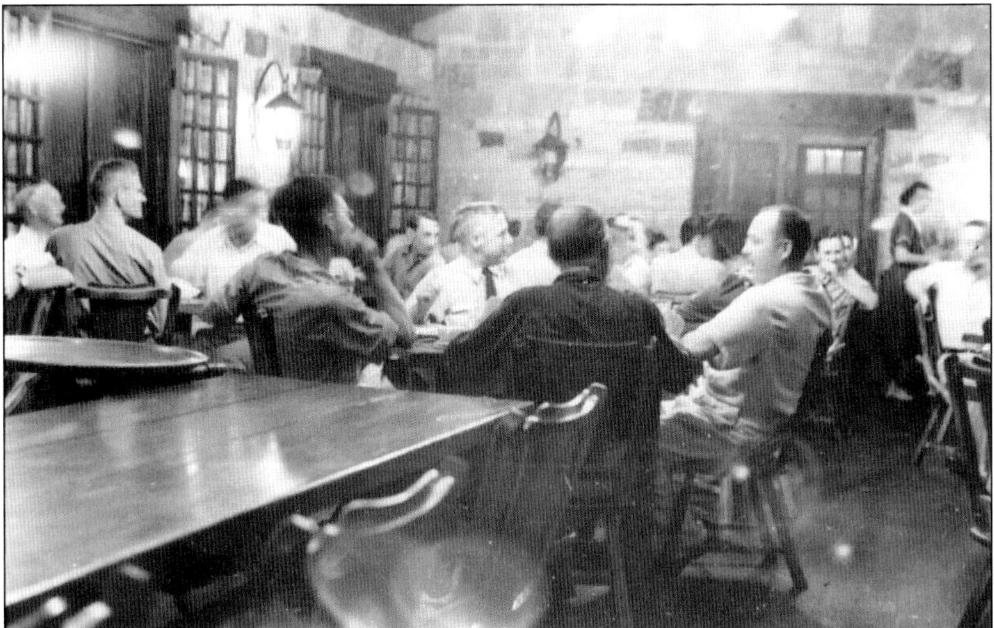

The 1939 Ozark Tour ate dinner on the first evening of the tour at Giant City Lodge in Jackson County. The meal was prepared by Clarient Hopkins and his wife, formerly of the Harrisburg Country Club. L.O. Trigg stated that Mr. and Mrs. Hopkins "know how to properly prepare and satisfactorily serve for such occasions as the coming of the Ozark Tour group."

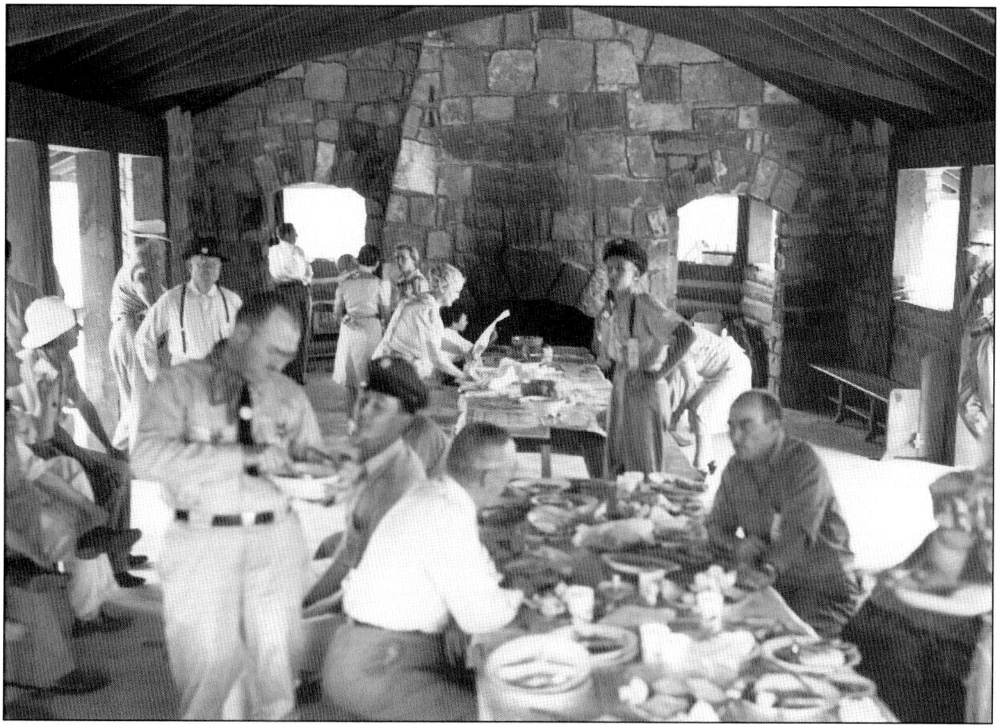

The first meal of the 1940 Ozark Tour was lunch served at a Lake Glendale shelter by the Dixon Springs Home Bureau Unit. The 55 registered members of the tour spent the morning touring Hayes Canyon near Eddyville. After lunch, the group viewed Tunnel Three on the Edgewood Cutoff rail line.

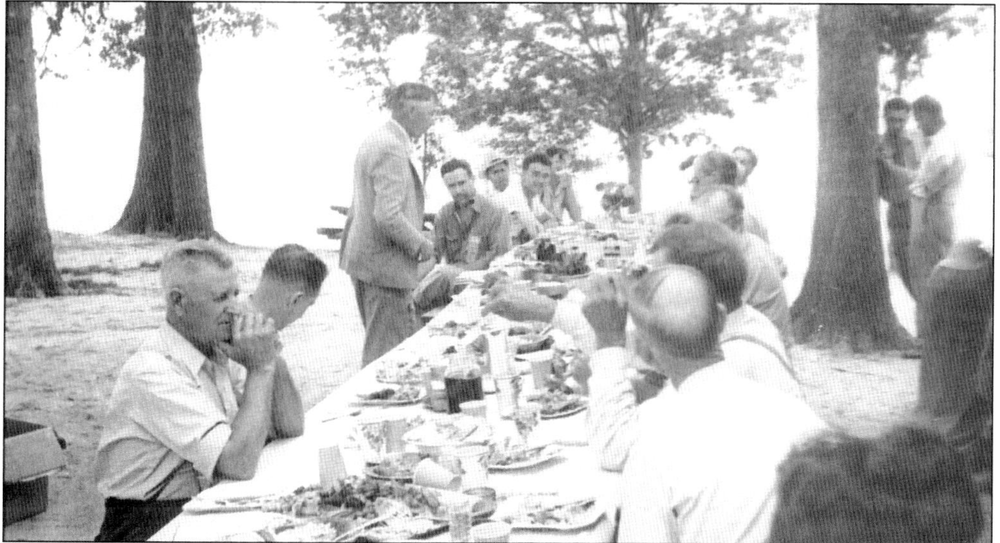

The final meal of the 1942 Ozark Tour was served on the north shore of Crab Orchard Lake. A fish fry consisting of more than a pound of food per person was prepared. Various Ozarkers expressed "pleasure of association together, the scenery enjoyed, the fine meals, and regrets that the event was to disband so soon." There were eight or nine new faces among the 39 registered for the 1942 tour.

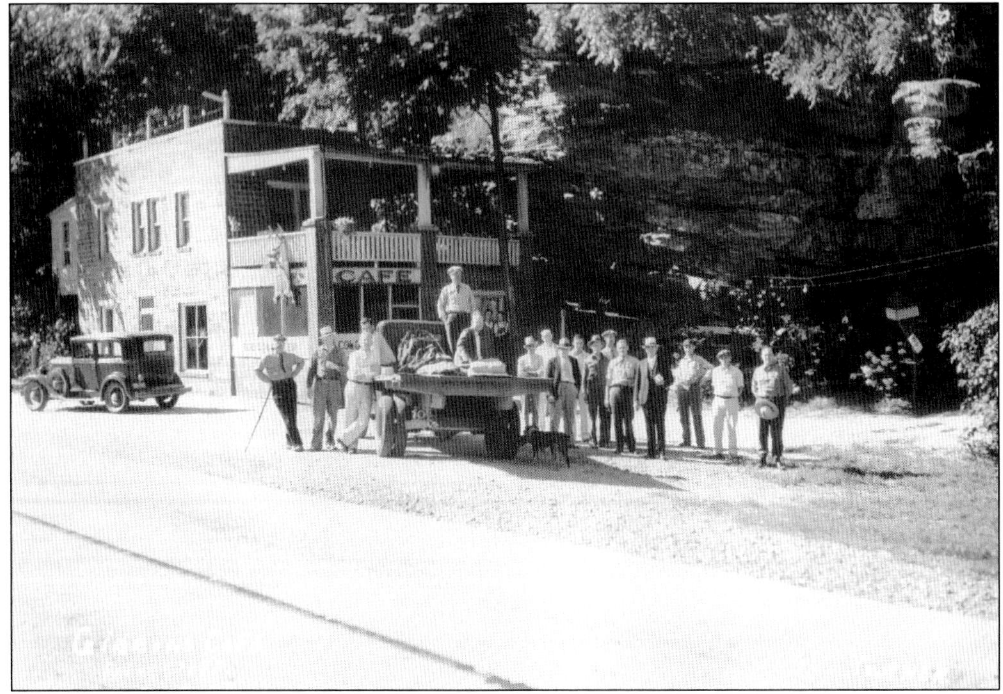

The 1933 Ozark Tour stopped at Gibbons Café at Fairy Cliff in Herod. The café was a favorite stop of L.O. Trigg's even when he was not on an Ozark Tour. The café hosted tour groups in 1941, 1944, and 1949, as well as celebrating Trigg's promotion to "colonel" in 1948. On one tour, rain forced the Ozarkers' meal to be moved into the shelter of the adjacent bluff cave.

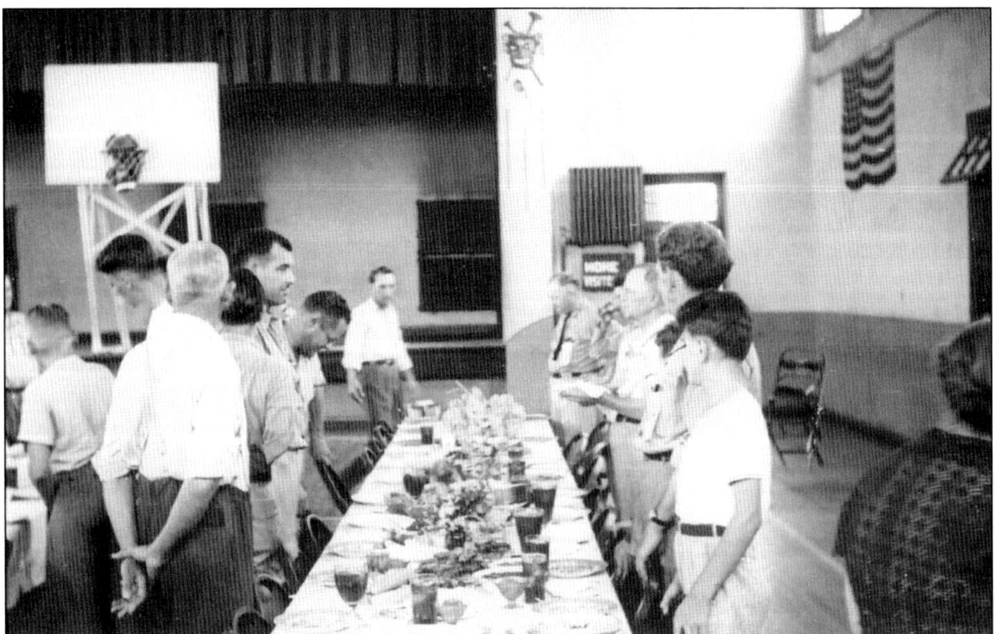

On the second day of the 1942 tour, lunch was served in a high school gym at Buncombe by the Baptist Ladies Aid. The Ozarkers spent the morning touring Ferne Clyffe Park and Cedar Bluff. In the afternoon, they toured the Sand Cave on the Miles Farm south of Goreville.

Five

Resthaven Farm

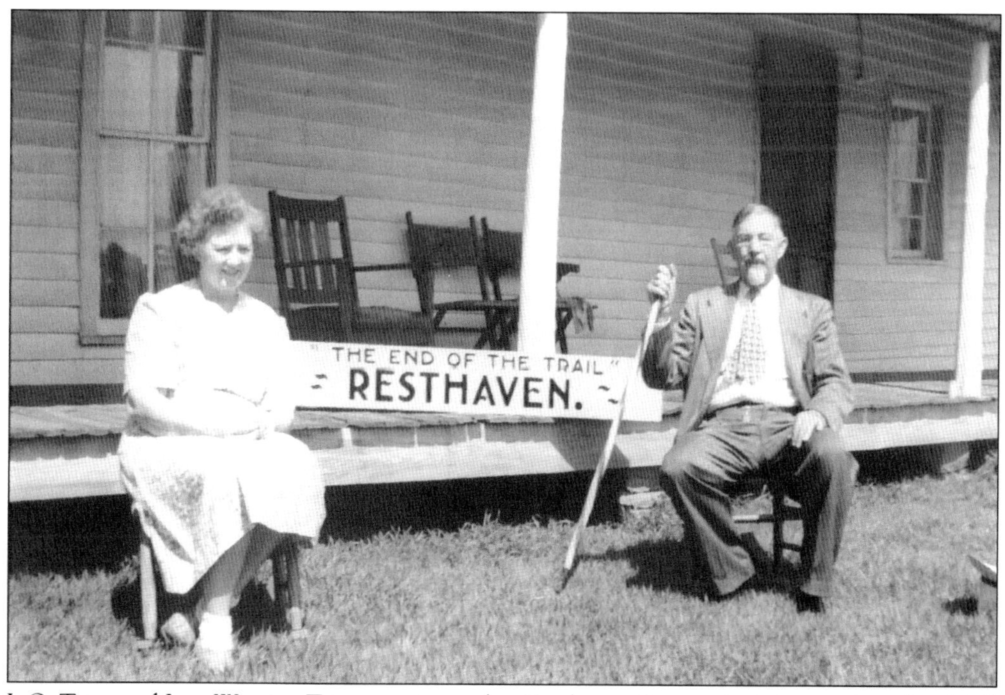

L.O. Trigg and Inez Wiggins Trigg are pictured at Resthaven Farm, which he purchased in 1937; the farm was located near the border of Gallatin and Hardin Counties. This picture was taken four days after the conclusion of the 1948 Ozark Tour. An Ozark Tour first visited the farm and Grindstaff Hollow in 1933.

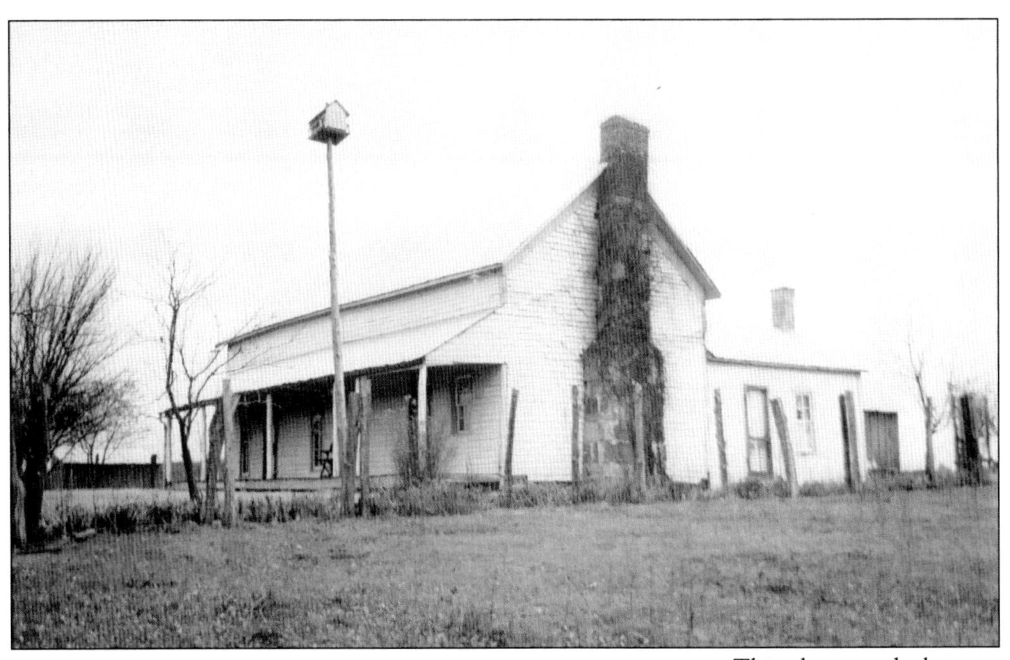

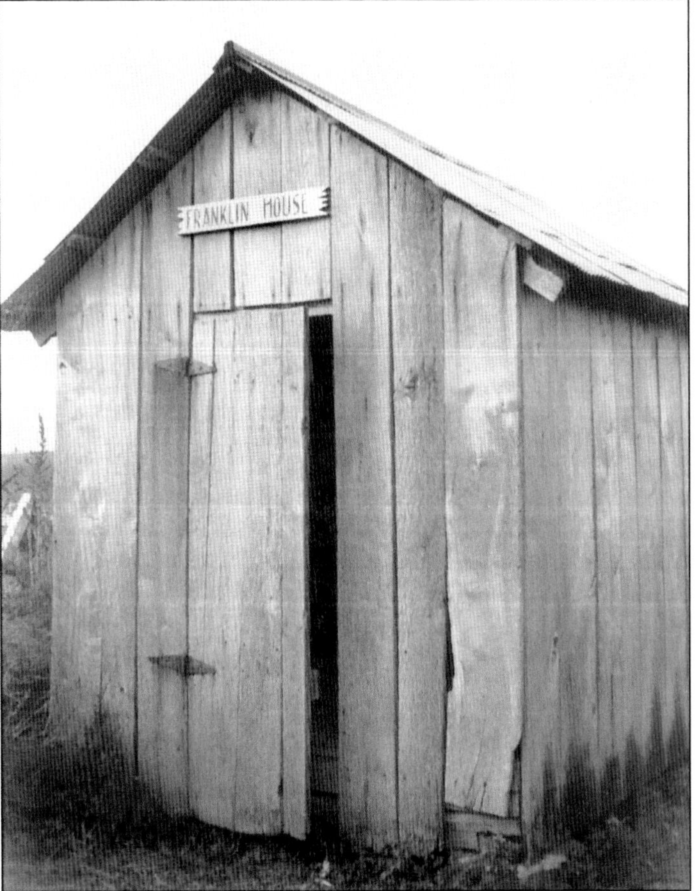

This photograph shows the old farmhouse at Resthaven. Some of the older parts of the house were log structures. At the time L.O. Trigg bought the property, the porch offered a clear view across Grindstaff Hollow to High Knob.

Trigg was a staunch Republican all his life. He named the outhouse at Resthaven the "Franklin House" after Pres. Franklin D. Roosevelt. Although Trigg did not care for the president's politics, it was Roosevelt who, on September 6, 1939, signed the proclamation designating the forest purchase units in southern Illinois as the Shawnee National Forest.

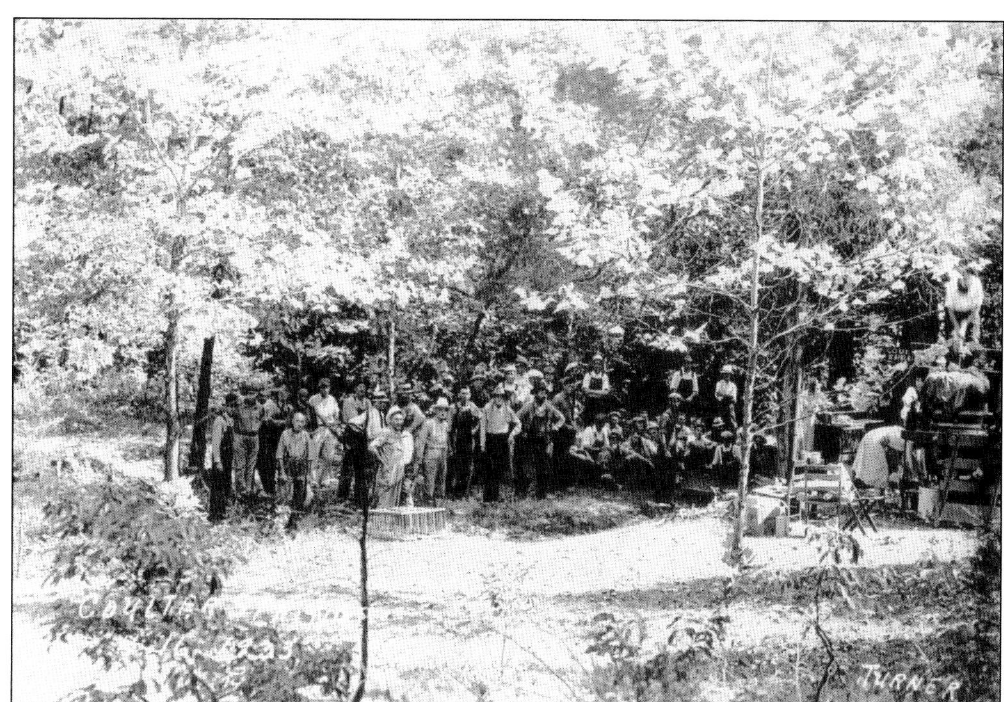

The 1933 Ozark Tour is pictured during the Ozarkers' first visit to Grindstaff Hollow to eat lunch at Coulter Spring. They had visited the Anvil Rock area that morning (as shown in the photograph on the cover of this book), and after exploring the unique sites in the hollow, they rode to Rosiclare for dinner at the YMCA.

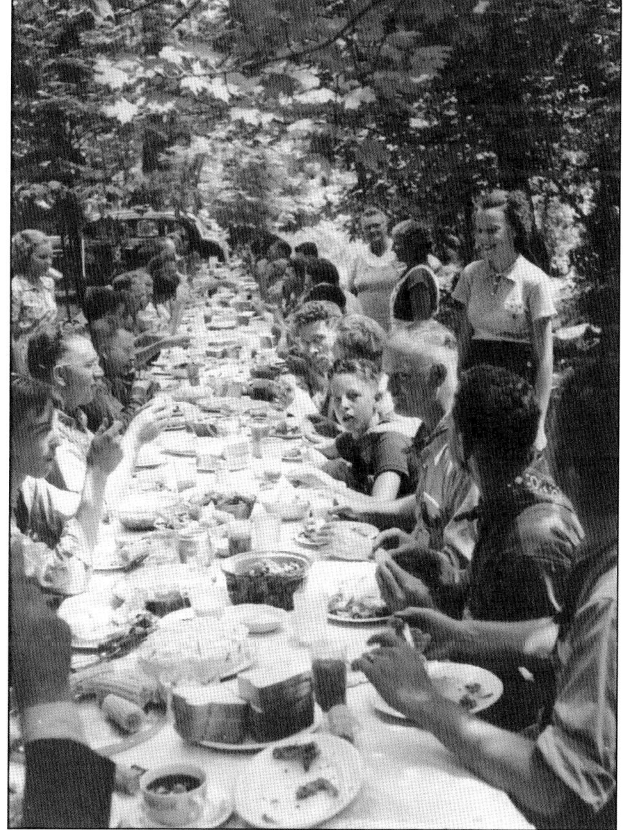

The 1938 Ozark Tour members eat lunch in the shade of the bluffs and trees of Grindstaff Hollow. Ozarkers passed the American Legion Auxiliary Memorial Plantation on their way to Resthaven Farm. They noted the roads were much improved since their visit on the 1933 Ozark Tour, during which they traveled an "abandoned road that hardly a wagon and team could traverse."

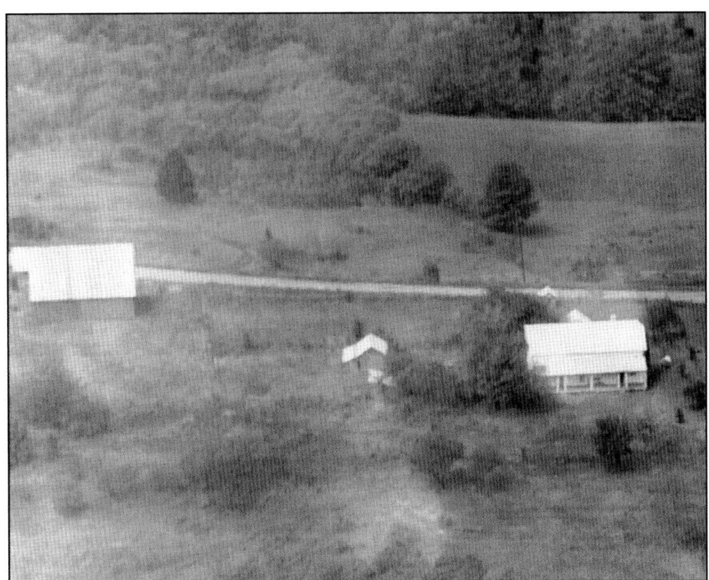

The house and barn at Resthaven Farm in Gallatin County are pictured in this view from the air. Across Grindstaff Hollow Road, in the empty field to the left, Trigg planted 4,000 shortleaf pines to create his own forest plantation. (Kenneth Price.)

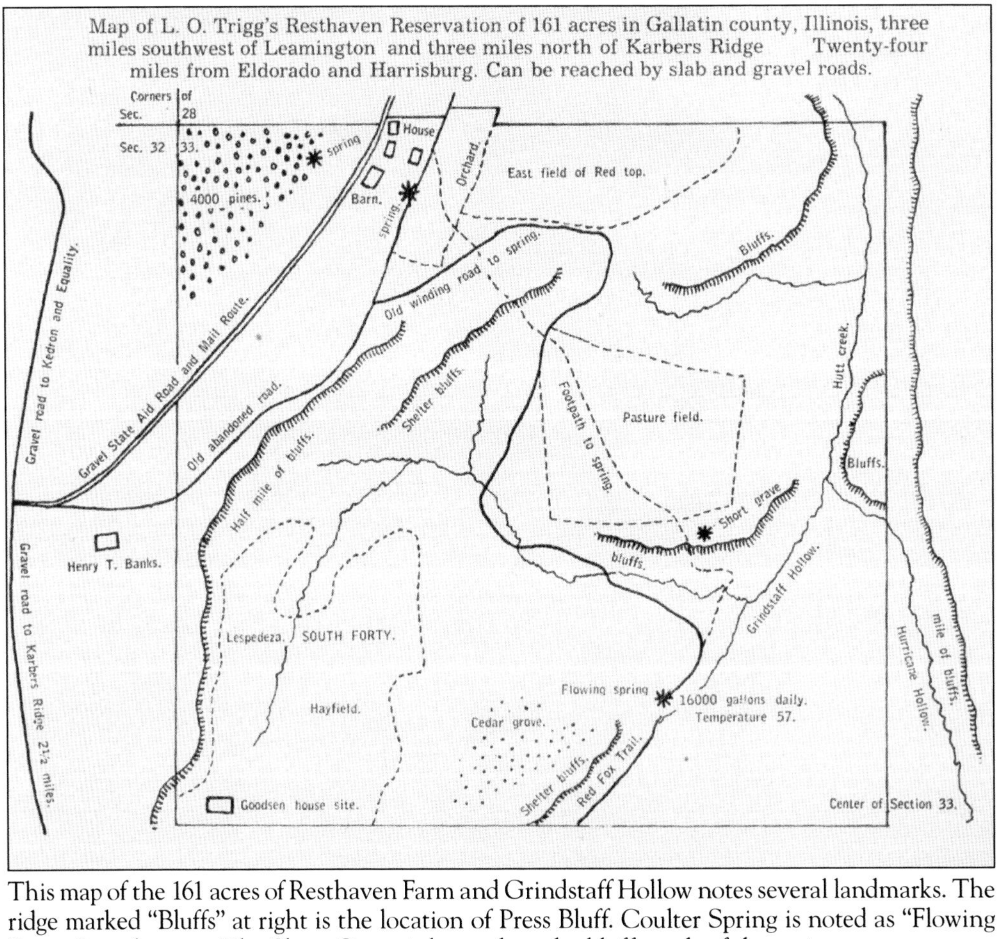

Map of L. O. Trigg's Resthaven Reservation of 161 acres in Gallatin county, Illinois, three miles southwest of Leamington and three miles north of Karbers Ridge Twenty-four miles from Eldorado and Harrisburg. Can be reached by slab and gravel roads.

Corners of
Sec. 28
Sec. 32 33.
House
spring
Barn.
spring.
Orchard.
East field of Red top.
4000 pines.
Old winding road to spring.
Bluffs.
Gravel road to Kedron and Equality.
Gravel State Aid Road and Mail Route.
Old abandoned road.
Shelter bluffs.
Half mile of bluffs.
Footpath to spring.
Pasture field.
Hutt creek.
Bluffs.
Short grave
bluffs.
Henry T. Banks.
Grindstaff Hollow.
Lespedeza. SOUTH FORTY.
Hayfield.
Flowing spring
16000 gallons daily.
Temperature 57.
Cedar grove.
Hurricane Hollow.
mile of bluffs.
Shelter bluffs.
Red Fox Trail.
Gravel road to Karbers Ridge 2½ miles.
Goodsen house site.
Center of Section 33.

This map of the 161 acres of Resthaven Farm and Grindstaff Hollow notes several landmarks. The ridge marked "Bluffs" at right is the location of Press Bluff. Coulter Spring is noted as "Flowing Spring" on the map. The Short Grave is located on the bluff north of the spring.

L.O. Trigg is pictured walking along the Red Fox Trail at Resthaven Farm on November 30, 1941. The trail leads from Coulter Spring through the shelter bluffs of Grindstaff Hollow.

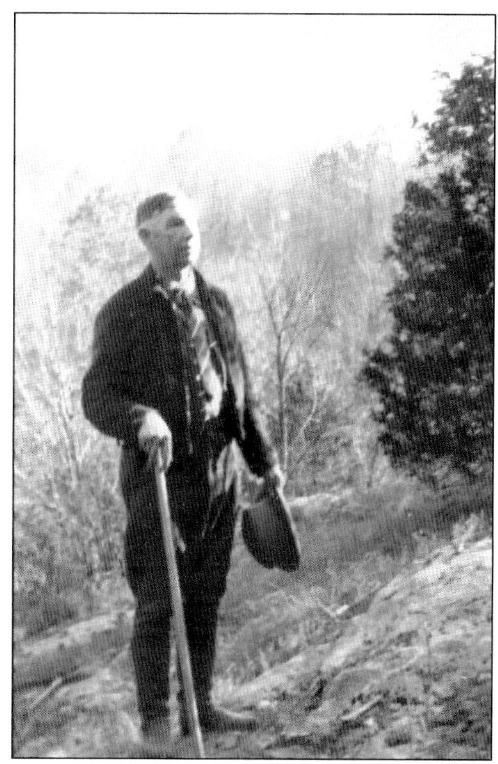

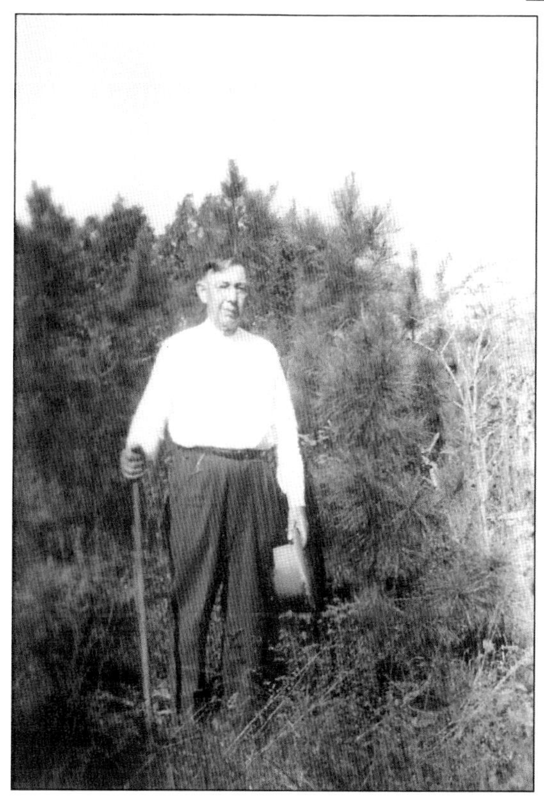

Trigg stands in his forest plantation in October 1946. He planted 4,000 shortleaf pine seedlings at Resthaven Farm in April 1941.

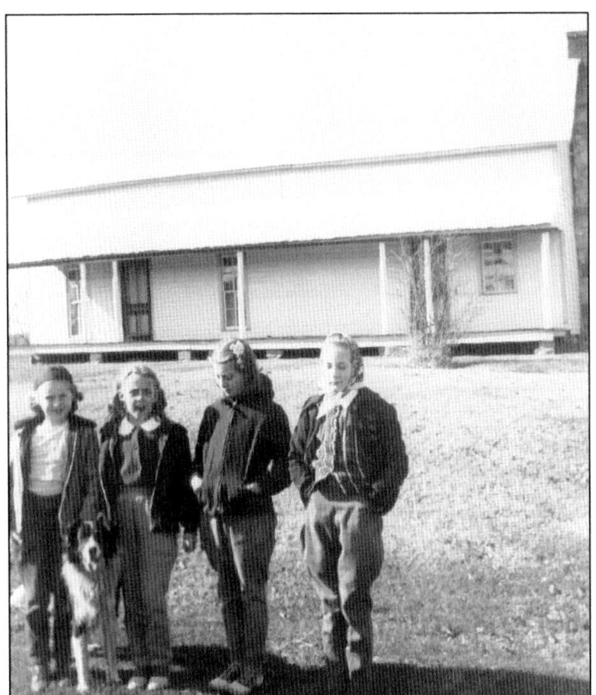

L.O. Trigg's granddaughters and Gerry the dog celebrate Thanksgiving at Resthaven Farm on November 20, 1941. Pictured are, from left to right, Janet Trigg, Jacquelynn Cook, Carolynn Cook, and Ann Erwood.

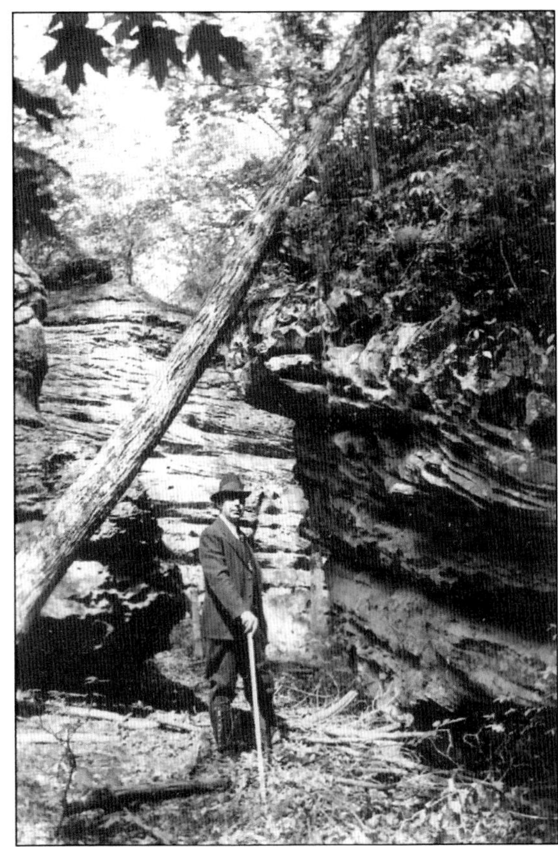

In this photograph taken on May 8, 1937, L.O. Trigg explores the shelter bluffs and cliffs of Grindstaff Hollow on Resthaven Farm.

Coulter Spring is named for Jonas Coulter, who had a cabin in the area sometime after the Grindstaffs moved out of the hollow. L.O. Trigg reported that the spring produced 16,000 gallons of 57-degree soft water per day, even in summer. Two grindstones at the spring were the only remains of pioneer Robin Grindstaff's mule-powered gristmill and home that once stood adjacent to the spring.

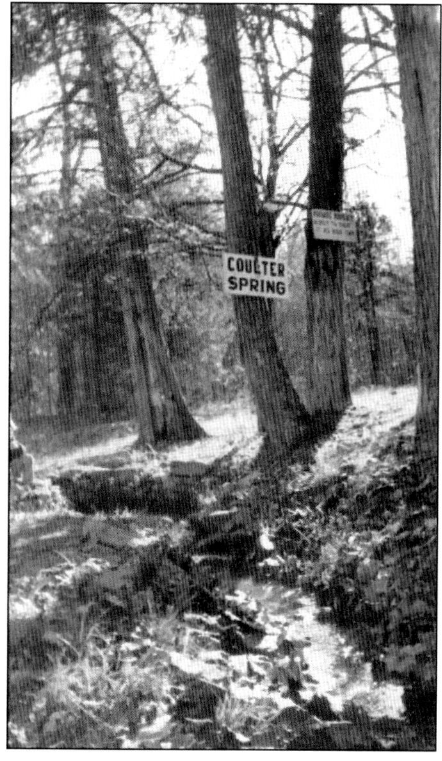

Dr. J.V. Ferrell (on his back at left) and other Ozarkers enjoy a "foot washing" at Coulter Spring prior to lunch in Grindstaff Hollow on the 1938 Ozark Tour. Visiting the hollow and spring became a "rite of passage" for Ozarkers.

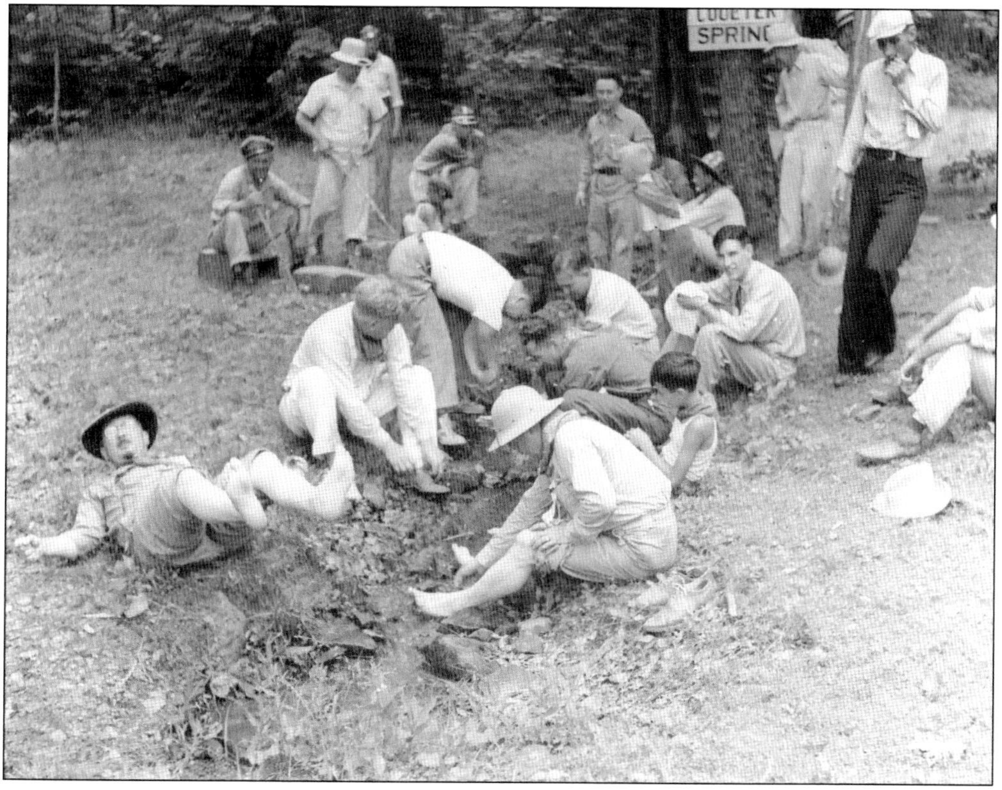

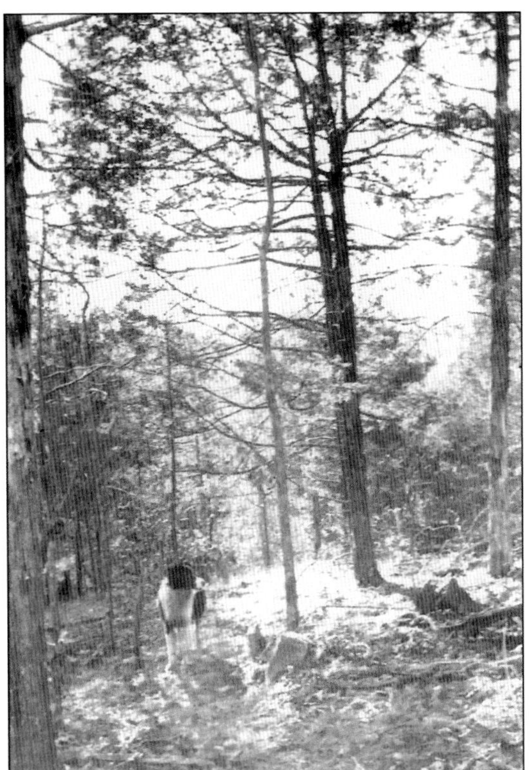

L.O. Trigg said that when Liz Grindstaff died, her neighbors used a stalk to measure the body to build her coffin. However, the resulting coffin was too short. With the effects of the heat on the body, there was no time for them to build a new one. Her husband, Robin Grindstaff, used a sledgehammer to fold his wife's legs under to fit inside the coffin—this is the origin of the Short Grave of Grindstaff Hollow. Pictured is Trigg's dog Gerry, standing next to the stone marking the location of the Short Grave.

On the 1938 Ozark Tour, the explorers used a rope to descend the bluff from the Short Grave to the valley. The stream below the bluff joins runoff from Coulter Spring to form Hutt Creek, so named for when Robin and Preston Grindstaff's homes (huts) were in the hollow.

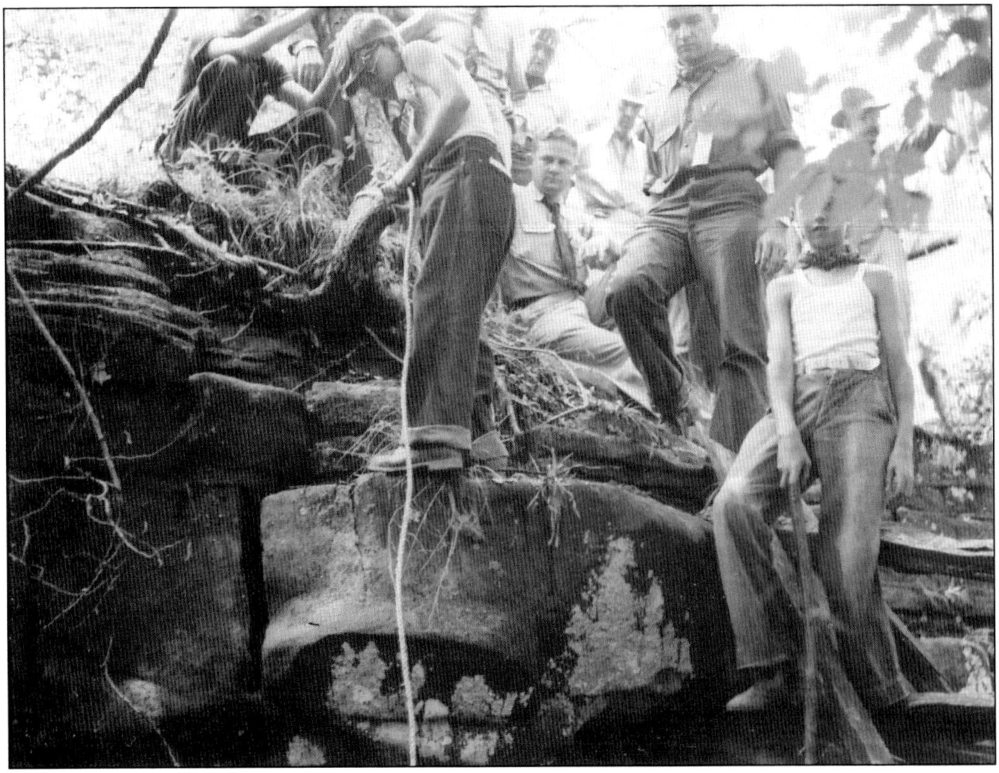

This shelter bluff is north of Coulter Spring in Grindstaff Hollow. Above the bluff, in the grove of cedar trees, is the Short Grave, the final resting place of Liz Grindstaff. At least one other unidentified grave is beside the Short Grave.

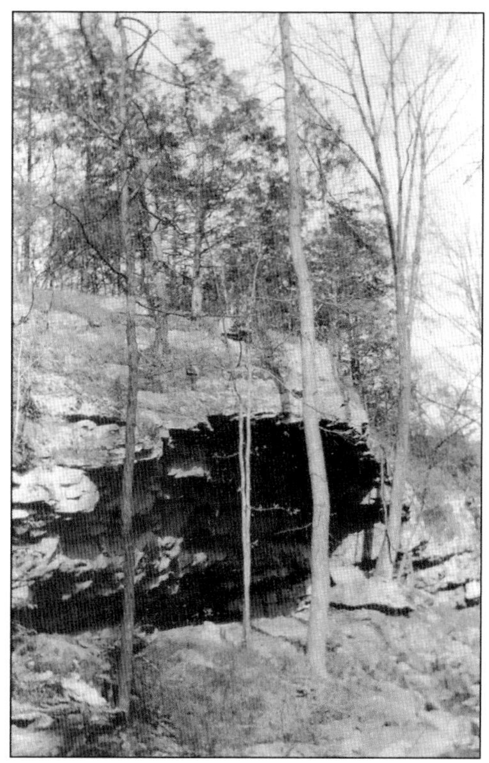

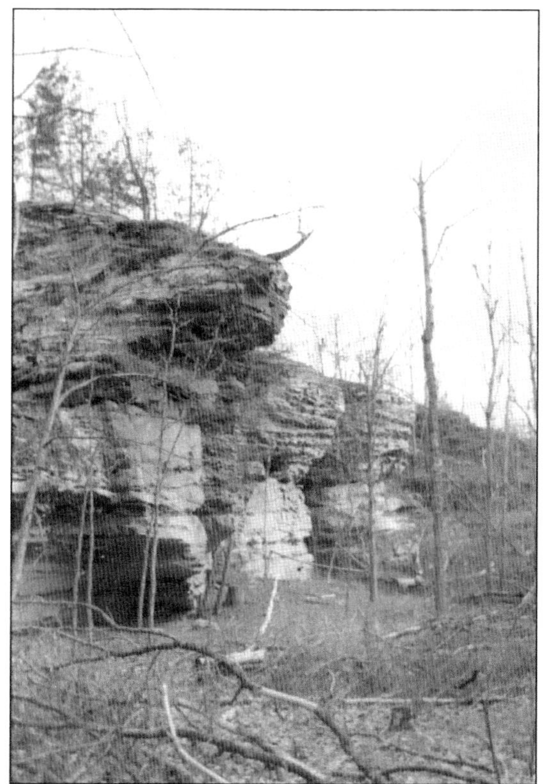

Press Bluff is located in Grindstaff Hollow. L.O. Trigg said that Preston Grindstaff built his home under this bluff. Grindstaff apparently was not well regarded and was driven out by neighbors throwing stones onto his home from the overhanging bluff above. Grindstaff died in the *General Lyon* disaster during the Civil War. His wife, Nancy Rawlins Grindstaff, died shortly thereafter, leaving behind two children—Leatha Elizabeth and Samuel P.—to be raised by her family. (Kenneth Price.)

The end of the Trigg Trails—Resthaven

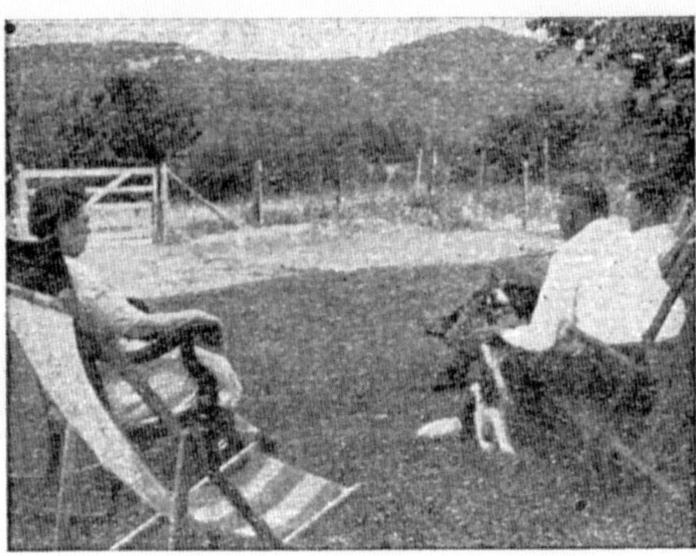

Relaxing on the lawn at Trigg's "Resthaven Farm" in Illinois Ozarks. The Eleventh Annual Ozark Tour camped here overnight enjoying scenery and pure spring water.

This is your vacation and your opportunity to REST at Resthaven. Or you can explore to the limit of your physical capacity.

On Resthaven Farm you will see old rail fences of pioneer days — taking your memory back to the time of Lincoln — back when he owned land here in Gallatin county.

If you are a writer and want to get material and a background for nature subjects, folk lore stories, etc., you should visit Resthaven. Suggestions: The squatters, pioneers, the Grindstaffs, the little grist mill, Casey's still, the shooting matches, the short grave, the buried loot of Cave-in-Rock outlaws, birds, trees, etc.

Fifty feet west of the big spring Robin and 'Liz Grindstaff settled as squatters, living in a cabin, building a little grist mill which was operated by mule power. Two pieces of the small (18-inch) buhrstone now rest beside the big spring.

On Resthaven Reservation is the famous cold water spring flowing sixteen thousand gallons of soft water daily. This and the shade of the two-hundred-year-old cedars make this a most inviting and restful place to visit even on a hot day in July. When its 98 this spring water is 57.

Years before a gravel road, electric lights and other improvements was brought to Resthaven it was a real hideout among cliffs, caves, shelter bluffs, etc. During prohibition days the extensive product of this farm was sold in terms of gallons instead of bushels. Of course those days now are only a memory. Today it is a haven for rest—a scenery farm, where you can rest in the shade and drink cold water from the big spring flowing sixteen thousand gallons daily, running a half mile through the woodland and on to the Ohio river. Here, too, you breathe the ozone of the Ozarks. Ask Jake and Dean.

This flyer advertises the 1944 Ozark Tour. Due to wartime restrictions on tires and fuel, the 1943 and 1944 Ozark Tours both headquartered in one place—Dixon Springs in 1943 and Resthaven Farm in 1944. The 1944 Ozarkers took day excursions to visit nearby locations "Little Garden of the Gods," a fluorspar mine, and boating and fishing on Pounds Hollow Lake. At Resthaven, they watched educational films and films of prior tours.

NATURE'S LANGUAGE

That nature in many ways reveals God is evident to anyone who knows his Maker and reads His holy Word. Detailed acquaintance with Bible language tunes man's ear to the voice of nature.

* * *

Wild flowers, returning song birds, rushing streams, blue lakes, fleecy clouds, creating pictures against the sky, a world beautiful, rich in joy-giving treasures—spring time.

* * *

In spring and early summer the great out-of-doors calls with an almost irresistible power. To walk among the flowers and trees by a clear cool stream is to move where nature herself speaks to us the language of the Creator.

* * *

Whoever has sat on the banks of a well-filled stream has observed the grass, the flowers, and the trees close to the water are more luxuriant and vigorous than elsewhere. The meadows and hills may be brown and sear, but near the water all life is fresh and beautiful . . . . The divine lessons to be drawn from this is recorded in the scripture.

* * *

The birds, the flowers, the mountains, the cattle on a thousand hills, the fish of the seas—all are His work. The rain is in His keeping, as are the snow and the winds. The stars, the sun and moon follow courses which He has determined.

* * *

What a basis here for all that man would study: Anthropology, biology, chemistry, geology, physics, astronomy, botany, psychology, zoology. There is not a phase of human learning but that it refers us back to the Creator.

* * *

O God, open our eyes to see also in nature all about us Thy goodness and wisdom, Thy power and majesty.

—Fourteenth Annual Ozark Tour reunion July 23-24-25, 1944.

The 1944 Ozark Tour started with Sunday services conducted by longtime Ozarker, Attorney Jacob Myers at Resthaven Farm. The printed bulletin *Nature's Language* was shared at Resthaven during the 1944 tour and is reminiscent of famed naturalist Aldo Leopold's writings in *A Sand County Almanac*.

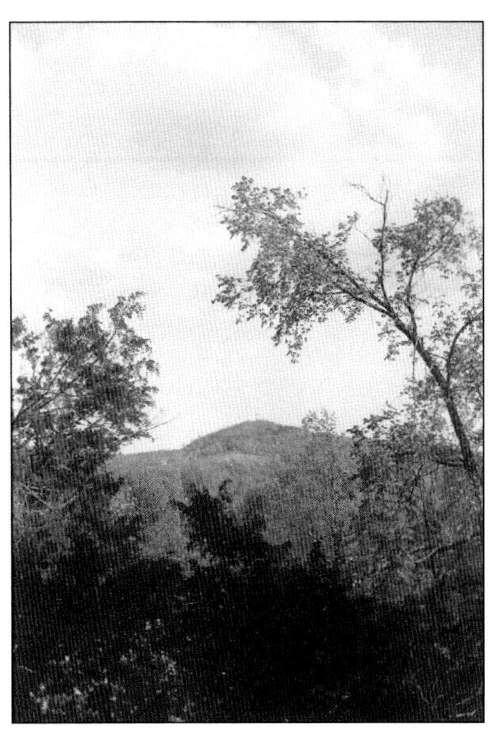

This image features a view of High Knob from Resthaven Farm. High Knob is the third-highest elevation in southern Illinois and was the location of a fire lookout tower. Between High Knob and Resthaven Farm is Grindstaff Hollow; all are within Gallatin County.

L.O. Trigg and his wife, Inez, relax around the fireplace at Resthaven Farm with their dog, Gerry. This picture was taken sometime after Trigg grew out his beard for the 1947 Saline County Centennial Celebration.

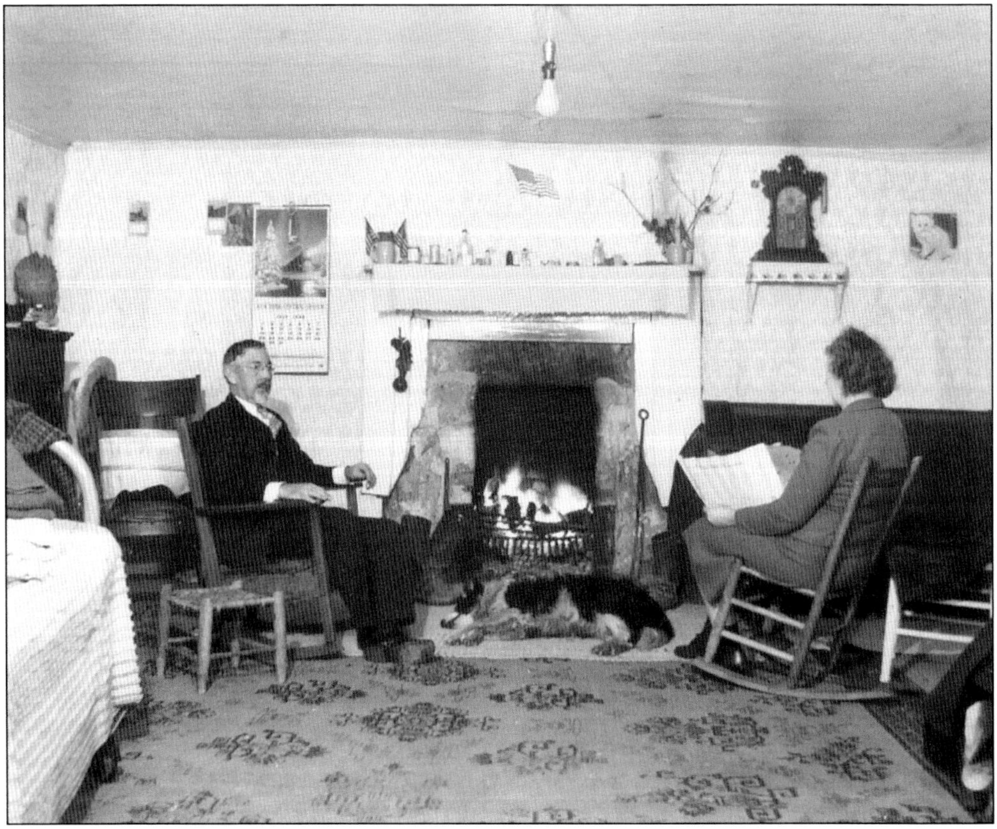

Six

On the Ohio and Mississippi Rivers

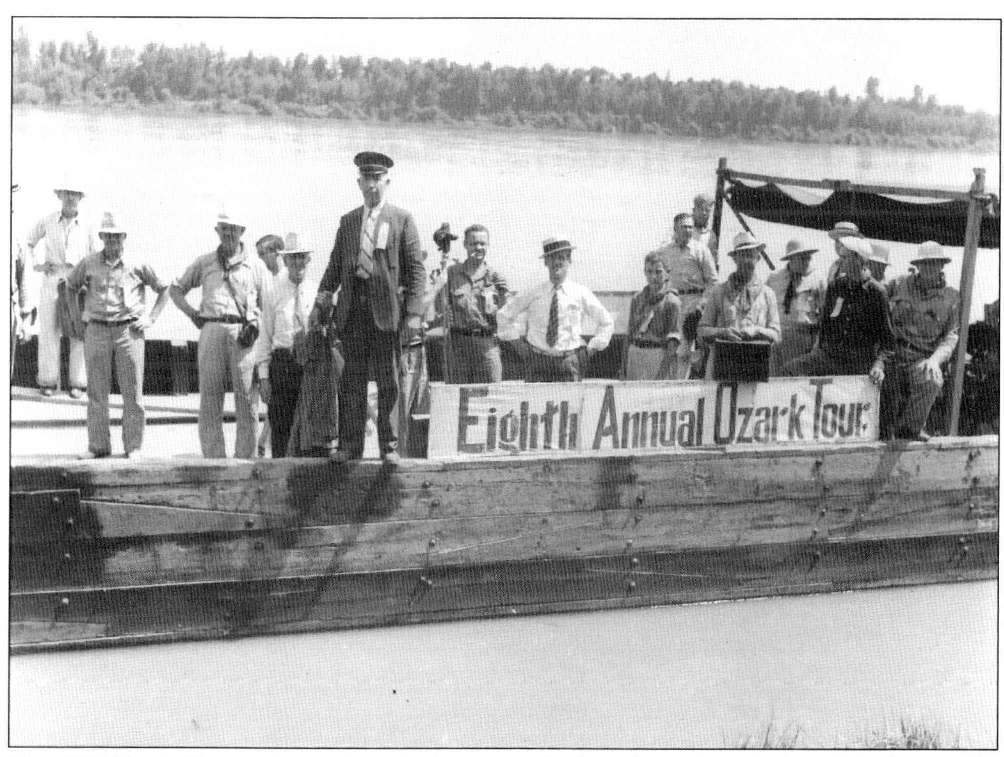

The 1938 Ozark Tour is shown aboard a barge attached to the tugboat *Hobo Bill* docked on the Elizabethtown riverfront. Ozarkers boarded at Shawneetown and made stops at Saline River, the Sellers' Landing paper mill site, Battery Rock, Ohio River Dam 50, the landing of the infamous Ford's Ferry, and "Pirate's Cave" at Cave-in-Rock before disembarking at Elizabethtown.

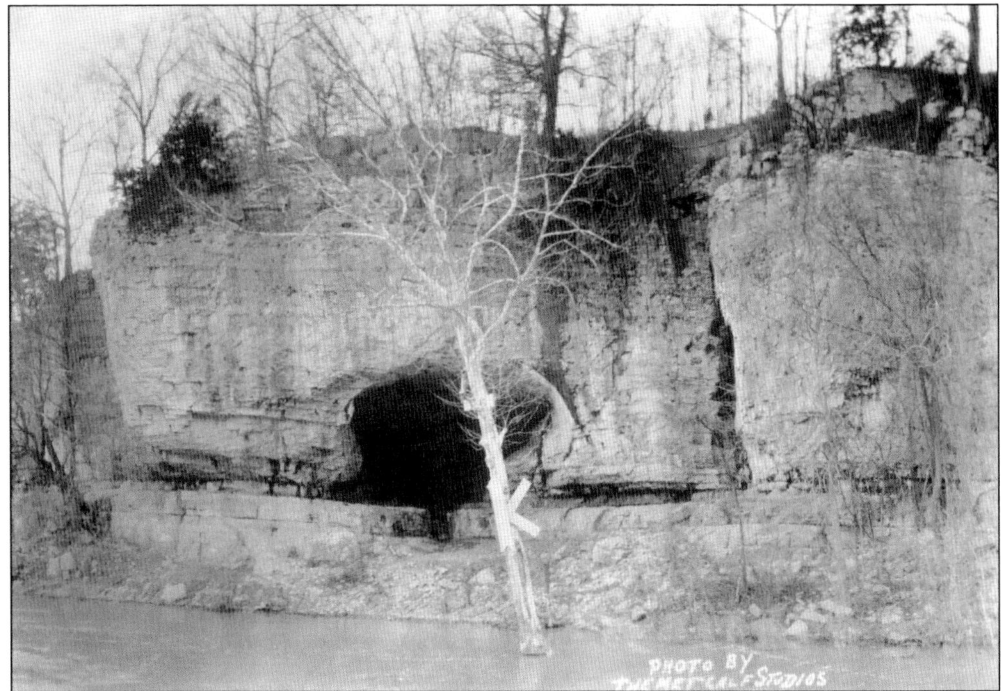

The cave at Cave-in-Rock was probably first discovered by Europeans in 1729, when French explorer Joseph-Gaspard Chaussegros de Léry called it *caverne dans le Roc*. The cave is also described by French explorer Pierre François Xavier de Charlevoix in his *History and General Description of New France* in 1744. Zadok Cramer gives the first detailed description of the cave in the *Ohio and Mississippi Navigator of 1803*. (Kenneth Price.)

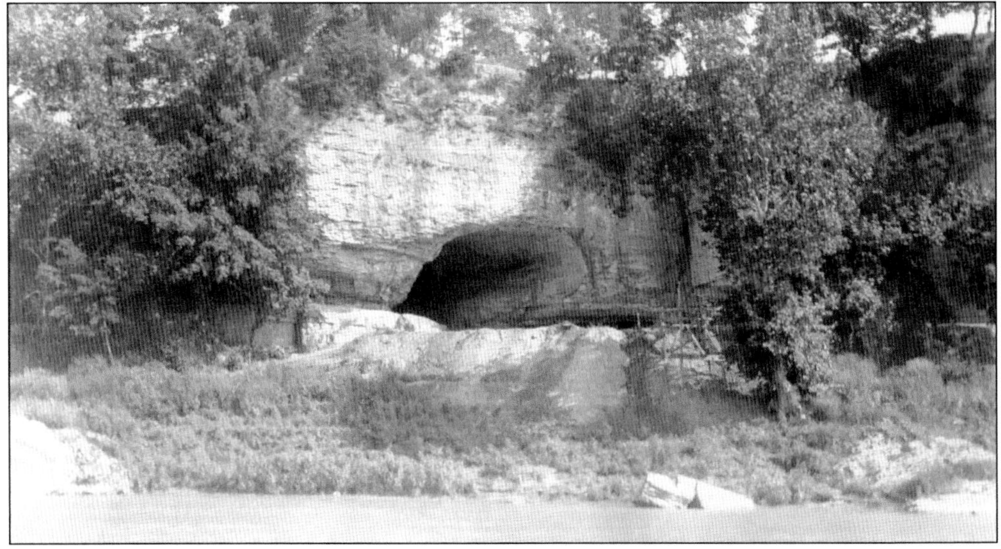

The cave is featured in this photograph taken from the *Katheryne* on the 1934 Ozark Tour. Dirt and debris from the rear of the cavern was removed as part of a Civil Works Administration project to return the cave to its size during the days of the river pirates. Two small chambers had already been discovered. Debris was first blasted then hauled out by mule and mining cart and dumped at the cave's entrance.

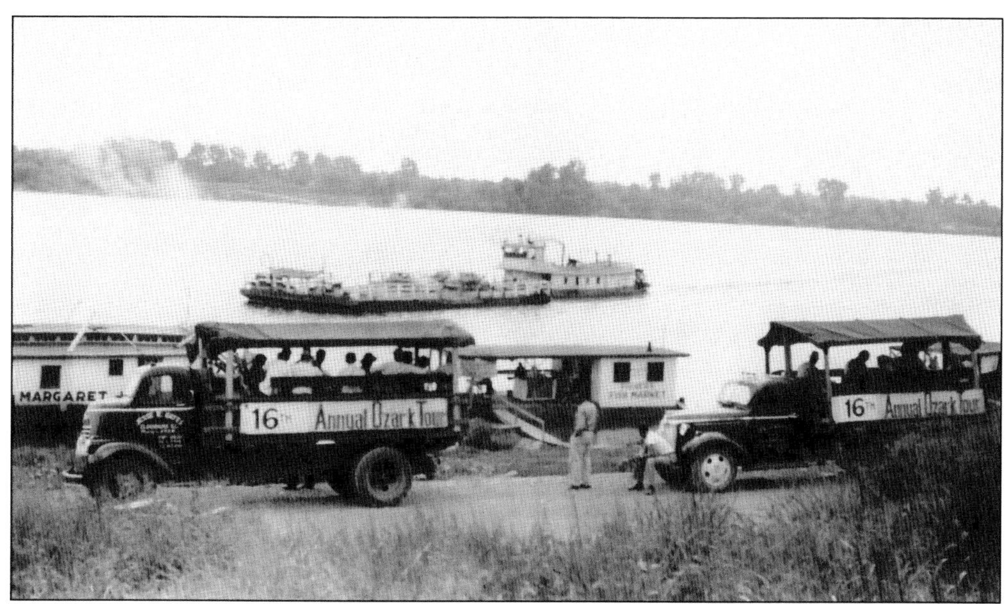

Covered trucks wait to cross via the ferry *Margaret J.* at Shawneetown for the first day of the 1947 Ozark Tour. Ozarkers finished lunch at the Posey Building and crossed the Ohio River to begin an afternoon tour of the Kentucky river towns of Blackburn, Caseyville, and Ford's Ferry. After a tour of Ohio River Dam 50, the trucks ferried back to Illinois at Cave-in-Rock for a fish fry prepared by L.O. Trigg's wife, Inez, daughter Mildred Erwood, and son-in-law Jack Cook. The Ozarkers camped in the state park for their first overnight.

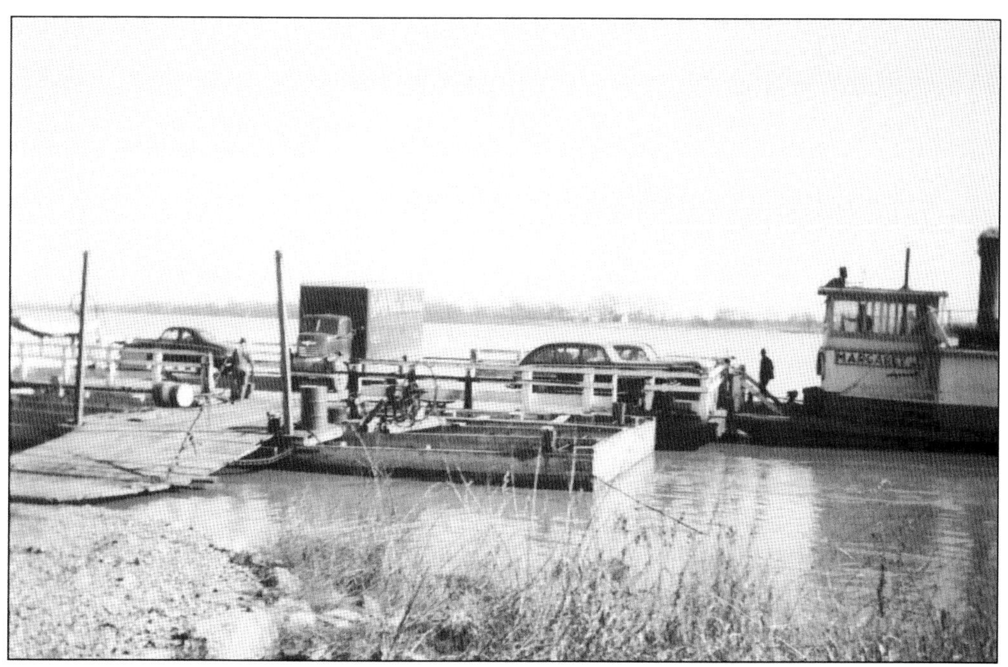

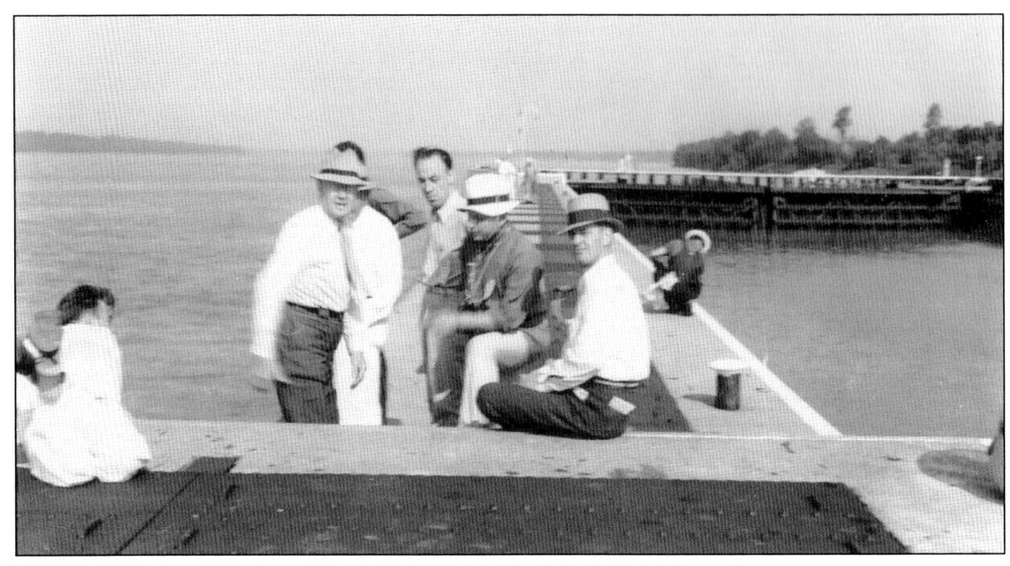

The 1936 Ozark Tour stopped at the locks of Ohio River Dam 52 in Brookport on the morning of the second day of the tour. Dam 52 was completed in 1928. The Ozarkers spent the previous night camping at the site of Fort Massac, downriver from Metropolis. Some of the Ozarkers purchased leftover Fourth of July fireworks in town and staged a new "Battle of Fort Massac" at midnight after everyone was asleep. As a consequence, L.O. Trigg banned fireworks from all future Ozark Tours.

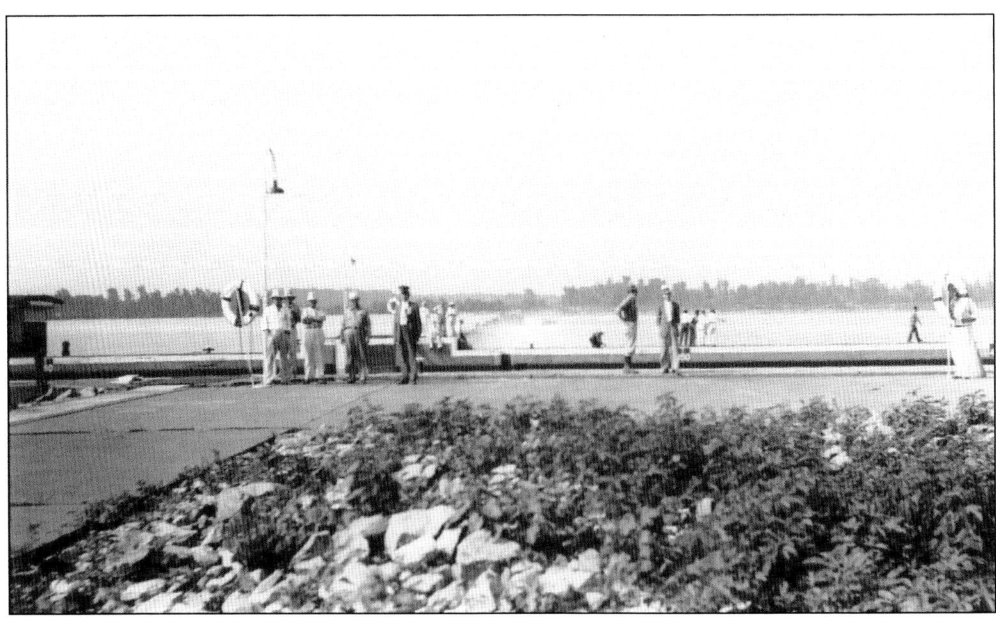

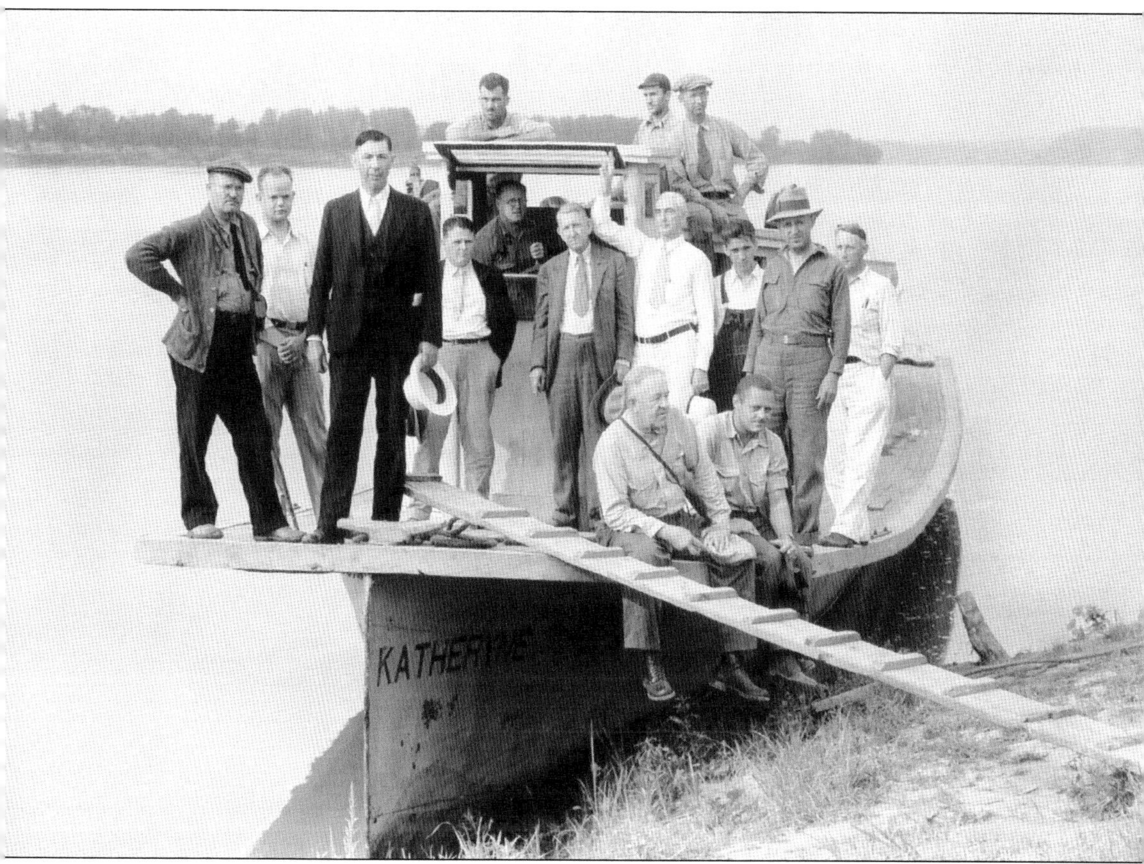

Members of the 1933 Ozark Tour are shown on their first river trip aboard the *Katheryne* mailboat. From left to right are attorney Jacob W. Myers of Harrisburg; attorney Victor Furman of Eldorado; "Captain" L.O. Trigg of Eldorado; attorney David Wheeler of Marion, Kansas; John H. Evans of Harrisburg (in pilothouse); attorney Walter W. Williams of Benton; banker Ed Wall of Elizabethtown; *Harrisburg Daily Register* reporter Casey Dempsey of Harrisburg; attorney Walter W. Wheatley of Harrisburg; Judge B.F. Anderson of Harrisburg; William F. Lodge and William T. Lodge of Monticello, Indiana (sitting on deck); forester L.E. "Buck" Sawyer of Terre Haute, Indiana (above pilothouse); Stanley Balloun of Harrisburg; and undertaker Earl Thornton of Stonefort. Tour members Norman Moore, Kendall Mecham, and August Zvara were not present when the picture was taken. Tour member H.O. Turner of Eldorado was the photographer.

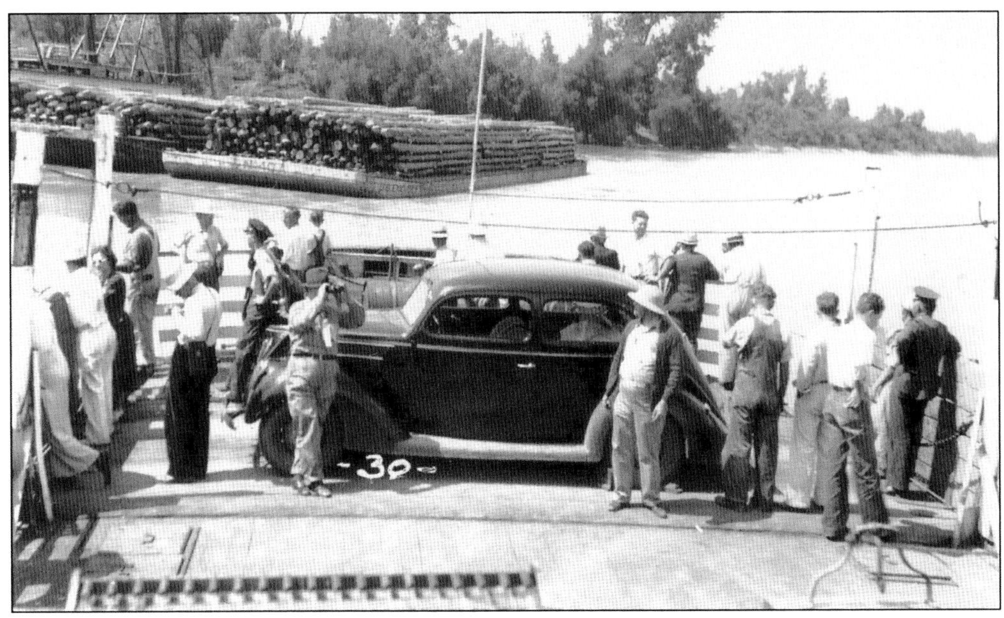

The 1937 Ozark Tour crossed the Mississippi River on the *Addie May* ferry at Thebes on the second day of the tour. The above image shows the Ozarkers viewing barges loaded with cut timber on the Missouri side of the river. The below image shows the Missouri side of the Mississippi River with the village of Thebes in the background. The historic Thebes Courthouse is visible to the right of center on the upper ridge of the town. (Above, Jeff Robinson.)

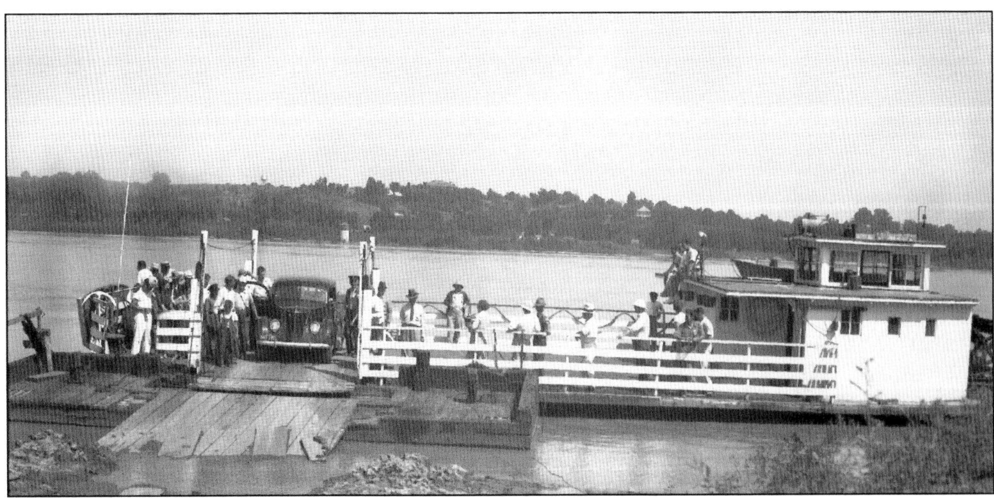

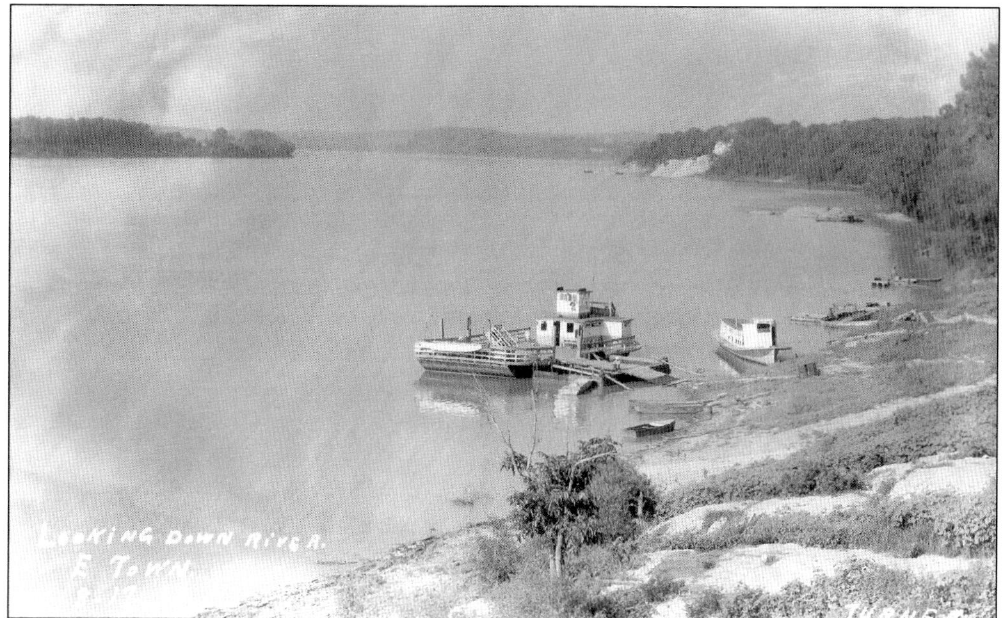

McConnell's Ferry docked at the riverfront in Elizabethtown in 1933. The ferry was used on the 1941 Ozark Tour. The mailboat *Katheryne* is moored nearby. In the near distance is Jack's Point. In the further distance, near the center of the picture, is the city of Rosiclare.

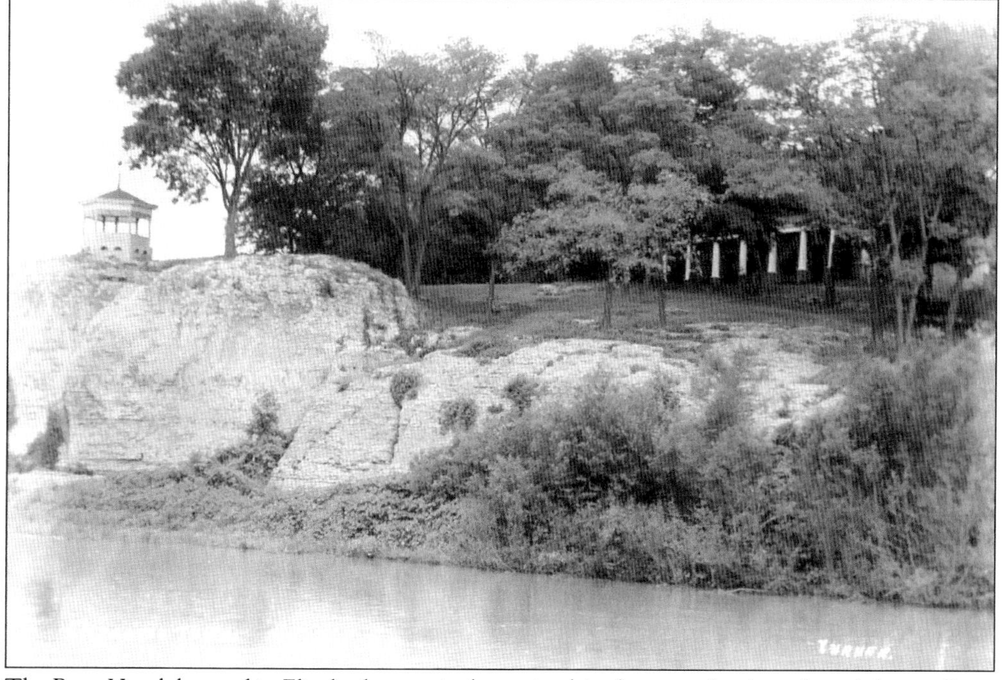

The Rose Hotel, located in Elizabethtown, is shown in this photograph taken aboard the mailboat *Katheryne* during the 1933 Ozark Tour. Town founder James McFarlan Sr. settled the area around 1808, and it is believed that he built the original portion of the hotel in 1812. During McFarlan's lifetime, the community was known as McFarlan's Ferry. When the town was platted and incorporated in 1840, James McFarlan Jr. renamed the town after his mother, Elizabeth.

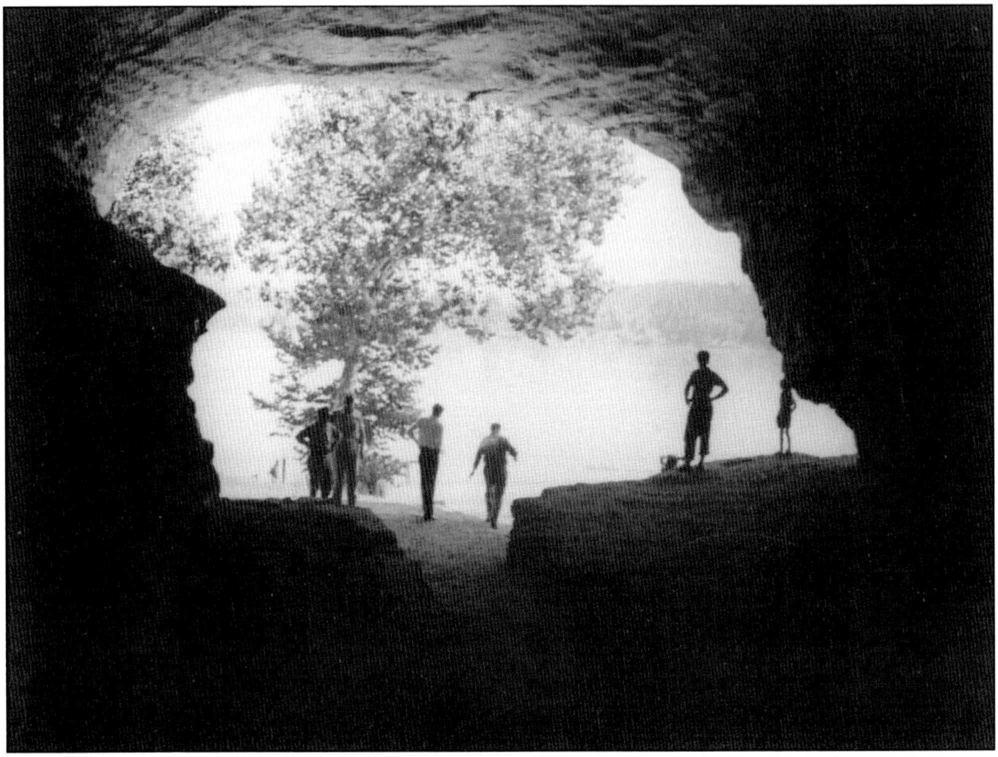

Ozarkers look outward from the interior of the cave at Cave-in-Rock State Park on the 1938 Ozark Tour. The park custodian provided a ladder so Ozarkers could view the upper chamber of the cave, which river pirates once used as a hiding place. The upper chamber was sealed off in later years and is no longer accessible.

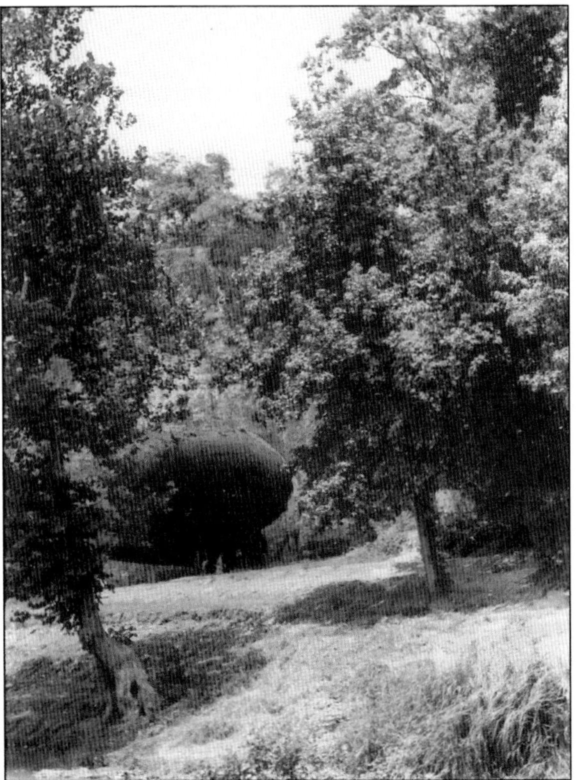

English tourist Thaddeus M. Harris wrote this description of the Pirate Cave at Cave-in-Rock during a visit in 1803: "Before its mouth stands a delightful grove of cypress trees arranged immediately on the bank of the river. They have a fine appearance, and add much to the cheerfulness of the place." According to legend, river pirates hung a sign outside that read "Wilson's Liquor Vault and House of Entertainment."

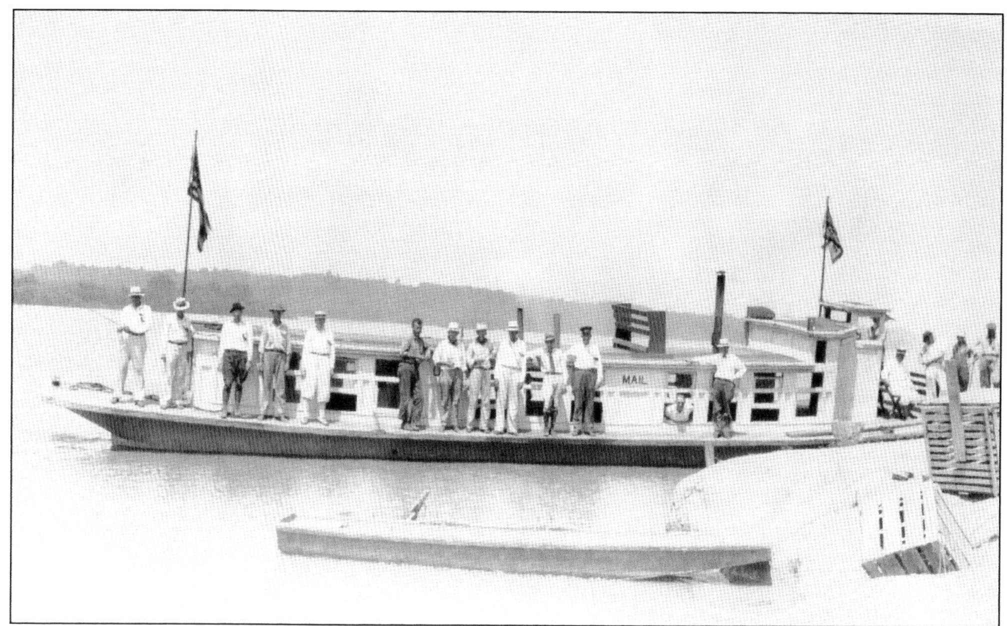

The 1934 Ozark Tour is shown aboard the mailboat *Katheryne* at Caseyville, Kentucky. This last day of the tour started with breakfast at Cave-in-Rock before a 14-mile cruise up the Ohio River to Caseyville. Later, tour members crossed the river to Sellers' Landing in Illinois and boarded trucks for the return trip to Harrisburg. Lunch was served at CCC Camp Kedron en route to Harrisburg.

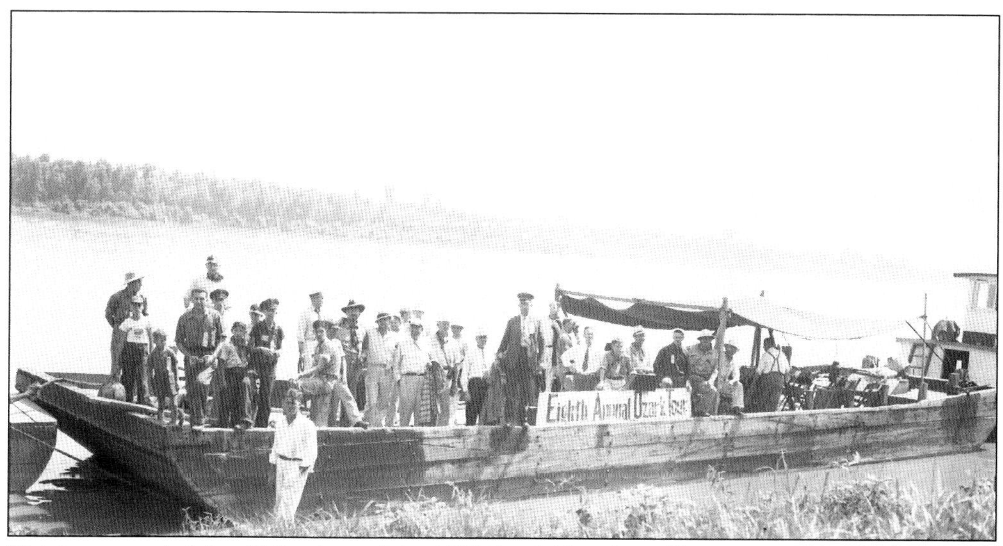

This barge carried the 47 Ozarkers of the 1938 Ozark Tour from Shawneetown to Elizabethtown. The tugboat *Hobo Bill* pushed the barge the 32 miles along the Ohio River. Lunch was served at the Rose Hotel. Trucks made the trip overland from Shawneetown to pick up the Ozarkers and return them to Harrisburg for the conclusion of the tour.

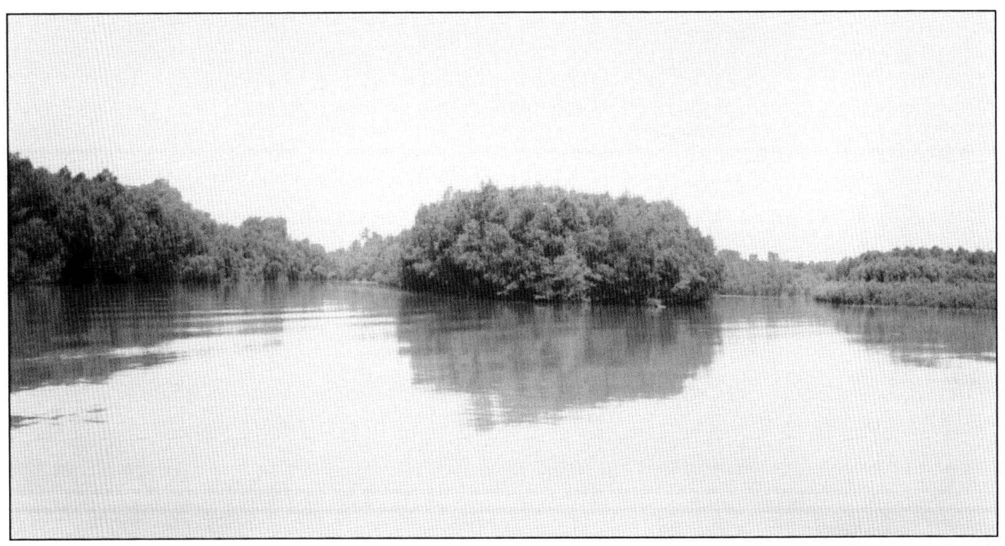

This view of the river was captured during the *Hobo Bill* excursion cruise during the 1938 Ozark Tour. On the left are Hardin County and the Saline River channel. In the center is the southeastern tip of Gallatin County. On the right are the Ohio River channel and Union County, Kentucky. The easternmost point of the Shawnee National Forest, located at Battery Rock, is south and downriver of this location.

This view is looking northeast to the bluffs of Cave-in-Rock State Park from across the Ohio River at the Kentucky ferry landing. The State of Illinois acquired the property and the infamous Pirate's Cave in 1929. Today, the Cave-in-Rock State Park Lodge and cabins and various picnic shelters dot the top of the bluff. (Kenneth Price.)

The flyer at right advertises the 16th annual Ozark Tour. The 1946 tour would begin, as usual, from Harrisburg and proceed to Old Shawneetown, where Ozarkers would board a boat for a three-day trip downstream to Metropolis. They would see several points of interest along the Ohio River. Initially planned for July, the tour was moved to September to overcome obstacles concerning meals and transportation. A few days before the tour's starting date, "the boat captain was warned not to attempt the trip without meeting some drastic requirements which he could not meet for weeks, even under favorable conditions." Pictured below is the notice sent to inform Ozarkers of the cancellation. The restrictions imposed by the "marine authorities" were wartime restrictions still in place following World War II. This was the only year between 1931 and 1949 that L.O. Trigg did not host an Ozark Tour.

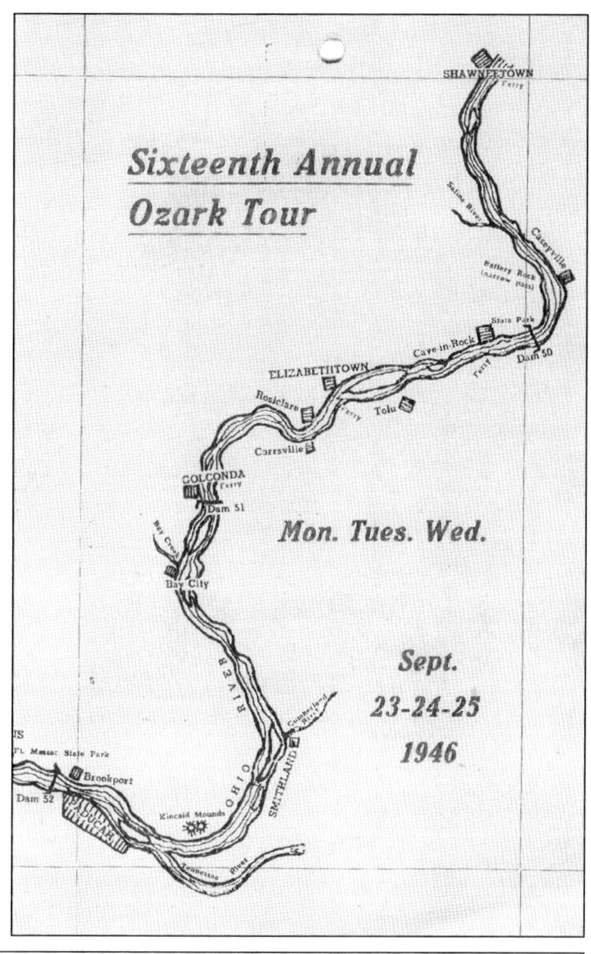

Harrisburg, Illinois
September 30, 1946

Dear Friend:

We know you share our disappointment due to the Ozark Tour having been cancelled, however, the spirit of our group continues with "high sail". The Captain spent endless hours in making preparations for a successful trip on the Ohio and plans were completed to a finished degree. However, the Marine authorities imposed last minute restrictions which were totally unforeseen and beyond our control. Thus the cancellation of the trip was a matter of regretful necessity.

Please drop the Captain a few lines of appreciation for his untiring effort. We will continue to work toward our being together next year.

Your Ozark Tour Committee

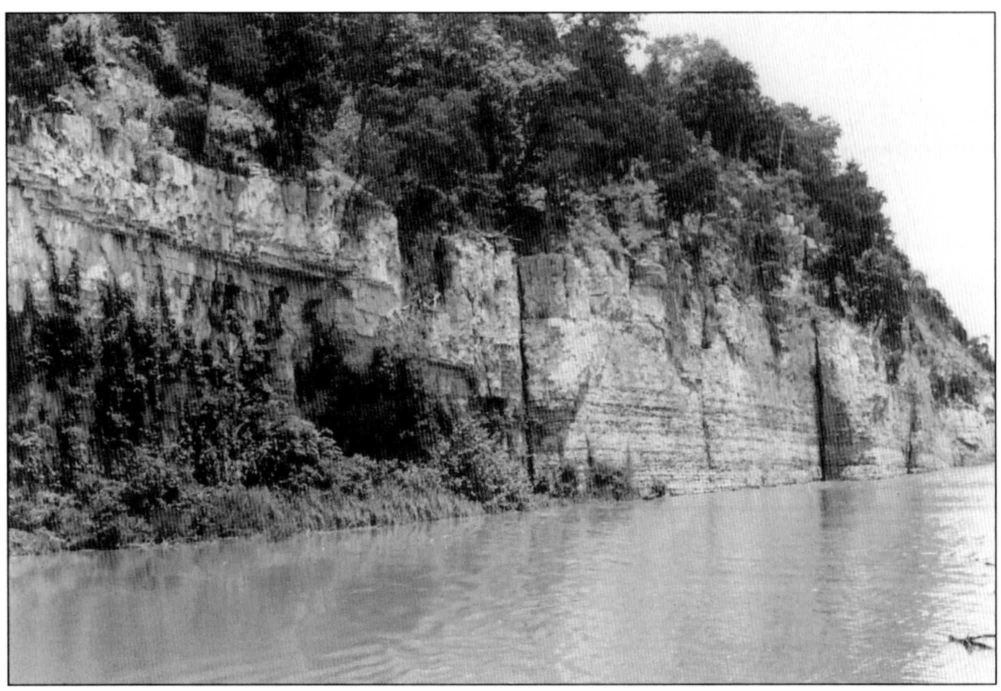

The scenic Ohio River bluffs upriver from Cave-in-Rock are pictured in this photograph taken aboard the *Hobo Bill* during the 1938 Ozark Tour.

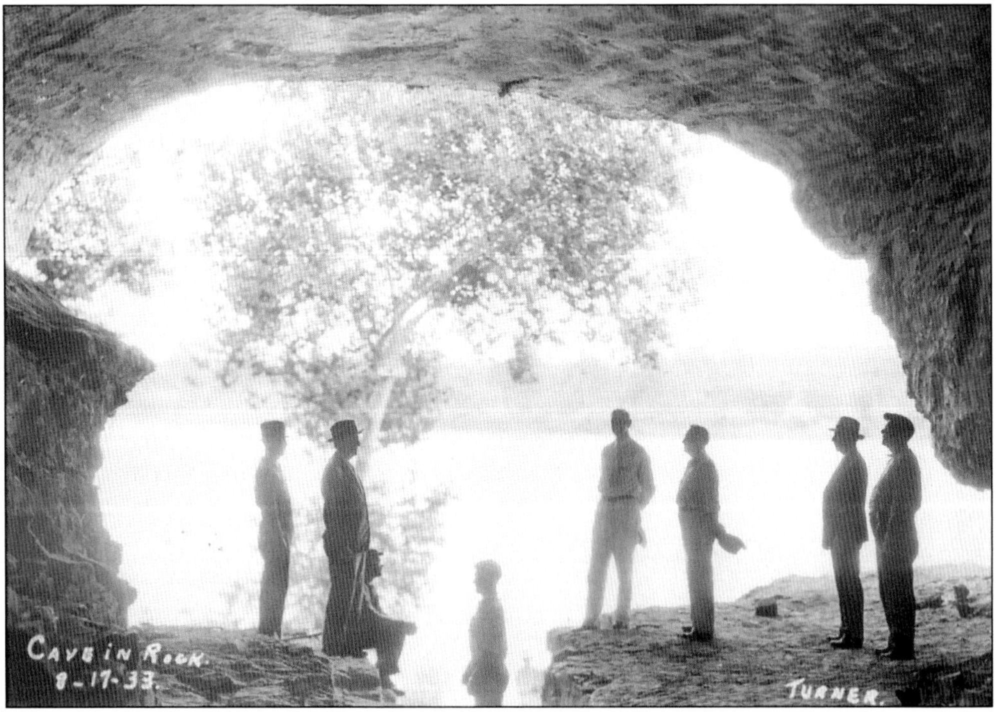

Ozarkers on the 1933 tour are shown looking out from the cave at Cave-in-Rock State Park toward the Ohio River. Pictured are, from left to right, Walter Wheatley, W.W. Williams, Jacob W. Myers (seated), "Buck" Sawyer, Ed Wall Jr., B.F. Anderson, L.O. Trigg, and William Lodge Sr.

Seven

Ozark Tour Legacy

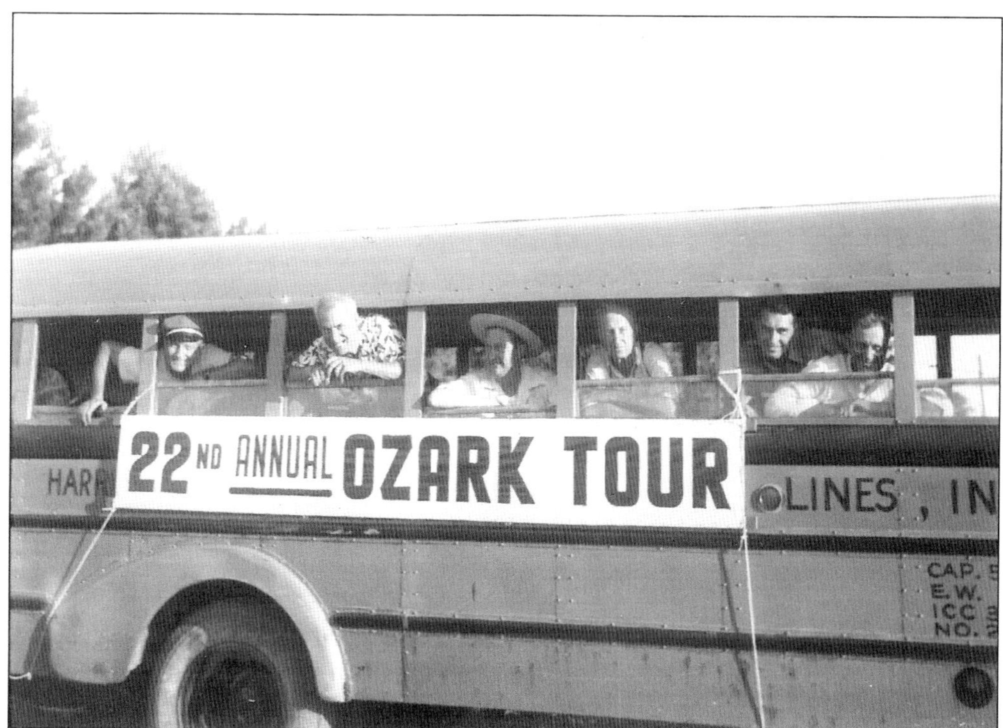

The 22nd annual Ozark Tour was conducted under the direction of Trigg's Ozark Tour heir William H. Farley. More than 300 miles were covered by 33 men traveling in a chartered school bus. The tour purposely avoided paved roads in favor of the rural roads of southern Illinois.

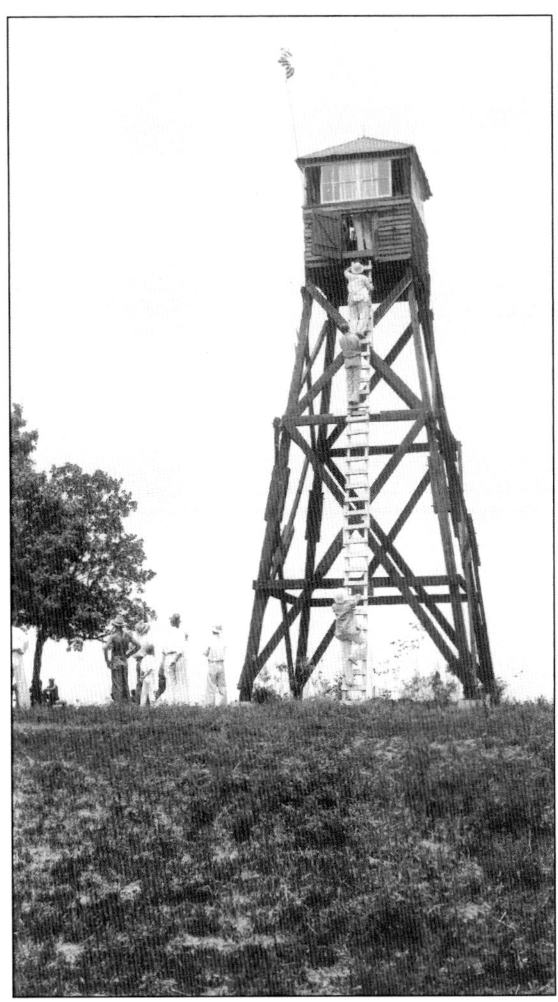

When US Forest Service officials began to plan for a lookout tower on Cotton Hill, located two miles north of Simpson, they decided to name it Trigg Tower in recognition of L.O. Trigg's promotional efforts for the Shawnee National Forest. The 1936 Ozark Tour visited the original 40-foot-tall wooden tower, which had a picnic area installed near the base. The tower was later replaced with a 90-foot-tall steel structure. When fire lookout towers were no longer deemed necessary, the steel tower was lowered to 40 feet but kept in place as a tourist attraction. Today, Trigg Tower is the only remaining lookout tower in the Shawnee National Forest.

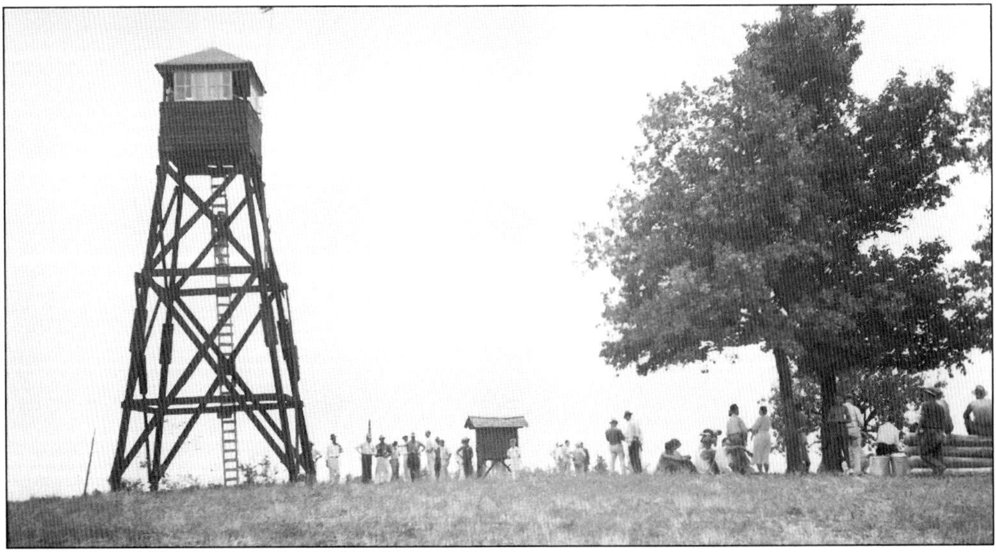

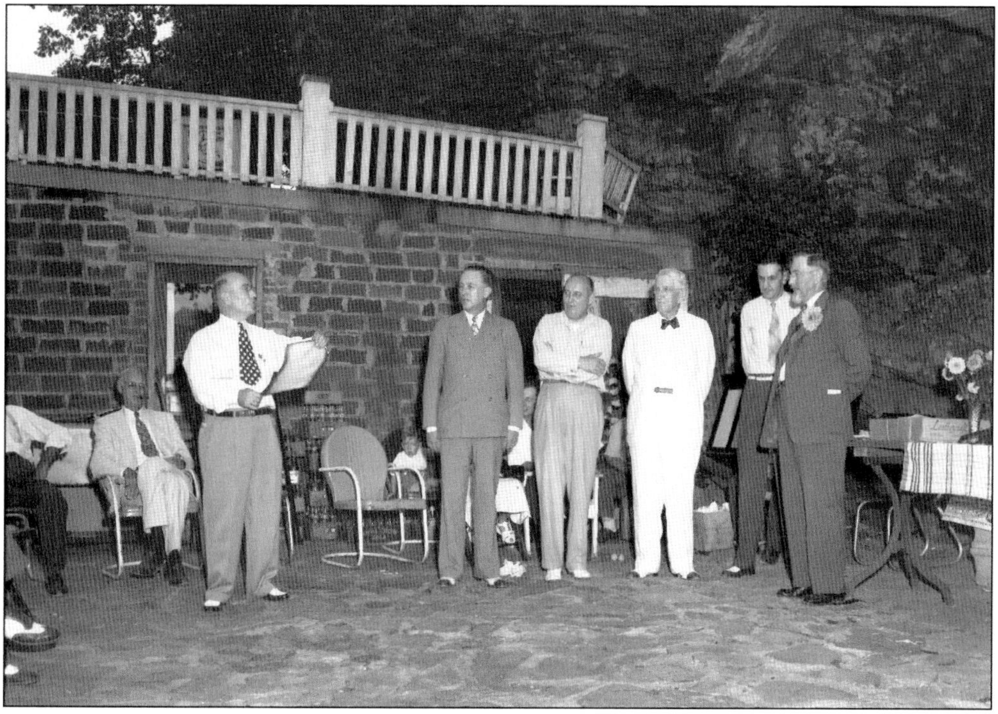

On August 2, 1948, L.O. Trigg's friends and family gathered at Fairy Cliff Café in Herod to honor Trigg for his efforts to promote southern Illinois. The attendees read letters from former Ozarkers who could not make it to the gathering. William H. Farley of Harrisburg read a list of names in memory of those who were deceased. Several in attendance gave short talks before the presentations. Above, Dr. John B. Ruyle, president emeritus of the Illinois State Archeological Society, based in Champaign, read from a hand-lettered scroll of linen parchment promoting Trigg from "captain" to "colonel" in the "Army of the Ozarks." Below, Ozarker Fred Wasson, a merchant from Carrier Mills, presents Trigg with a leather briefcase gifted to him from his Ozark Tour friends.

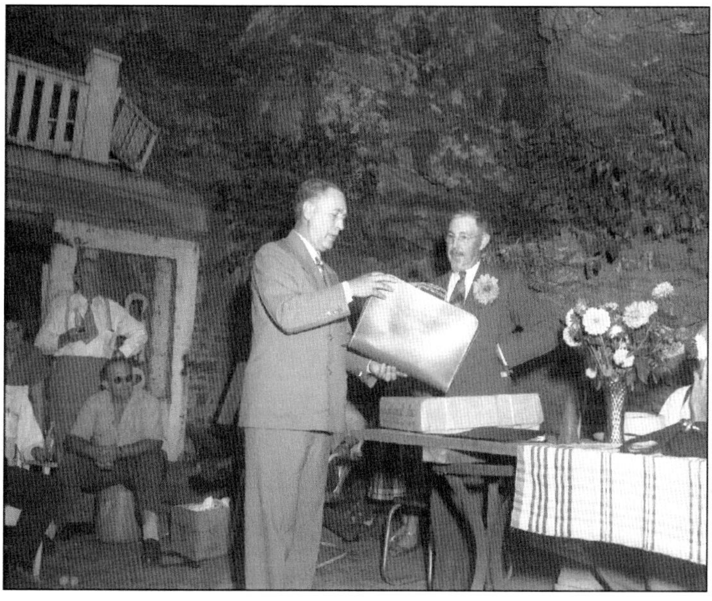

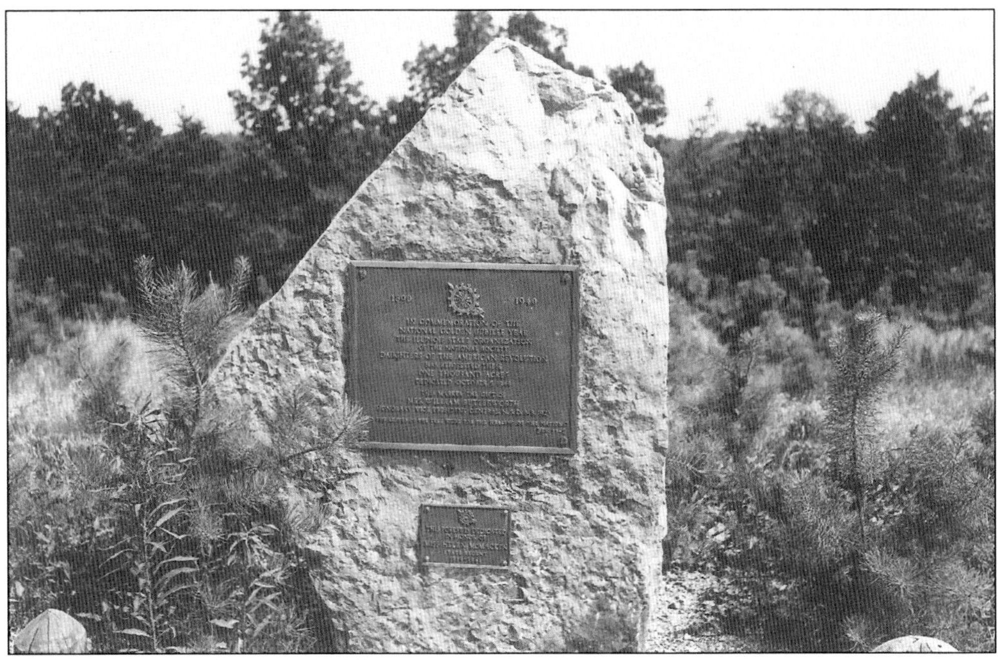

Pictured above is the dedication marker for the DAR 1,000-acre Golden Jubilee Forest near Pounds Hollow in Gallatin County. Note the increase in foliage around the marker between when it was dedicated in 1940 (above) and 2016 (below). (Above, US Forest Service, Shawnee National Forest; below, author's collection.)

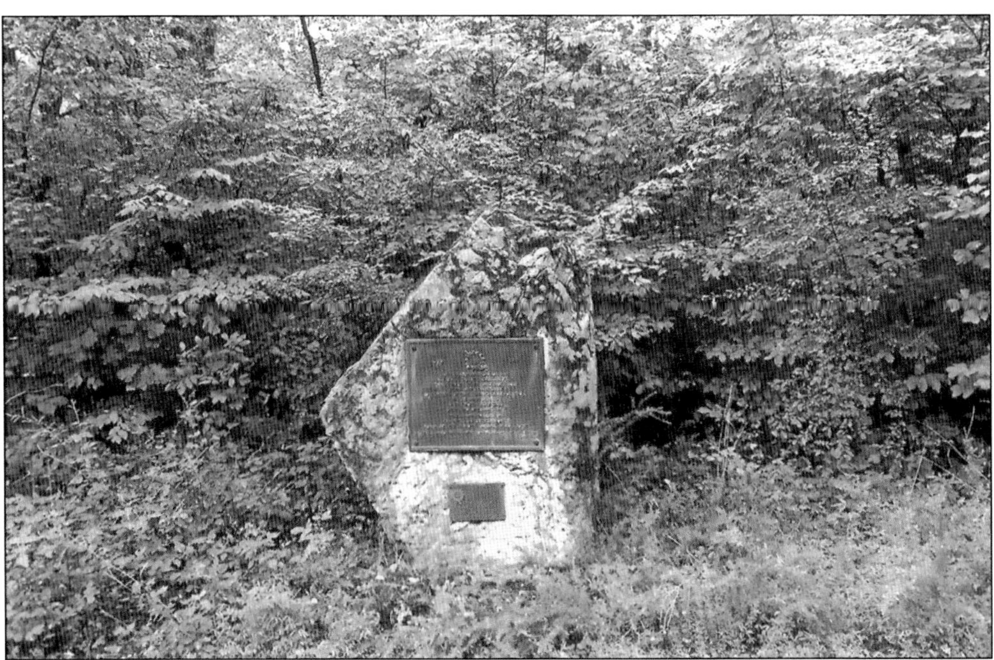

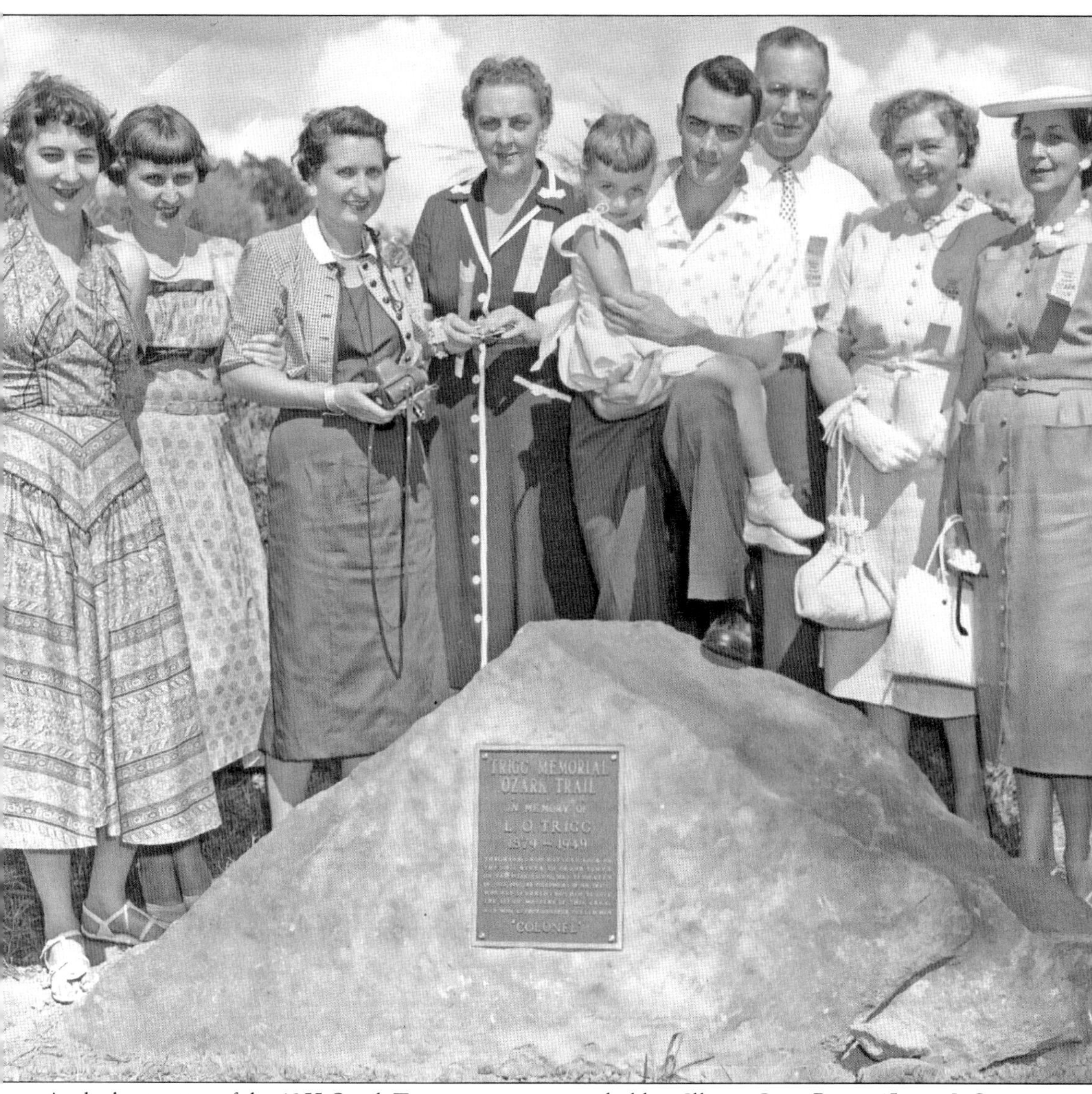

At the beginning of the 1955 Ozark Tour, a ceremony was held on Illinois State Route 45 near L.O. Trigg's birthplace of Ozark to dedicate what supporters hoped would become a memorial highway named in Trigg's honor. Speakers included Ozarkers who had traveled with Trigg on his Ozark Tours. Several members of Trigg's immediate family were in attendance. Pictured are, from left to right, Trigg's granddaughters Ann Erwood and Janet Trigg Tierney, daughter-in-law LaHoma Trigg; daughter Ethel Cook, great-granddaughter Beth Tierney, grandson-in-law Bob Tierney, son Kenneth R. Trigg, widow, Inez Trigg, and daughter Mildred Erwood. The plaque reads: "Trigg Memorial Ozark Trail in memory of L.O. Trigg 1879–1949 This road, from Battery Rock on the Ohio River to Grand Tower on the Mississippi, was dedicated in July 1950, by followers of Mr. Trigg, who had learned from him to love the scenic wonders of this area, and who affectionately called him 'Colonel.'"

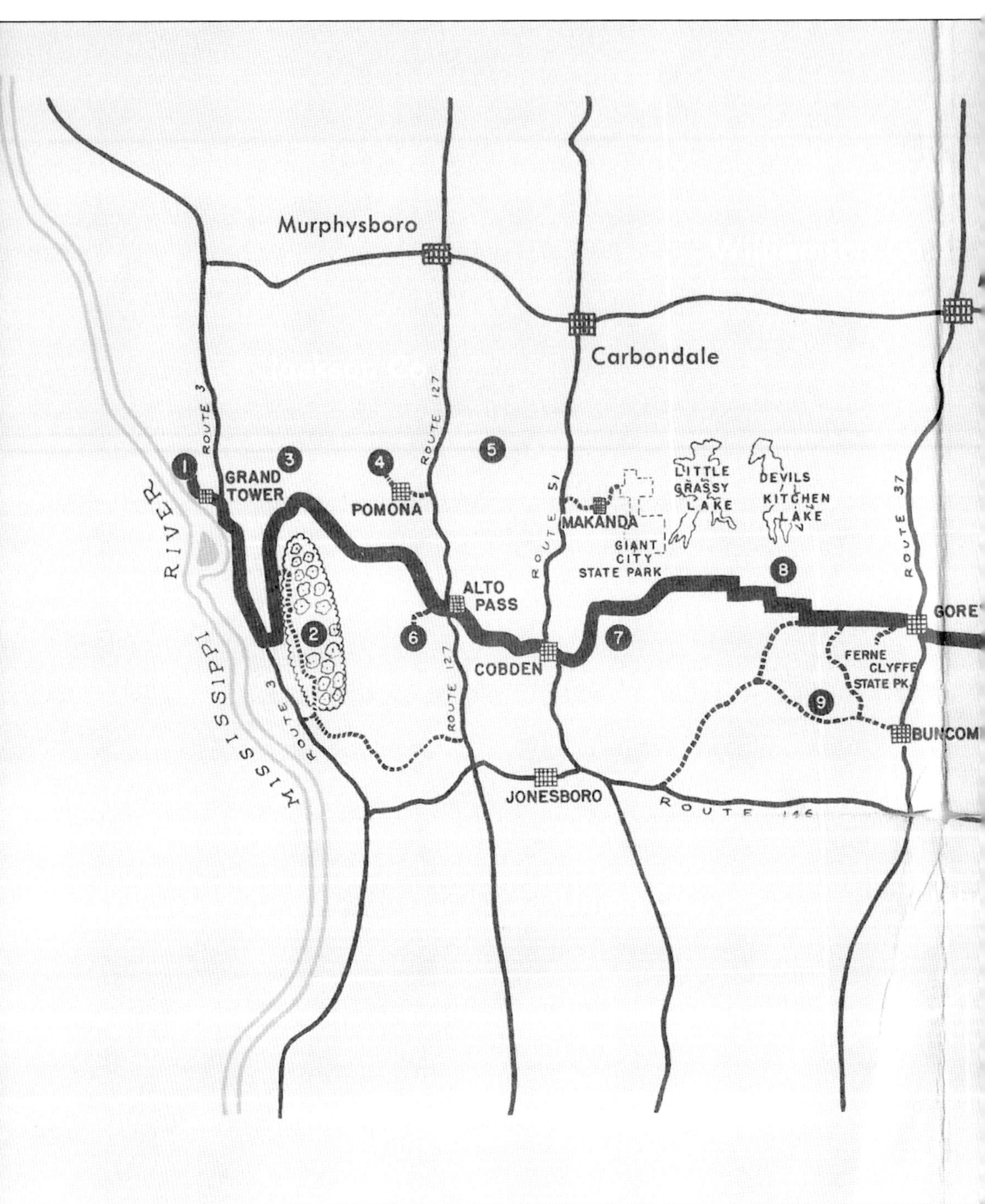

The Trigg Memorial Ozark Trail was dedicated during the 1955 Ozark Tour. In the late 1950s, Boy Scout Ney-a-ti Lodge of the Order of the Arrow marked an automobile, camping, and hiking trail generally following the route and called it the Ozark-Shawnee Trail (map pictured). The Boy Scout council offered special badges for successfully completing the trail. By the mid-1960s, the highway was still under consideration, but its name had been changed to the George Rogers

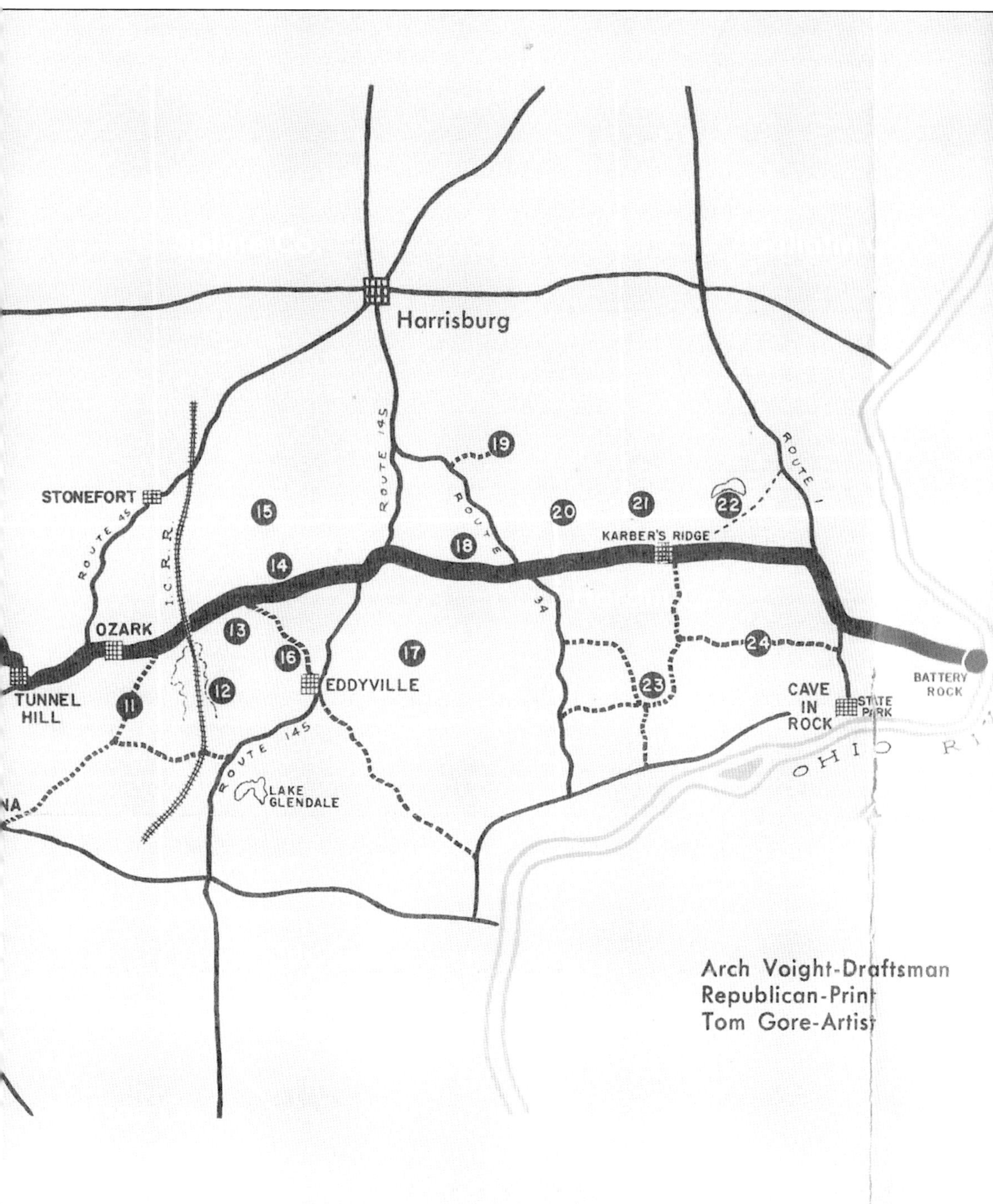

Clark Recreation Way. The scenic highway was last considered in the 1980s under the name River-to-River Road. Today, largely through the efforts of the River-to-River Trail Society and local equestrian groups, the 160-mile river-to-river equestrian and hiking trail roughly follows the original route and is a leg of the coast-to-coast American Discovery Trail.

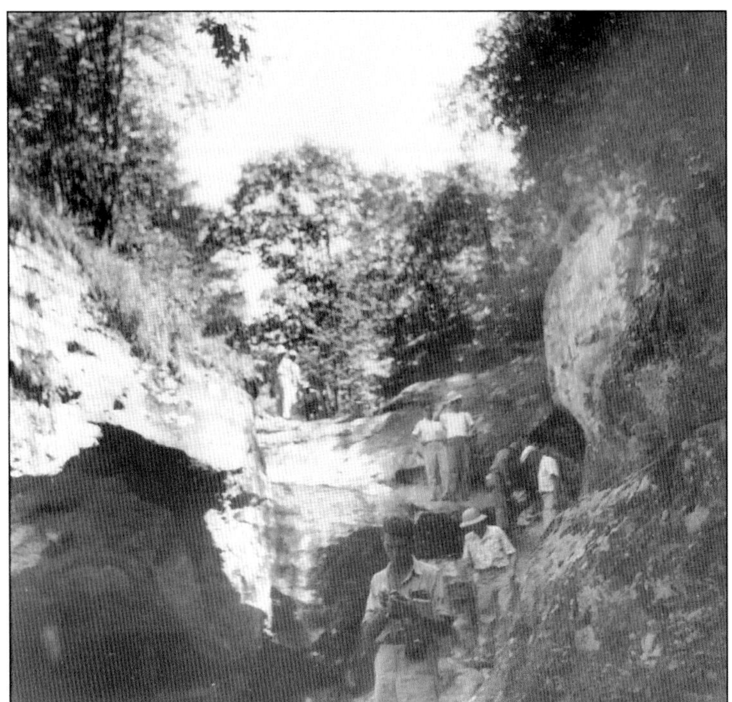

After L.O. Trigg's death, the Ozark Tours continued from 1950 through the late 1970s. Pictured here are Ozarkers of the 1952 Ozark Tour as they descend into the Little Grand Canyon of southern Illinois, a recreation area seven miles south of Murphysboro. At the time of this tour, a lookout tower stood on Hickory Ridge at the trailhead of the box canyon. Little Grand Canyon was designated as a National Natural Landmark in 1980.

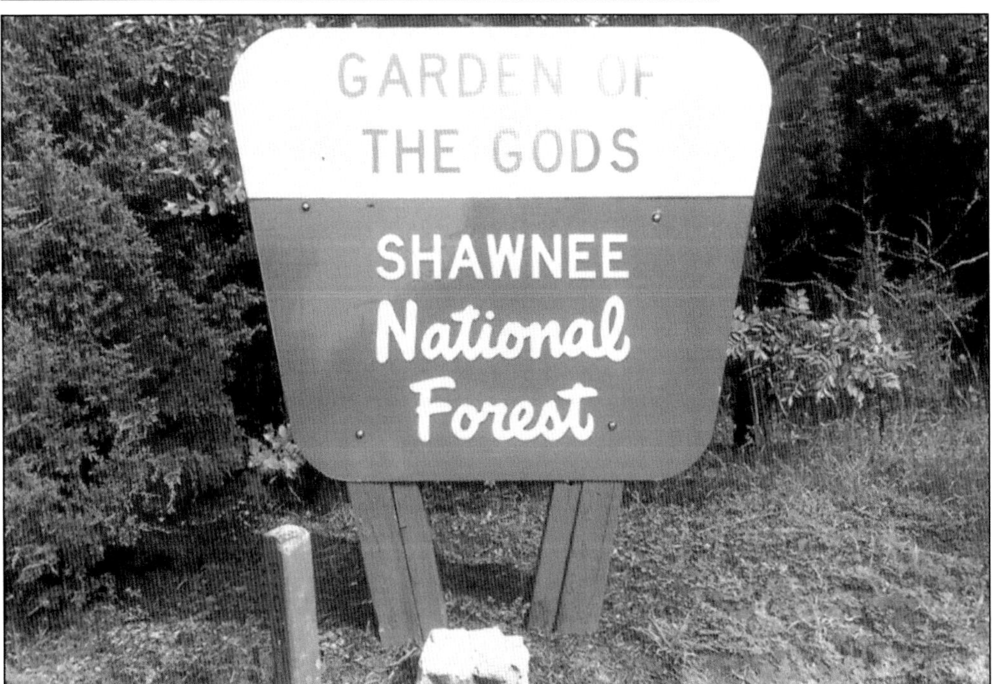

Garden of the Gods is a 3,000-acre wilderness area in Gallatin, Hardin, Pope, and Saline Counties. The scenic overlooks of the observation trail make this one of the most visited attractions within the Shawnee National Forest. The image of Camel Rock, a sandstone bluff believed to be 320 million years old, represented Illinois on the US Mint's "America the Beautiful" quarter series in 2016. (Author's collection.)

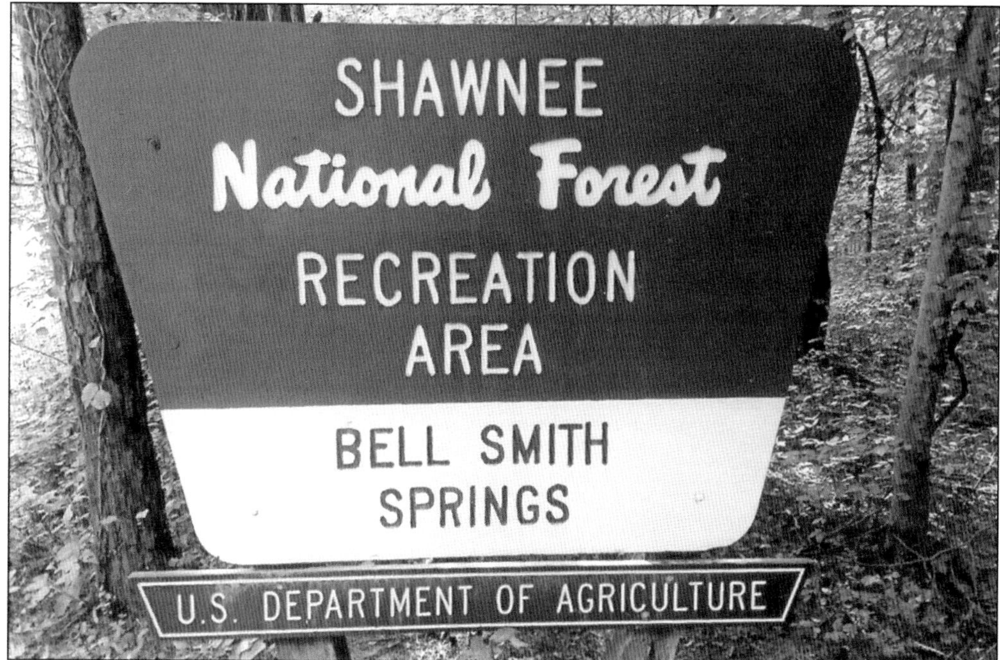

One of the first recreation areas in the Shawnee National Forest was improved in the 1930s by the nearby CCC Camp Eddyville. Scenic sandstone cliffs surround four meandering forest streams and rock formations such as Devil's Backbone, Boulder Falls, and the largest natural bridge in the forest. Bell Smith Springs was designated a National Natural Landmark in 1980. (Author's collection.)

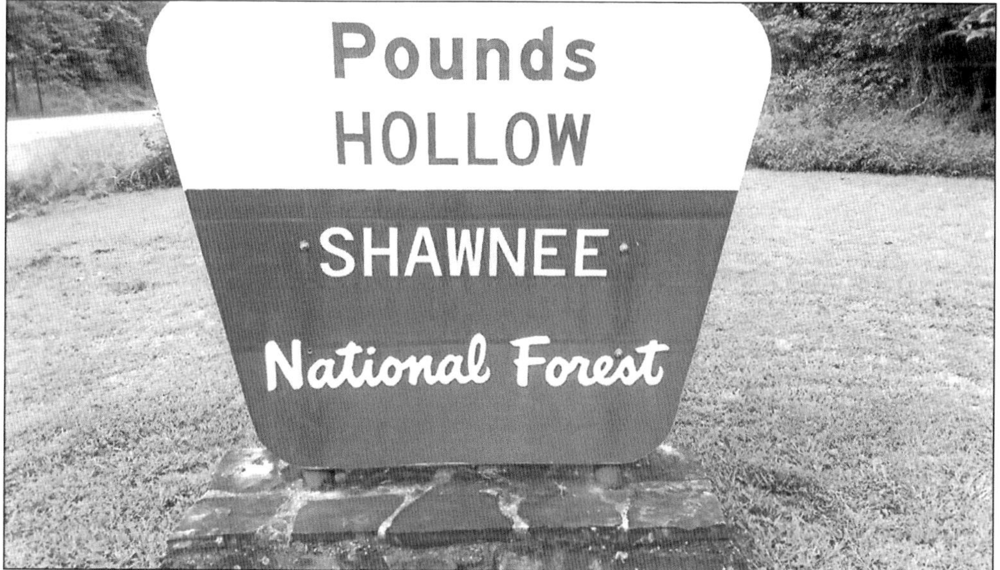

CCC Camp Cadiz made improvements to Pounds Hollow Recreation Area in the 1940s near the end of the CCC program. Pine Ridge Campground sits on the hill overlooking Pounds Hollow Lake, a popular kayaking spot with a swimming beach, a fishing dock, and picnicking facilities. The "Beaver Trail" connects with nearby Rim Rock National Recreation Trail and the impoundment from which the hollow gets its name. (Author's collection.)

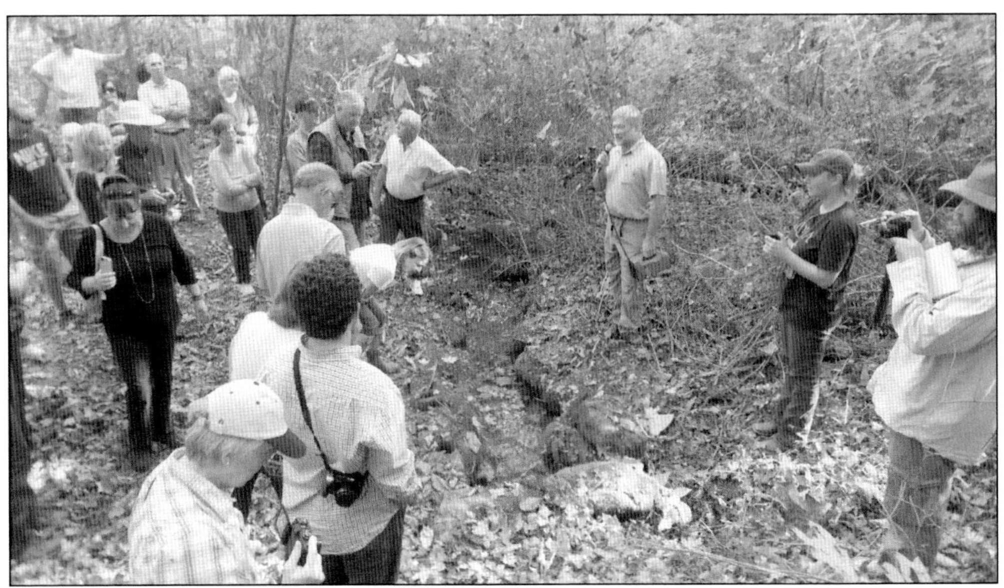

Local historian Mark Motsinger shares the "Legend of Billy Potts" with participants on the 2014 Fall Ozark Tour at the Potts' Inn spring near Illinois State Route 1 in Hardin County. An old pioneer forest road, Ford's Ferry Road, runs between the spring and the site of Potts' Inn. According to local legend, many early pioneers lost their lives to highwaymen while drinking from the spring. When Trigg's Ozark Tours were brought back in 2013, women were allowed to participate for the first time. (Author's collection.)

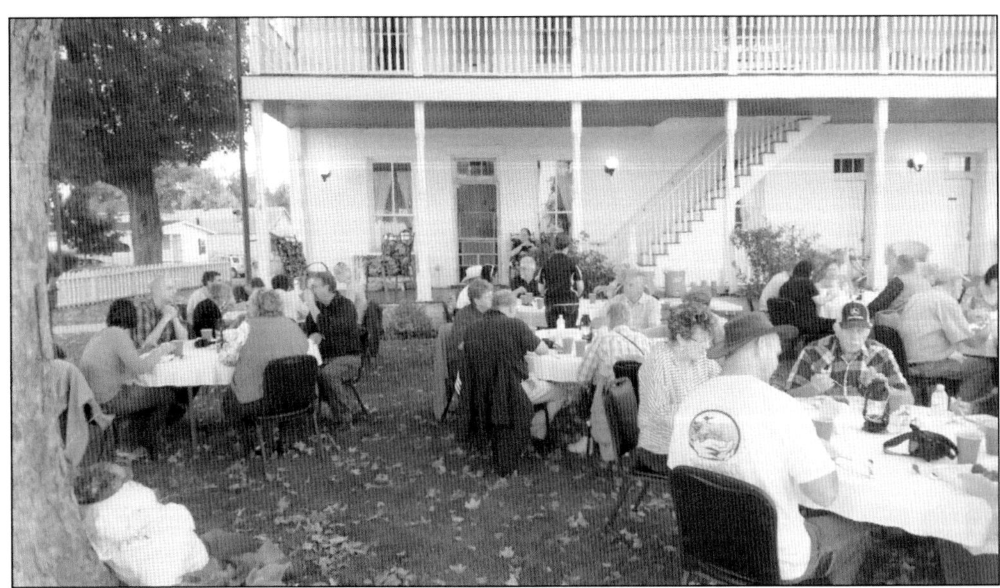

Ozarkers on the 2014 Fall Ozark Tour were treated to a pork chop and catfish dinner on the front lawn of the historic Rose Hotel in Elizabethtown. The Rose Hotel was extensively renovated by the State of Illinois in the late 1990s and is now run as a bed-and-breakfast under contract with the Illinois Historic Preservation Agency. (Author's collection.)

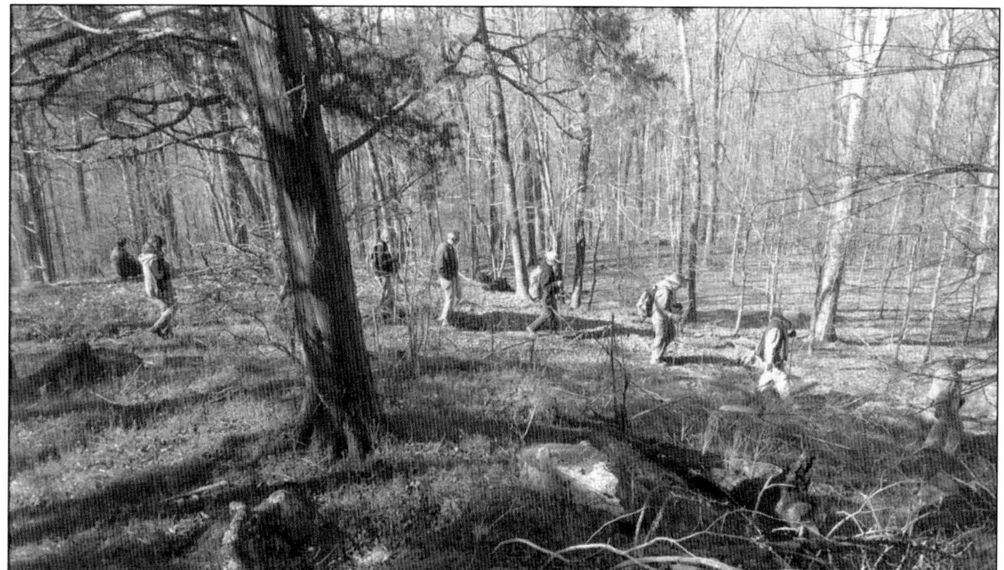

Ozarkers on the 2016 Spring Ozark Tour took a waterfall and wildflower hike around Dutchman Lake in Johnson County. Other sites visited on this tour included Bork Falls, the Double Falls of Happy Hollow, and Ferne Clyffe State Park. In 1963, the Shawnee National Forest began acquiring parcels of land to connect the originally noncontiguous Illini and Shawnee Purchase Units; Dutchman Lake is in this area. (Author's collection.)

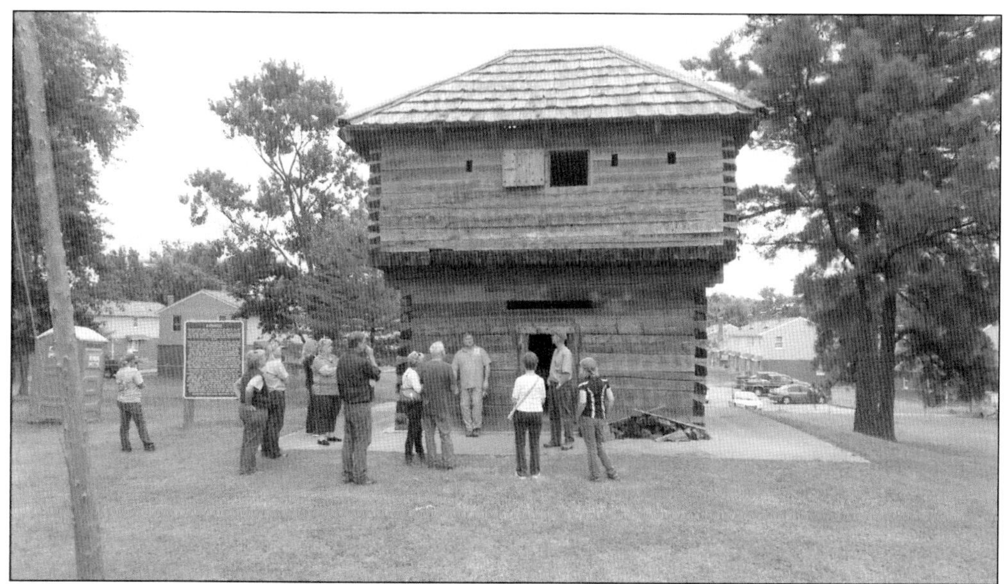

On the 2015 Fall Ozark Tour, local historian Gillum Ferguson led a discussion near a replica blockhouse on the grounds of the Saline Creek Pioneer Village and Museum in Harrisburg. Several of these blockhouses lined the Kaskaskia and Goshen Trails in southern Illinois in the early 1800s, providing gathering places and protection for early pioneers. (Author's collection.)

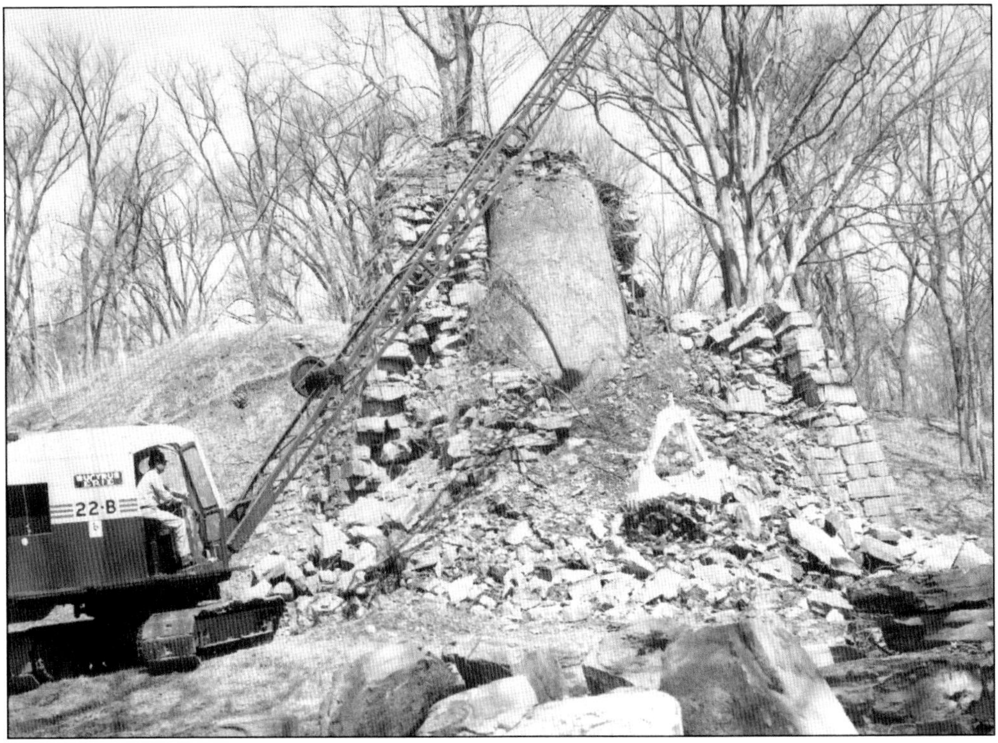

The above photograph shows the Illinois Iron Furnace, located four miles north of Rosiclare near Elizabethtown, being demolished before reconstruction could begin. The Golconda Job Corps Center rebuilt the furnace in 1967. A picnic area was established as part of the improvements. An old-fashioned swimming hole is located in a deep area of Big Creek adjacent to the site. In 2016, new interpretive signage, which is pictured below, was added to provide a history of the community that arose around the early industry and explaining how pig iron was made at the site. The Illinois Iron Furnace was listed in the National Register of Historic places in 1973. (Above, Hardin County Historical and Genealogical Society; below, author's collection.)

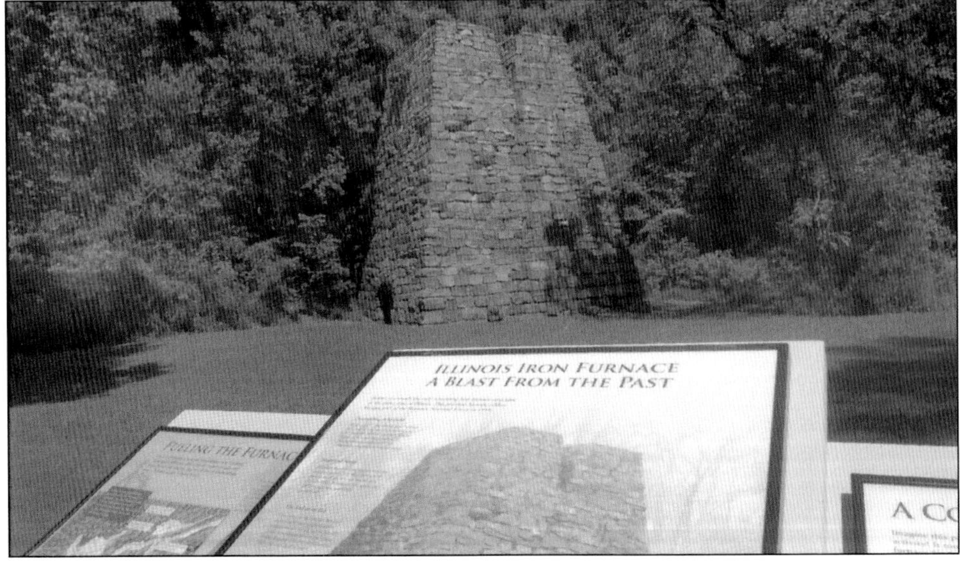

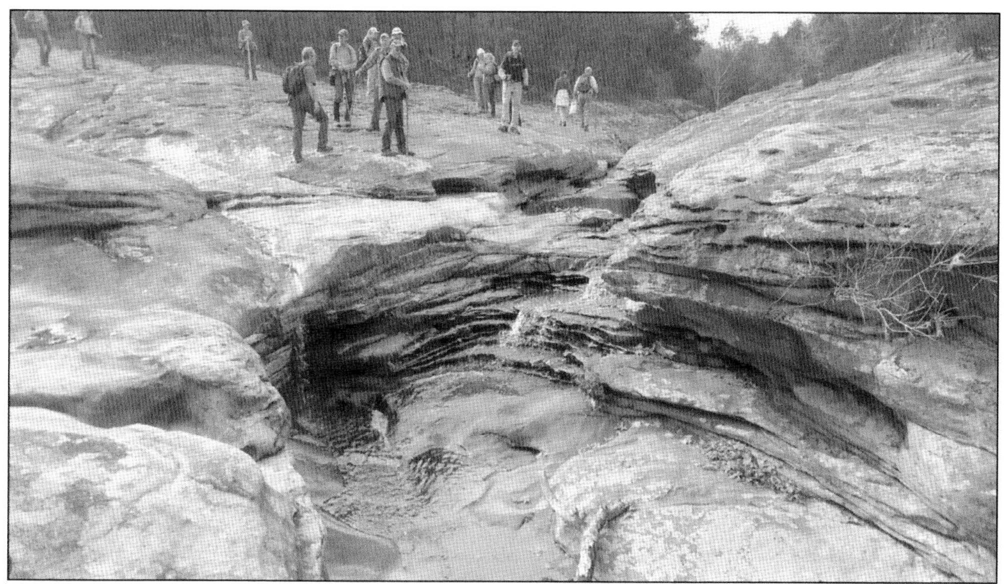

The River-to-River Trail Society leads organized weekend day hikes to some of the more remote or lesser-known areas of the Shawnee National Forest. Hikes are publicized on the society's Facebook page and in southern Illinois newspapers. Above, hikers view the Hill Branch Barrens of Bell Smith Springs in Pope County. An early gristmill was located downstream of the barrens area near where Hill Branch and Hunting Branch join. Below, hikers cross Bay Creek while hiking from Sand Cave to Bell Smith Springs. Sand Cave, said to be the largest sand cave in the United States, is a large sandstone cave and an Underground Railroad site near Miller's Grove, site of a freed-slave village in Pope County. (Both, author's collection.)

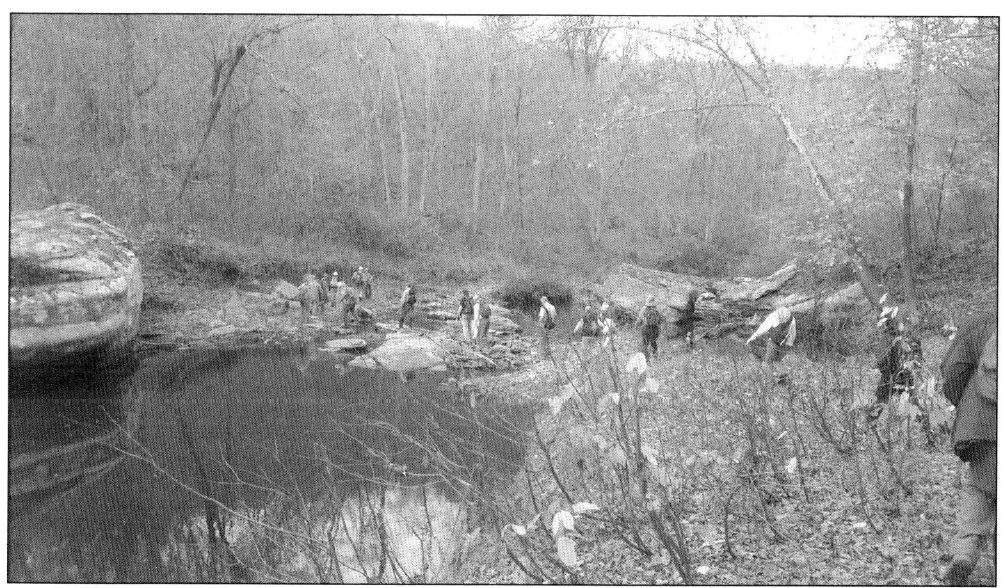

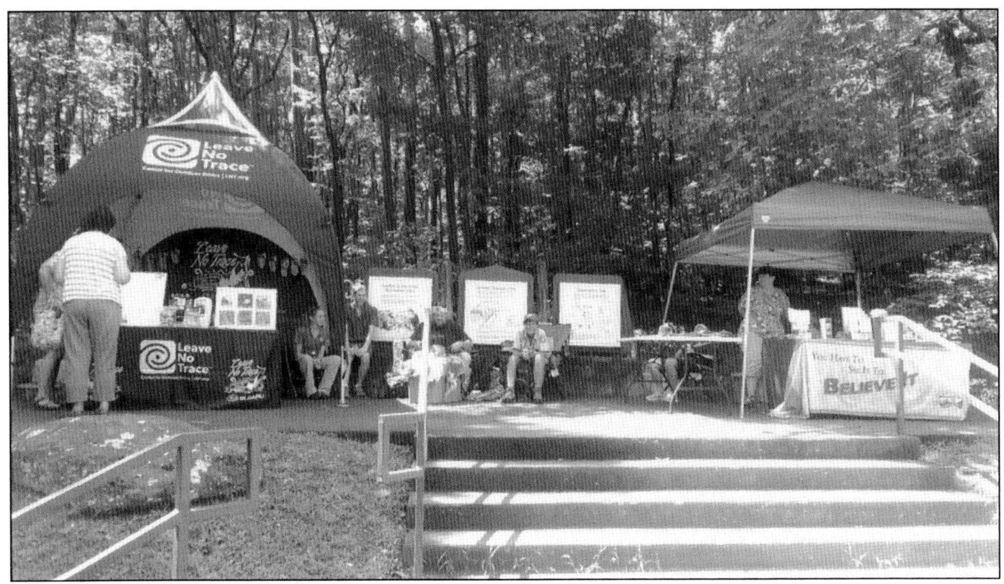

Friends of the Shawnee National Forest is a not-for-profit organization that supports and promotes land stewardship, responsible recreation, economic sustainability, and connecting people and communities to nature—especially kids! Above, Friends of the Shawnee National Forest and Southernmost Illinois Tourism Bureau partner with the Shawnee National Forest to promote the Center for Outdoor Ethics' "Leave No Trace" event at Garden of the Gods in Saline County. Below, volunteers with the Southern Illinois University Touch of Nature Environmental Center lead activities on the Observation Trail at Garden of the Gods to teach the seven principles of "Leave No Trace." (Both, author's collection.)

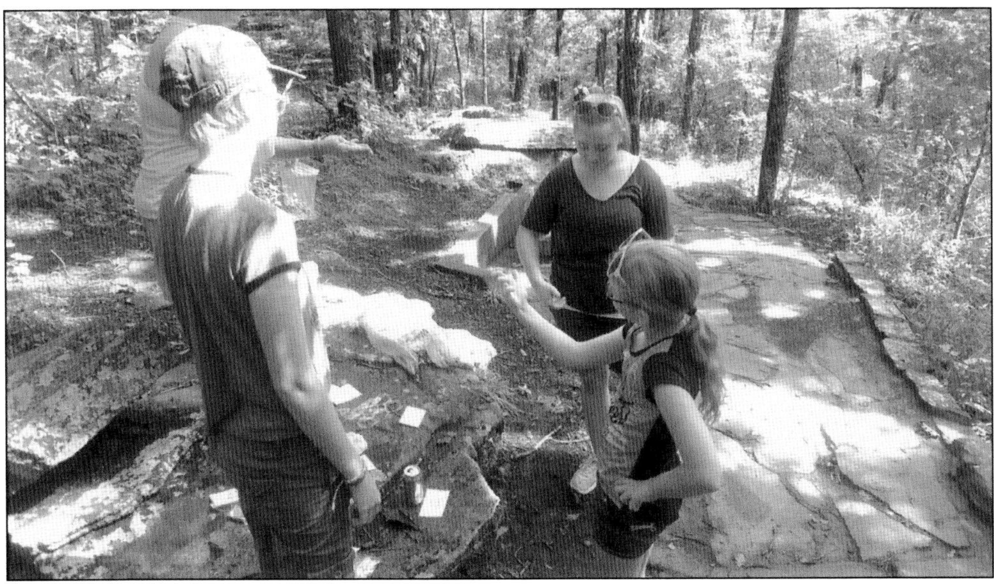

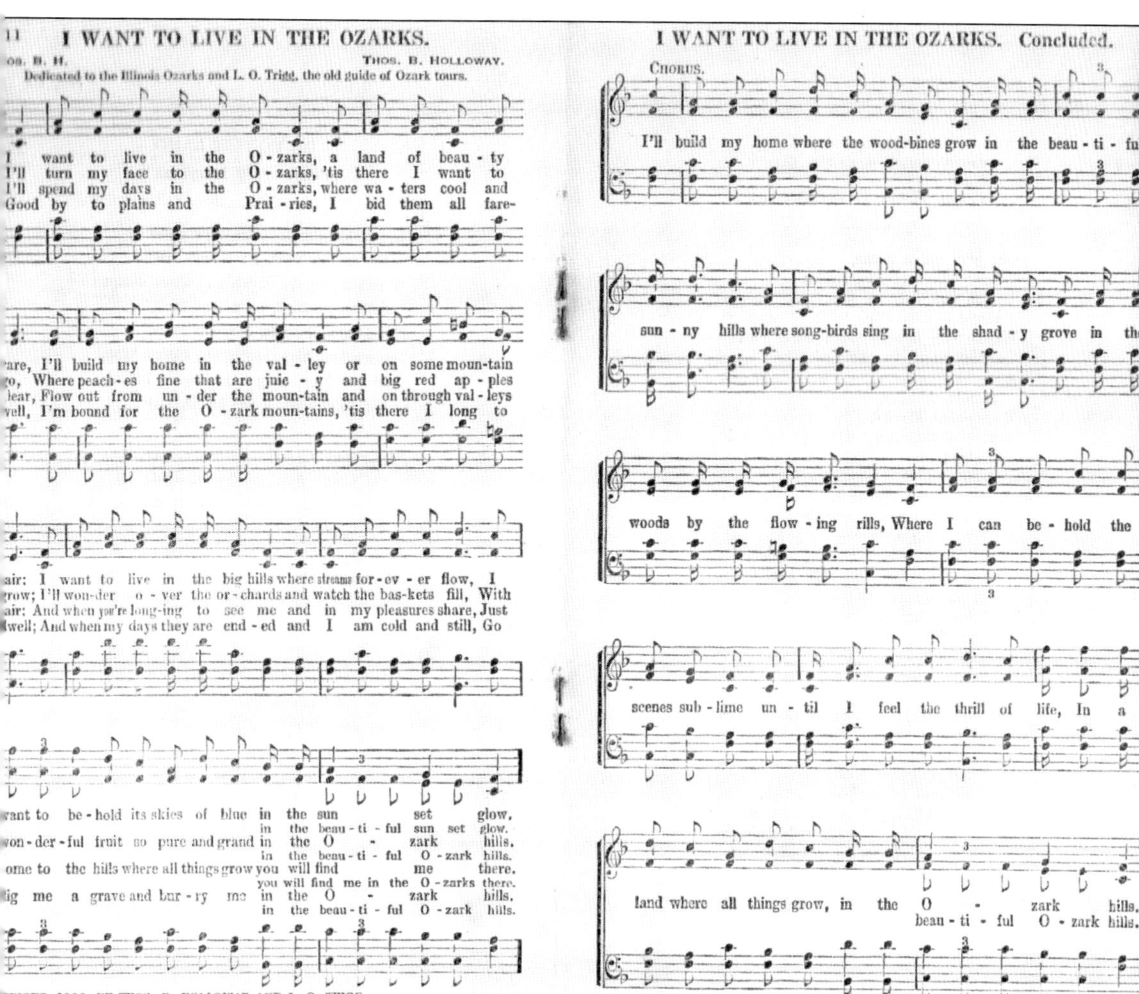

The lyrics and music to "I Want to Live in the Ozarks" were written by southern Illinois native Thomas B. Holloway of Eddyville. Holloway was a graduate of four music colleges and taught at over 600 singing schools during his career. Holloway presented the song to L.O. Trigg in 1936 and dedicated it "to the Illinois Ozarks and L.O. Trigg, the old guide of Ozark tours."